Open
Boundaries

Open
Boundaries

*Creating Business Innovation
Through Complexity*

Howard Sherman and Ron Schultz

PERSEUS BOOKS

Reading, Massachusetts

Library of Congress Catalog Card Number: 99-65118

ISBN 0-7382-0155-3

Cover design by Peter Blaiwas
Text design by Jean Hammond
Set in 10-point Meridien by Argosy

1 2 3 4 5 6 7 8 9-   -02 01 00 99

Perseus Books are available at special discounts for bulk purchases in the U.S. by corporations, institutions, and other organizations. For more information, please contact the Special Markets Department at HarperCollins Publishers, 10 East 53rd Street, New York, NY 10022, or call 212-207-7528.

Find Perseus Books on the World Wide Web at
http://www.perseusbooks.com

The soul contains in itself the event that shall presently befall it.
The event is only the actualizing of its thought.
Ralph Waldo Emerson

This book is dedicated to
Camilla Jewell and Laura Sanderford

Contents

Acknowledgments

At the heart of this book are its interactions. As collaborators, we decided before ever writing page one that we would write this book not as a linear progression, but as an organic process. That meant we allowed the complex process to self-organize and unfold. The ideas could interact with each other and produce new ideas. We would combine and recombine, doing our best not to get locked in to a word, an assumption, or a belief that might limit what would follow. Having followed the principles and ideas about which we were speaking, we realized that something blossomed forth that neither of us had anticipated.

Producing a book, as anyone who has done so knows, requires the efforts of many people. Since this was a collaboration, there were many people who directly helped the process and those that were of constant support to us individually.

Since I, Ron, am writing first, I get to acknowledge my partner first. This project could not have been conceived without the efforts, thinking, and generosity of Howard Sherman. I stand at the end of a long line of people for whom Howard has been a mentor, and I'm sure plenty more will follow me. But in this experience, as those who know him would tell you, I have found my ways of thinking, my understanding, and my ever-shifting perspective to have been changed in ways that were inconceivable when this idea began taking shape. Howard Sherman, though he will deny it all, has a way of opening thought, of making it absolutely safe to venture into new ways of thinking. He makes us better thinkers, better able to understand and comprehend what we encounter in this complex environment. As a reader, you will be able to recognize for yourself this quality that both challenges and opens. It has changed me forever, for which I am forever grateful.

This relationship didn't simply spring forth from Santa Fe's Las Chivas coffee shop in which many of these ideas took form, but from an introduction by Cathy Allen. Cathy's ability to recognize successful partnerships before they exist is remarkable. She has been a valued ally, support, and friend.

As in any complex mixture of relationships, events take place that, like the initial conditions of the universe, allow new combinations to expand and spiral out. Henning Gutmann's editorial instinct launched this project, and we are greatly appreciative of that. Good editors have one thing in mind when they read drafts of a book—to make it better. Nick Philipson found himself thrust into a situation he had not expected. His input and his willingness to advise and consent has had a profound and positive impact on this book. We would also like to thank Janet Rasmussen for her hours of labor in transcribing what must have seemed like endless conversations and interviews. And also to Kathy Fares for her efforts and understanding.

For germination and generation to take place, I have been fortunate to have the love and support of my partner and wife, Laura Sanderford, and the patience and love of our children, Johana and Emily. I would also like to acknowledge the education, humor, and caring I received from three people without whom the marathon process of producing this book would have been very difficult: Barry Milner, Jo Eatonson, and Steve Tinkler.

No matter how clear an idea is in its formulation, sometimes its written articulation leaves something to be desired. We have received tremendous feedback, both critically and morally, from Richard Carlson and Norm Levine, who read drafts and made copious notes, and from Peggy Levine, Jeremy Sherman, Sam Schultz, Kyle Radaker, Charles Smith, Bob Samples, Cheryl Charles, and Kristina and Richard Paoff at the Las Chivas Coffee Roaster, who even turned down the music so we could work in their comfortable space. We were also fortunate to work with colleagues like Michael Lissack, Lynda Woodman, Ken Prokuski, Bill Barr, and Richard Rothwell, who provided important contributions to the formulation of these emerging ideas, and were not afraid to tell us when they thought we'd gotten it wrong, or agree with us when we'd gotten it right.

In addition, we would like to acknowledge the information and exploration of ideas we gained from those we interviewed and with whom we worked: Bruce Abell, Mike Simmons, Mike McMaster, Brian Arthur, Murray Gell-Mann, Stuart Kauffman, John Holland, Colin Crook, David Whyte, Hatim Tyabji, John Seely Brown, Sam Cruce, Jennifer Self, Laura O'Dell, Colonel Tony Woods, Curt Lindberg, John Hiles, Jay Keyworth, Paul Abrams, Pam Sampel, John Chambers, and Doyne Farmer.

None of these efforts would have made any sense, because the book would never have found its way into print, if Peter Miller and Yuri Skujins had not first recognized that there was indeed a book here. As agents they were the best—perceptive, open, loyal, and aggressive. Simply, the best.

In the preceding acknowledgments, Ron speaks for both of us (including the personal acknowledgment of his lovely wife and partner, Laura). In addition, I, Howard, would like to acknowledge several people who have contributed to my work.

First, of course, is Ron, without whom this book would not have been written. He created the title, the idea of the book, and the format, and he conducted all the interviews for the numerous case studies, sensitively allowing novel ideas to emerge as he did so. He struggled throughout to bring the book into existence, with perseverance, clarity, insight, and integrity. He never lost faith that this could be done. The readers and I must share our indebtedness to him.

Bruce Abell and Mike Simmons, my two partners in the Santa Fe Center for Emergent Strategies, have contributed greatly to the ideas and the content of the book. In our work together we have lived, in our seminars and with our clients, the ideas and values found in the book. I thank you both for your presence in my life. Magdalena Romero, our administrator, has provided invaluable support to me for the last five years through periods of transition and confusion. Thank you.

Mike McMaster is an old and dear friend and colleague. It was Mike who first interested me—and perhaps the academic and business worlds as well—in organizational intelligence as a frame of reference different from individual intelligence, and in what he called knowledge-based development. Through his books, lectures, and consulting he has become the world's foremost teacher to organized business. Thank you, Mike, for your inspiration.

Camilla Jewell, my most precious friend, has for many years participated in all my creative work. She has been conscience, critic, and guiding spirit, sensitive always, in relation to any moment of creation, to truth, to beauty, and to goodness. Thank you, Camilla.

Throughout my adult life I have derived inspiration, stimulation, and guidance from Barbara Chavez and from my three children, Miguel Sherman, Deborah Sherman, and Alex Sherman. They are also my closest friends. I am also indebted to two other close personal friends, Don Cox and Suzanne Miller, for valuable editorial assistance.

Finally, I would like to acknowledge a group of people without whose influence this book would have not been possible—the Santa Fe Institute. As a member of their Business Network and as one of several cocreators with them of the first international conferences on complexity and business, I learned from them the enormous potential for productive applications of their research into complexity science. I would like to acknowledge one of the cocreators of those two pioneering conferences: Monib Khademi, for his valuable contributions in making those conferences possible.

This book, then, has been a collective effort.

Authors' Note

The reason the chapters aren't numbered was to reinforce the idea that they form a nonlinear pattern, which, because of the limitations of a two-dimensional book, defy the holographic dimensions of its topic.

Preface

Business success or failure in today's world is essentially cognitive success or failure. *Cognitive* has two equally significant meanings: "to know" and "to beget." Taken together these two meanings suggest that all birth is an awakening to knowledge. To know and to generate are inseparable.

This book will demonstrate—by examples, case studies, histories, and analyses—that knowledge is power and that there is no power without knowledge. We will show how businesses coevolve with an environment of ideas as fully as they coevolve with an environment of things and behaviors. That is, ideas influence the environment as much as the environment influences ideas. The ideas provide both context and methodology for the complex interactions of a business and for the feedback mechanisms so critical to modern business performance. Companies are telling us, "We know how to operate our businesses and we know how to make our products. We need to know the new ideas and strategies out of which we can operate creatively."

Understanding the ideas that influence the business is limited to the formulations of those ideas—as models, metaphors, and theories. Most formulations tend to be repetitive and are often accepted and followed without question. Yet it is only when these formulations are questioned at their inception that they will inform what a business is and does. The formulations may take the form of requests, commands, and questions. They serve to define problems, provide solutions, and declare intentions. They are used to recount or tell stories, prescribe, proscribe, evaluate, and judge. Whatever the form, they occur as various levels of abstraction and delineate frames of reference.

Ideas contain all possibilities and at the same time may limit those possibilities. They provide for both direction and novelty. They can reveal sources of innovative behavior or constrain that behavior.

This is not a "how to do it" book, it is a "how to think it" book, or, more precisely, a "how to be right" book. Its intent is pragmatic: to enable businesses and organizations to be powerfully generative in everything they and the agents or actors constituting the organization do. This is not science, but it "learns" from science, and it may contribute to science (and probably will to the extent it is "right"). We agree with Einstein when he says, "I am not of the opinion that there exists an essential difference between concepts and methods in the fields of 'common sense' and science," and when he says, "The whole of science is nothing more than a refinement of everyday thinking," and when he says, "The use of numbers does not involve a difference in essence between scientific and commonsense methods."

From a commonsense frame of reference, we give you here some of our ideas about the cognitive sources of business achievement. We claim no originality, but of course accept responsibility for these ideas. They have developed over a period of five years of participating with the Business Network of the Santa Fe Institute and with many other Institute participants, especially Brian Arthur, Stuart Kauffman, and John Holland. Bruce Abell and Mike Simmons, from the Santa Fe Center for Emergent Strategies, have been instrumental in defining these ideas. A good deal of their thinking has contributed directly to many aspects of this book.

Some formulations will develop inductively throughout the book, from case studies of business that either survived or failed, or ideas, that turned out, in retrospect, to be right or not right, and through studies of businesses struggling in today's hypermodern world to be right.

Open
Boundaries

The Myth of the Closed System

Our thinking creates problems which the same level of thinking can't solve. • Albert Einstein

When businesses get stuck in old ways of thinking, they limit their possibilities. This chapter will serve as an introduction to a new way of thinking. It provides a basic understanding of how what we think directly influences the actions we take. It also opens our thinking to the interactions that can drive today's businesses forward or backward. What issues forth are the strategic elements necessary to understand today's complex business environment.

We are a world of wall builders, partitioners, and dividers of space. We long for the security of safe places. We construct these barriers in a vain attempt to control the elements, to keep the rain from dampening the fire, the wind from covering our lives with the inevitable dust. Many of the walls we build are essential for our survival. Many, however, are not. By fortifying the unnecessary walls, we in business and industry huddle in the systems we have closed. The consequence: Thinking decays and novelty vanishes.

It's not enough, however, to say we simply need to change, to tear down what's unnecessary so that we can usher in the new. We also need to understand why it is necessary to change, what we are changing, and what we're changing into. The objective of this book is to see our place in the world as it is today, based on our current knowledge, not as it has been in the past or as we might wish it to be. Once we understand and integrate the ideas that form today's thinking, then we can act according to those ideas, opening our organizations to real novelty and innovation.

The Myth of the Closed System

Over the last two hundred to three hundred years, we have seen a radical shift from closed systems of thinking to open systems in a broad range of disciplines. This has been a shift away from the medieval *weltlich* (world spirit) notion of a closed universe which dominated Western Europe for a thousand years. In this finite, simple system all the answers were somehow known or knowable. The universe was seen as creator-designed and knowable in terms of certain limited models that God had in mind when He made it. Its nature did not change. It was to be exactly what it was forever. This image of a closed universe was reinforced by Newtonian science, whose clockwork-style representation reduced the whole universe to a simple mechanism.

In stark contrast to the Newtonian closed system, open systems are not mechanical but emergent. They can arise only out of that which has directly preceded them. As we will see, there is continuity, but not determination.

A surprising amount of closed-system thinking still prevails in the way we think about and do business in the contemporary world. The roots of that world are firmly planted in a closed-system structure that came to characterize the early period of the Industrial Revolution. As we proceed through and past the industrial and postindustrial period, we can see that this approach no longer supports the evolution of today's business climate.

When we try to close systems that in fact cannot be closed, we create a radical incompatibility with nature and business. The consequences of this incompatibility are severe: a retardation of coevolutionary development, a gross limitation of novel innovation and new possibilities, and an eventual and untimely death of the system.

The difference between closed and open systems is like that between a fish in a fishbowl and one swimming in the open sea. The fishbowl fish may be safe in its walled habitat, and it may breed for a cycle or two, but when conditions change, it will be completely unprepared to meet any variations in its environment. The fish in the sea may be subject to greater danger, more predators, but the choices and new possibilities available are virtually unlimited. Its ability to change and adapt as needed is also greater.

People also get stuck in a similar kind of repetitive thinking behavior. They continue to formulate the same things in the same way, adapting to the relative safety of their environment. They also continue behaving and evaluating their behavior in the same way, without significant regard to life outside the bowl. The mistaken impression in doing so is that they are safe and stable and will lead comfortable lives. Nature, however, points to a different conclusion: stagnation, oxygen deprivation, untimely death.

In many cases, business operates in a similar way when it gets locked into closed-system ideas. One example is business's inability to tolerate and deal with any kind of ambiguity. In a misguided desire for order and certainty, business would much rather stamp out ambiguity than see it as a necessary precondition to influence potentiality.

Businesses are always operating under conditions of ambiguity. There is no way to avoid it, because there are no clear-cut answers to any of the questions that arise. There are always elements of the unknown, the unpredictable, and the uncertain. The way most businesses try to stamp out ambiguity is by putting together contingency plans. We plan on A, but if A doesn't work, we do B. These companies think they are eliminating the ambiguous. What remains, however, is that no matter which of the many alternative plans are put together, they always arrive in a context of ambiguity.

Colin Crook, Citibank's former senior chief technology officer, offers an example about ordering computers today for a need that will arise a year from now. This is a very ambiguous situation. He couldn't be sure that the computers he ordered today will be the right ones in the future, because they could be obsolete by the time he receives them. What Crook did was incorporate this ambiguity into his decision making as a necessary precondition to influence potentiality. Whenever possible he didn't buy computers, he leased them. He then negotiated terms within the lease to be able to replace them if the technology was upgraded by the time he received them.

If a company tries to eliminate ambiguity, if it is unwilling to maintain a place for the inevitable unknowing, it will fall into a sad state of affairs, because this limits the possibilities that are available to it. The question becomes, How do you decide what to do while at the same time keeping all of your options open? If an organization closes itself down in a way that cuts it off from changes that occur—from new possibilities—it finds itself making decisions that are inappropriate to the state of affairs from which it has cut itself off. What takes place when ambiguity within an organization is avoided becomes a matter of sheer luck. "Maybe computer technology won't change significantly in a year."

Another faulty line of reasoning an organization falls into arises from its inability to see the issues that are beyond the very tight boundaries of its limited definition of its industry and consequently to see clearly how it conducts business within them. By trying to operate within those very restrictive boundaries, the organization inadvertently drives itself toward huge problems that it is incapable of anticipating, because its vision is so limited. Out of this myopic perspective, the business proceeds blindly to make changes to alter the system, but they all conform to its limited definitions. In so doing, it makes terrible mistakes that will be very expensive to fix in the future.

When the models that drive our businesses are built on a closed-system perspective, the radical incompatibility between the way the world actually operates and the way we are thinking about it forces an organization to come up with ideas and make decisions that are based only on partial information. Businesses tend to deal with interpretations as if they were matters of fact when they are nothing more than choices we make.

An excellent example of closed-system thinking is one that states that things are either true or false, that there is a certain objective determination that can be made as to what constitutes a fact. A fact functions as something to which absolutely all thinking and behaviors must somehow conform. It defines what is. What an organization takes to be a fact sets up and determines all the boundaries of what it can and cannot do, what is admissible and what is not admissible, what is possible and what is not possible.

A business might assume that there is some separate, static, external reality that exists outside the business, and makes its decisions on the basis of that assumption. Many companies do this all the time. Doing so, however, locks the business into a highly risky situation, because there is no "there" out there. We are speaking about ongoing processes that are molded by the actions, ideas, and languages of all the interacting agents (participants), not stationary forces that can be diagnosed and torn into pieces.

To understand this, we need to see that it is through language that adaptive agents interact with each other in human organizations—and through those interactions changes occur and interactive behaviors take place that continually remold the environment, which is always changing and being molded in this cognitive process. An organization that assumes that a reality exists out there independent of its own actions, formulations, and ideas has missed the point. A concrete example is that there is no point in looking for the truth about what consumers want as a guide to making decisions, because this is changing all the time. In doing so, we are attempting to set up an either/or situation, effectively eliminating alternatives.

As we unlock the doors of closed systems, we find that the distinctions we make are not really distinctions at all. They are two sides of the same whole. In closed systems, there are very rigid dualisms: Something is either this or that. For example, in the Cartesian model of reality, something is either subject or object, known or knower. It can't be both. This dualistic thinking goes back to the distinctions made in medieval thought between God and the created universe. Any concept attributed to one couldn't be attributed to the other. They were different in their very nature. God was eternal and perfect and the universe was temporal and imperfect. In contrast with this is one of the early precursors of open-system thinking, the dialectical process, in which two things that seemed utterly different and incompatible can really be understood only in relation to each other. Neither can exist without the other. The classical example of this dialectic is the thesis and antithesis of being and nonbeing, which are synthesized into becoming, which is not one or the other, but both.

The dialectical aspect of open systems is very important, implying, in effect, that anything designated as an "either" or an "or" is really part of an ongoing process in which, inevitably, the two aspects are going to have to come together in ways that lead to new formulations that are neither A nor B, but that simply integrate them in some other fashion. Plato said twenty-five hundred years ago in laying the groundwork for scientists to come, "Existence is a process of everlasting becoming."

As might be expected, we must tread in the areas that business cannot fence or separate, that are neither an either nor an or. The author John Holland suggests that these areas have for centuries been marked on the map with the label "monsters exist here." On any heroic journey—and what more heroic journey can there be than doing business in today's blisteringly paced marketplace—the uncharted and ambiguous must be entered to emerge in the new world. But we can never really leave where we are unless some of the walls that we have built come down.

Recognizing the Complex Environment

In order to open the system, we need to understand how a business operates. An organization's behaviors and its business propositions emerge in the following ways:

1. Within the complex interactions of the individuals that make up the company.

2. Within the interactions of the individuals in their departments.

3. Within the interactions of the departments.

4. Within the interactions of departments with the company's divisions.

5. Within the interaction of its divisions.

6. Within the interactions with stockholders, competitors, and consumers.

But this is a cursory appraisal, and the interactions are actually far more complex than this. For a deeper context, we must comprehend four basic elements that drive these interactions.

Principles, Models,
Rules, and Behaviors

Every interaction in a business operates within a given set of principles. Sometimes unstated, these principles are enduring, surprisingly abstract, germane to the enterprise, and fundamental to its success. The models, rules, and behaviors, each operating at a different level within an organization, are more arbitrary than principles and even emergent. When the interactions between principles, models, rules, and behaviors are right (in the Hawking sense stated earlier) an organization can enhance adaptation and innovation. If they are wrong, companies invariably fall behind as the environment changes.

Today's businesses know they must innovate to survive. But innovations that are incompatible with a company's principles often produce confusion rather than growth. Successful innovation is very much the product of a company's cognitive structure. As we will illustrate more completely in the chapter, "Principles, Models, Rules, and Behaviors," what is required is a framework for thinking deeply about what a company is and is not. This framework demands an examination of the critical connections among principles, models, rules, and behaviors. As we will see, serious problems arise when, for example, a rule is mistaken for a model or a behavior is based on a principle and not on a model.

Ideas based on principles drive models. Relationships based on ideas influence behaviors. Rules are routines for carrying out the models. Yet rules often loom as the most restrictive element, becoming confused with principles, distorting and reinforcing inappropriate behaviors, and compromising the company's ability to deliver value, to prosper, and especially to innovate. As we will demonstrate, a startling implication of this perspective is that rule-generated behaviors don't work.

Adaptation and innovation occur within the interaction of models and behaviors. Recent research in complexity and complex systems has provided significant insights into how this emergence of adaptation and innovation takes place. These insights demonstrate how the fundamental elements of an enterprise—its people—are often best positioned to sense the multiple environments they encounter, try alternative solutions to problems, and, like nature, sort out the better solutions. Yet all too often we find that companies want to close their systems, and unnecessarily constrain behaviors; and in so doing, they constrain the best source of creativity available to them—the distributed knowledge of their workforce.

Developing New Ways of Thinking

Einstein stated, "Our thinking creates problems which the same level of thinking can't solve." The English philosopher and mathematician Alfred North Whitehead (1861–1947) said the same thing. If we continue using our old ways of thinking to describe our current situations we get nothing more than "orthodox experiments disclosing orthodox novelty." This is what closed systems produce—more of the same. We would like to clothe this orthodox novelty in the trappings of the new, and have everyone hail it as such. Unfortunately, the system doesn't work like that. As will become evident in the chapters that follow to be truly innovative and to survive, companies must step outside their outmoded perspectives, reevaluate their models on the basis of their new understandings, and then adjust their behaviors accordingly. When these steps are integrated as a continual part of the process, emergent novelty becomes characteristic, not inconceivable.

The Challenge of Nature's Process

It is evident that evolution is unstoppable. With or without our intervention, emergence occurs. But what does this mean? The word *emergence* comes from the Indo-European root "to dive." From this context, *merge* then means "to dive in." *Submerged* means "dive under." *Emerge* is literally defined as "dive out," to come out of the depths. *Er* is also the root for the French word *mer* or ocean, literally meaning to rouse or rise up. Thus, *emergence* refers to what arises out of the depths of complex interactions. Since there is also a connection to the French word for mother, *mère*—out of which all human life emerges—emergence could also be said to be an idea brought to life. The problem for business is that the natural process of emergence—for example, in humans the nine months of gestation of a child—takes too long. Evolutionary time periods may be insignificant wisps in the time frame of the universe, but to businesses—for whom FedEx's next-morning delivery is too slow—change has to be faster, immediate, hurried, and in some cases even forced.

Why the great hurry? There's good reason. Some companies in the marketplace today bring product to the shelves, from concept to release, in time frames of months rather than years, let alone historical epochs. The pace of business has skyrocketed. To be perceived as leaders setting that pace, businesses are always looking for that extra step to keep them ahead of the pack. In an effort to change before the competition changes, business leaders inevitably turn to science.

Fortunately, business's need for rapid change coincides with the growing understanding of complex systems and how they can naturally adapt to changing conditions. Both the emerging science of complexity and the requirements of business have been fueled by profound changes in the way we acquire, process, distribute, and use information.

The marketplace, and the companies functioning successfully in that marketplace, are moving toward a world in which their operations and responsibilities are increasingly spread out across both periphery and core in what is known as a distributed system. Such a system's agents—entities that interact with other such entities—are, for the most part, semiautonomous, able to act without centralized approval. In large measure this is because distributed systems can respond and adapt more quickly than centralized systems to external changes. By opening systems in this fashion, organizations can also offer more means and incentives for innovation, while allowing solutions to problems to emerge from the interaction of the distributed parts of the enterprise.

Companies close their systems because they fear that allowing for autonomy and distributed management is a direct line to chaos. While we will define these concepts in more depth later, it is important to note that even though chaos and chaos theory have gotten a tremendous amount of press and are often associated with complexity thinking, it will play a very minor role in this process. Simply stated, chaos is a place in which no patterns of organization can be found. Mistakenly, organizations think they can stave off chaos by closing their systems. Unfortunately, building stronger walls in a vain attempt to solidify a position invites chaotic dissolution. The problems that invariably force a company into chaos are often brought about when the flow of information becomes dammed by the impediment of too much infrastructure.

Closed systems lead to entropy, which is total security. No changes occur. But, as John Holland said, "Equilibrium is death."

The Ratio between Infrastructure and Information

The way to avoid chaos is by establishing and sustaining the proper relationship between an organization's information and infrastructure—the

network

ratio of information to infrastructure. Infrastructure means everything from physical support systems and structures to philosophical constructs to psychological preconceptions. Information is not simply data, the accumulation of more facts. (Information means the gathering of models, patterns, and ways of informing and learning) This information makes it possible for infrastructure to (work more efficiently at a lower output of resources) Thus the optimal relationship between infrastructure and information is a high ratio of information to infrastructure. When a company gets trapped by its infrastructure, paying greater attention to infrastructure than to its flow of information, the company has lost the opportunity for real growth and may have difficulty surviving.

We have mentioned this ultimate danger a number of times. Are we being alarmist? No. As we view nature, it becomes evident that death is a process of weeding out that which can no longer adapt or that which has run its natural course. No judgment is made here beyond that ultimate conclusion.

(The critical factor for operating and surviving in a world of complexity is access to information.) This access is the (linkage to our models and principles.) What is not needed is more unnecessary walls that only block information rather than truly support the required infrastructure. To avoid building needless impediments, organizations need to examine carefully the models they construct, which influence their behaviors, as well as the ideas that drive those models. When people continually call into question the assumptions and beliefs an organization holds sacrosanct and eliminates those that no longer serve it properly, innovation that was previously inconceivable emerges out of a level of thinking different from the one that created the problem.

What follows then is a detective story that is fraught with possibilities. We will look for clues in large and small companies that are finding new applications for complexity thinking. We will include case studies from companies—Midas International, Xerox PARC, Coca-Cola, Citibank, Lucent Technologies, NeoRx, Thinking Tools, Hewlett-Packard, VeriFone, the Prediction Company, Perkin-Elmer Corporations's Applied Biosystems, and the U.S. Marine Corps and the nonprofit VHA hospital organization.

It is our mission to make business organizations aware of the nonlinear dynamics of their organizations, the complex interactions that take place throughout a company that affect the way they do business. Such awareness can lead an organization immediately to recognize the limitations of its outmoded linear assumptions and belief systems. This in turn helps it recognize new ideas that can drive its strategies and decisions and allow it to build new models that reflect today's business world. By taking this step, companies will be enabled to think in previously inconceivable ways that may be more productive in generating the results they seek to create.

In reality, we may be looking for something that does not exist. But if we can learn anything from business history, it's that no one asks for that which does not yet exist. However, twenty years after its arrival, no one can live without it.

A New Way of Thinking

People like to think that businesses are built of numbers (as in the "bottom line"), or forces (as in "market forces"), or things ("the product"), or even flesh and blood ("our people"). But this is wrong. . . . Businesses are made of ideas—ideas expressed as words."
  * James Champy,
    Re-Engineering Management

Our businesses are only as successful as our ideas. If our ideas are out of date, the behaviors they drive will be out of date. The ideas that emanate from a mechanistic, Industrial Age perspective influence behaviors very differently than the ideas that emerge when we see our businesses as the complex adaptive systems they truly are. This chapter introduces the ideas of complexity thinking and its constituent complex adaptive systems. It also unveils how businesses get stuck in outdated ways of thinking, which keeps them from recognizing what is truly innovative. When businesses become locked into orthodox novelty they propel themselves toward cognitive failure.

If Albert Einstein had lived long enough and had had the inclination to capitalize on his theories and discoveries, he would, in today's market, be the president and CEO of the largest company on the face of the earth. His ideas have led directly to the invention of such products as photoelectric cells, TV cameras and televisions, optical sound tracks for movies, devices that carry telephone calls over fiber-optic cables, solid-state devices like calculators and computers, drugs produced via the fusion process, lasers, and consequently, bar-code scanners, power generators, precision clocks—and the list goes on.[1] Einstein's new way of thinking made these technological breakthroughs possible. They could not have existed without it.

In order to understand how to operate within a business climate that embraces new ways of thinking, it's imperative to grasp just what business is. As James Champy says, "Businesses are made of ideas—ideas expressed as words." Complexity thinking provides us the capacity to deal with those ideas, which in turn makes possibilities possible.

Prior to complexity thinking, Galilean, Newtonian, and Cartesian (GNC) ideas influenced the world mentality to such a degree that we didn't even question them. These ideas operated as a transparent—functionally invisible—overlay to every action we took. These ideas were a perfect match for the linear, materialistic, predictable world of the Industrial Age. But things have changed. The Postindustrial/Information Age fueled by our new technology cannot operate only under those old rules. Business leaders from both large and small organizations find themselves caught with their feet in two worlds, trying to hold on to their old GNC ideas, while wanting to live meaningfully with the new science and its new ideas but not being clear on how to incorporate them.

The difficulty is giving up the mechanical, logical progressions of the Industrial Age and having to enter a world of nonlinear thinking. For hundreds of years, business has assumed that the target it was trying to hit, as mentioned earlier, was something "out there." All a business had to do was aim at the target and progress along a straight and narrow path until reaching it.

One assumption we hope to dispel is that there is an "out there" called the marketplace. Most companies think they need to look out there, and they tailor their activities to what is perceived to be the nature of the marketplace. Executives see this marketplace entity as if it were independent of what that company does. That's Newtonian thought—the dualism of the observed and the observer. From the frame of reference of complexity thinking, this is a limited perspective. The observer and the observed are not independent of each other. They are both part of the same ongoing process. The idea that if a company wants to be successful it had better gather more objective data ignores the truth that there is *no* independent objective reality out there. This way of thinking also disregards where innovative ideas originate.

The problem that arises within today's complex business environment is that business and the target are constantly modifying each other and coevolving. What was once directly in sight and would remain so has left the screen by the time a business tries to take the linear path to it. The balance, order, and simplicity of Industrial Age processes are lost today, because the elements are continually changing. In the complex environments of the Postindustrial Age, balance is no longer even part of the equation. If, as John Holland pointed out, "Equilibrium is death,"[2] then within the nonlinear confines of business, the identification must be with relationships and ratios rather than balance.

In a previously unpublished letter dated January 8, 1955, written by Albert Einstein to a former Princeton student, Einstein writes, "I still believe that one cannot distinguish, in principle, between primary and secondary qualities. It is basic for all physics that one assumes a real world existing independently from any act of perception. But this we do not *know.*"[3]

The unfortunate side to thinking in a new way is that companies would rather be lied to than give up their old GNC ways of linear thinking. For example, management by objectives was one management technique that basically said, "Let's agree to lie to each other." In order to meet an objective, it was necessary to come up with a profit projection that usually bore little or no resemblance to reality. Why? Because a number was needed so that a conclusion or an outcome could be agreed upon. A+B=C, even though C would probably look more like when all was said and done. Unfortunately, today's Postindustrial Age businesses are more complex, and cannot tolerate having old arcane ways of linear thinking forced upon them.

This is the power of complexity thinking. What scientists call complexity is the integrating aspect of all living systems, like humans, and all organizations of living systems, like corporations and organizations. Complexity is the attractor that brings together all the various bits and pieces of these systems and enables them to interact as a whole. In doing so, it opens this larger system to the unlimited possibilities generated by the distributed interaction of its parts. Within these open boundaries, complexity thinking provides an underlying understanding of organization and a new way of thinking about how systems organize. This understanding allows business to rethink, reframe, and reinvigorate its organizations so that the competitive process of innovation can flow freely.

Complexity

Before we explore further how complexity works in an organizational world, we should offer some simple definitions—a foundation from which to view this expanse of new perspectives. *Complexity* can be characterized as a deep sea of vast possibilities. In the watery depths of this complex ocean, entities combine in unpredictable ways that affect the way other entities combine and change. This is called coevolution. Out of this coevolution something new emerges—dives out of the depths. All the entities involved in this process are living and all are themselves complex adaptive systems. Complexity is the study of complex adaptive systems.

A more precise definition would be, "A complex adaptive system *(a business)* is composed of interacting 'agents' *(employees, managers, board members, customers, suppliers, competitors,* and *regulators)* following rules *(blueprints, values, ethics, laws, economics, organization/political, friendship, profit-maximizing)*, exchanging influence *(goods, ideas, money, trust)* with their local and global environments *(from the cubicle to the global market)*, and altering the very environment they are responding to by virtue of their 'simple' actions."[4]

Complex adaptive systems of all kinds, from ecosystems to multinational corporations, share many fundamental characteristics and processes, from "frozen events" to coevolution. These common features make the study of one pertinent to the understanding of the other.

Some of the processes that characterize natural complex adaptive systems include the following:

- Agent-driven interactions

- Interchanges with external environments

- Distributed information processing and problem solving

- Sustained coevolution

- Adaptation to changing environments

- Instability (never really at equilibrium)

- Perturbation by probabilistic (unplanned and unpredictable in detail) events—both internal and external in origin

- Emergent phenomena

- Self-organization of structures (relationships) and rules for interaction at all levels

- Occurrence of events that have altered the course of evolution: "frozen history"

- The ability to innovate

- The existence of memory/expectations/predictions

- Nonlinearity: the condition that small events may have no effect, or may create an avalanche of change

Our human-influenced systems have some additional characteristics that emerge in large part from our cognitive processes and that distinguish us from other natural systems. Before we can apply the idea of complexity within our business activities, it is crucial that we understand the consequences of those differences.

First, we are not bacteria with a simple repertoire of actions. For the most part, we humans have extensive cognitive abilities that can address multiple objectives simultaneously. These are sometimes referred to as "fitness" objectives, pertaining to the evolutionary notion of organizational fitness. In other words, we can carry on a variety of unrelated tasks with different motivations and rewards at the same time. Second, the rules and culture within which we operate are more complex than a colony of bacteria, and because those rules are embedded in practice, we are more resistant to change than the members of a colony of bacteria. This resistance is also greater within organizations (for example, a political party), especially when it comes to finding new solutions to problems. At the same time, this resistance means that those who are more flexible have a great opportunity to form new organizations that can identify, fill, and expand emerging niches. We have seen evidence of this in everything from cults to high-tech spinoff companies to political caucuses. However, as we will discuss in the chapter "Language, Narrative, and Metaphor," whether social organization or spin off, these are all specific forms of complex adaptive systems that we will call *purposeful* complex adaptive systems.

In addition to these social organizational qualities, businesses (another form of purposeful complex adaptive system) have further complex refinements that must be taken into account if they want to realize the benefit of complexity and innovation. Businesses have limited, defined objectives and deliver measurable value. They have strongly imposed structures and rules, but because of their close coupling to markets, they are subject to radical change. Businesses are also inherently unstable, operating in an increasingly volatile environment that has a much higher mortality rate than that associated with other social organizations. They have to contend with "unnatural" time scales, mismatches of internal and external paces, as happens when customers demand a product whose delivery is held up by an interrupted supply chain. In addition, they are both victims and beneficiaries of perceptions and can manipulate perceptions to get market share. In today's market, they are usually dependent on technology, either as producers or users. Furthermore, and in marked contrast to most social organizations, businesses are property, owned by a defined group.

Chaos

Chaos, according to the author and consultant Mike McMaster, is that unlikely circumstance in which patterns cannot be found nor the details understood. Without patterns, we cannot project what will happen, analyze the circumstances, or make any plans to deal with the totally unpredictable conditions. All we can do when we are in a chaotic situation is to "clear an island of certainty," as McMaster suggests, "and make small efforts to move forward." Another alternative is to get rid of the chaotic situation in its entirety.[5]

If complexity can be characterized as watery depths, chaos would be like a gas state, dissipating in all directions without shape or form. It is a state in which little or no pattern can be discerned. Complexity, though unpredictable, has shape, form, and pattern.

In the early 1990s, when IBM was looking for a new CEO to deal with its impending chaos, management interviewed Apple Computer's former CEO, John Sculley. Sculley's recommendation was for IBM to get rid of its ancillary businesses amounting to over half the company and return to the core business. IBM decided that this was too radical. They were so locked into their frame of reference that it had become sacrosanct. As we will demonstrate, unless Big Blue does something to knock down its ever more strangling infrastructure, IBM will inevitably return to the silicon from which it sprang.

Why Is Complexity Thinking Important for a Business?

It should be noted that it is not adequate to say there are ideas developing in the sciences of complexity that relate to business without seeing these ideas as part of a larger process. There is growing evidence coming out of institutions such as the Santa Fe Institute and others that these ideas are becoming pervasive and are being discussed in many different areas within our overall society. It is also true that there is a sense in which business has to do for itself something analogous to what science has done by developing this new way of thinking. It is crucial because the issues affecting business are exactly the same as those that have been limiting the sciences.

The reason understanding the science coming out of complexity is important is not because business can't discover the same things for itself, but because the sciences have already indicated what that process looks like. They have come to certain "conclusions" and understandings regarding what has been holding back science from getting its job done better than it has. Business can save a great deal of time and energy by looking at what the sciences have already accomplished, rather than reinventing the wheel.

If, as we will discuss at length throughout this book, our ideas shape our behaviors, and if our ideas are outdated and no longer relevant, then behaviors shaped by those ideas will be outdated and no longer relevant. In order to bring our ideas into the present, we need to understand what we presently know about how organizations and businesses fundamentally operate. What we intend to offer is a snapshot of what complexity looks like and how that work can be built on to further business.

Why did the sciences and ultimately business have to take this journey into complexity? They did it because too many of the ideas with which they were working were derived from limited ways of understanding the world and how it functioned. These ideas made it difficult to break through to new ideas that are more consistent with the changes that are emerging.

Science could no longer remain stuck in the ways it was formulating ideas and the way those formulations were impeding its capacity to get its job done. Scientists have their work just as business has its work, and that is to develop ways of predicting behaviors.

Scientists discovered that they were doing a brilliant job of predicting the behaviors of physical entities in motion, in space and time. Unfortunately, when it came to applying those same methodologies to individuals in societies and cultures and to the behavior of groupings of individuals in organizations, methodologies did not hold up as well. Scientists could not quantify what they found. They could not use the same methodologies that predicted things. The mathematics that they were using was not very useful. The predictions that they were making about behavior, based upon these proven methods of quantification, were not productive. To this day, their usefulness is still questionable.

The reason why science now must start to contend more effectively with individual and social behaviors is that a shift began to occur in the sciences away from the behaviors of things to the behaviors of organisms. Scientists had to confront the fact that not all of the knowledge and methodologies of physics worked. They still don't completely work. So complexity thinking emerged. There has been a radical change of direction for science to one that is now capable of asking how we can expand our capacity to deal with phenomena other than the limited traditional phenomena which were the objects of study of the science called physics—everything else being an offshoot of physics.

Businesses also have had to confront the fact that they are moving away from the Industrial Age, when they did a beautiful job of dealing with the mechanisms by which things get put together. These mechanisms included the functioning of the marketplace and economics, which were all influenced by the Newtonian worldview. Within that context, they worked beautifully. However, once the closed systems of human societies began to break down, and the phenomenon of globalization emerged, which the sciences themselves made possible through new technology, these Newtonian-based methods no longer worked very well.

This idea that organizations have to change and people have to change is not new to business. Business has been hearing this for decades now. Why is this different?

This is not change for the sake of change. It is waking up and seeing that a different kind of world has emerged and is emerging rapidly. It is not just a matter of keeping up with the change. It is a matter of rethinking and reformulating what this change is all about. We are not simply addressing an outdated model that has changed in certain ways but that still allows us to use the same ways of locating and positioning things in relation to it as we once did. We are looking at something new and different.

What has changed are the logics, the formulations, the quantifications, the ways of dealing with probabilities and predictions. Planning doesn't work well in relation to unanticipated behaviors because it is essentially linear. It looks at a flat plane of existence and tries to set a course for an organization that itself is nonlinear. Still, businesses tend to look at planning in the same way that we once naively assumed was perfectly adequate. The difference in the formulation of change is that in today's business world we must look away from the "orthodox novel" to the "emergent novelty." Rather than seeking more of the same, we begin to realize real innovation.

Recognizing Adjacent Possibilities

How does a complex organizational system develop an emergent way of thinking? A clue might be found in looking at how Einstein was capable of conceiving the inconceivable. It is generally agreed that Einstein had a highly inventive mind capable of making great leaps. He did not, however, have the freedom to make *any* leap whatsoever. His innovative sojourns were part of a developmental process that in today's complexity thinking would be called an ability to see the *adjacent possibilities*. The Santa Fe Institute's Stuart Kauffman, suggests that these adjacent possibilities never existed until a previous possibility had been realized. He explains, "If we consider the species of organic molecules now on the earth, we can also consider those species of organic molecules that do not exist, but that are one reaction step away from molecules that currently do exist." What Kauffman is describing, in terms of physics and biology, is that nothing comes from nothing. He then points out that "since the number of possible molecules with several tens of thousands of atoms per molecule is vast, the Universe has not had sufficient time to make each such molecule at least once since the Big Bang."[6] In other words, there are limitless possibilities that have never even been considered before and, as Plato said, everything that occurs in the universe is part of a process of everlasting becoming. These are the pragmatics of innovation: Until a previous possibility has come into existence, an adjacent possibility couldn't exist.

The question that organizations must ask is, What are the adjacent possibilities within an industry that allow for the creation of something new? In highly competitive markets this is vital information, because once an adjacent possibility becomes possible, it will occur. Someone will discover it. There's no way to predict when, but it will happen.

The businesses that succeed are those that are first within an industry to see an adjacent possibility and act upon it.

An example that closely involved one of the authors came from a small company that was the first to see the possibilities of car mufflers as a viable consumer product. Midas International Corporation created a consumer brand product that had never existed before, and they have dominated the muffler replacement industry ever since. How did that happen? Up until the early 1950s, Midas had been a muffler supplier to auto repair businesses. Not being an original equipment manufacturer, Midas was able to take a different view of its industry and saw the potential for an innovative way of doing business. They never looked back.

The key is to develop the capacity within an organization to step outside the industry, view from that vantage point the way business is conducted, and imagine other possibilities. We call this innovation. To be truly innovative, a business must maintain a level of consciousness and focus within its industry that exposes how that industry has changed through the coevolution of its members and customers and how its character has consequently been altered.

The founders of Midas saw people waiting in service stations and garages for mufflers, while the owners of those businesses were overloaded with repairs ranging from blown gaskets to engine overhauls to oil changes. Midas came up with an adjacent possibility that hadn't existed until those lines formed—they created a consumer brand identity and a specialized system of distribution for a car muffler, a previously anonymous auto part. The possibility was recognized and Midas acted on its discovery; that's what we call innovation.

ord *innovation* comes from the Latin root *novus*, meaning to cre-
ing new. It also derives meaning from the root *nu*, the source
of the word *now*. In this relationship, something new is something now.
Therefore, innovation is something that doesn't lie in memory or anticipation of the future. It is now and absolutely new.

In contrast to this idea of innovation is that of institution. Even the
most innovative people take great pride in their institutions without
understanding what it is they are supporting. The word *institution* is
derived from the Indo-European root *sta*—that which stands and is
unchanging. From this root, words like *stable, stasis,* and *static* arise. Our
institutions have been designed and developed by their very root structure as a way to keep change out, to maintain the status quo. *Innovation
and institution, at their core, are at odds with each other.*

Barriers to Innovation

Lynda Woodman, the president of the International Center for Information Technologies, in her paper "Barriers to Innovation," delivered at the
Santa Fe Seminar "Complexity and Strategy in Action," asked why some
business organizations adapt easily to certain changed circumstances in
their environment but have problems adapting to other changes? "Why is
it that some organizations either don't adapt at all or do so in very limited
ways? Why are some organizations far more innovative than others? Why
do obvious threats go unseen? Why are obvious opportunities missed?"
And finally she asked, "What are the barriers to adaptation and innovation?"

As examples, she posed a list of questions about some specific unseen
threats and missed opportunities. It is important to point out that the con-
verse of these threats and missed opportunities is examples of organizations that recognized adjacent possibilities and acted on them.

Unseen Threats

Why did the big three auto makers not see the impending threat of
the Japanese before they had stolen significant market share?

Why was IBM so late in entering the personal computer market,
and why did they then give away the personal computer software
market?

Why did Sears not see the impending threat of Wal-Mart?

Why was Encyclopedia Britannica so late in publishing their product on CD-ROM?

Why did Wang fail to see the personal computer as a multifunction work station with word processing as just one application of many?

Why did Citibank not see the threat of AT&T getting into the credit card business?

Why did Emery Air Freight fail to see the threat of Federal Express when it was originally launched?

Why, before deregulation, were the three major U.S. airlines—Pan-Am, Eastern and TWA—forced to file for Chapter 11, and why did two subsequently disappear?

Missed Opportunities

Why did IBM turn down the opportunity to acquire Xerox in its early days, saying the demand for photocopies was insufficient to warrant the investment?

Why did Xerox miss out on the personal computer revolution when they had so much invested in their Altos machine?

Why did Merrill Lynch fail to capitalize on their Cash Management Account Services?

Why did Compaq miss the opportunity of just-in-time personal computer assembly exploited by Dell?

The cognitive failures these companies experienced, Ms. Woodman believes, were not simply normal accidents, but fell into a fundamental pattern.

To see the impending threat or opportunity would have required the people in the organization positioned to take action, to challenge the assumptions or rules that had previously made their organization rich.

My hunch is that it wasn't just hard for these people to challenge the assumptions that had made their organizations rich. It simply wasn't possible—the beliefs of the people positioned to take action in these organizations limited the space of possibilities visible to them and prevented them from seeing what is now obvious. They were blind to any possibilities that challenged their organization's identity, beliefs and consequent view of the reality of the world. They weren't stupid or lazy, just blinded by their beliefs.[7]

The Peril of the Cognitive Failure

Champy's observation that businesses are made of ideas implies that business failures, by most conventional definitions, are *cognitive* failures, failures in dealing effectively with ideas. The way businesses organize can contribute substantially to their cognitive effectiveness. An organization, in this sense, always reflects fundamental concepts that shape it and influence its capacity for the creation of new ideas. If these ideas are flawed and are held on to because it's the way things have always been done, they become a negative influence and accelerate an organization's demise.

The reality is that cognitive failures are unavoidable, but the ability to adapt and change rapidly allows an organization to avoid the potential devastation of its occasional wrong thinking. What often happens, however, is that rather than having the courage to discard obsolete ways of thinking, organizations make these ideas sacrosanct. They are turned into *the truth* as a way of maintaining the system. In the name of maintaining security, organizations lose the ability to adapt cognitively. They close down the open boundaries of unlimited possibilities, deny the complexity and change that are integral parts of all living systems, and sanctify their old ways of doing business. This primary cognitive failure sounds the death knell for an organization. This is an unfortunate characteristic of individuals, but it is devastating in organizations, particularly large organizations.

General Foods thought it had a lock on the American coffee market, but Starbucks had a new way of thinking. The impact has meant billion-dollar swings for both organizations—Starbucks on the plus side, General Foods in the loss column. Sears thought it was invincible with its historic presence in American family life until Wal-Mart came up with a new way of thinking about the market. Wal-Mart now generates six times the profit of Sears. Getting stuck in old ways of thinking or applying outmoded abstractions about an industry or business can leave an organization unfit to survive.

Why are ideas and abstractions so important to an organization? First, let us define abstraction: It is the distilled essence of an idea, its heart, its raison d'être. To paraphrase the English philosopher and mathematician Alfred North Whitehead: We cannot think without abstractions; accordingly it is of the utmost importance to be vigilant in critically revising our modes of abstraction. This is essential to the healthy progress of any business. A business or industry that cannot burst through its current abstractions is doomed to sterility after a very limited burst of progress.

Peter Drucker, the noted business and leadership authority, concurs with Whitehead's statement: "The large organization has to learn to innovate, or it won't survive. . . . It also requires something that is most difficult for existing companies to do: abandon rather than defend yesterday."[8]

Many organizations have no process for questioning assumptions and beliefs and therefore suffer from their lack of innovation. Xerox PARC's John Seely Brown sees this questioning as an integral part of his job.

> I constantly question the assumptions and beliefs of the organization. One of my main roles is to set the stage for there being deep engagement in terms of what are those assumptions. Are they any longer valid? What are the trends and context that they are operating on? What is the limit to those trends and context? What would be different if those trends were followed out to their logical conclusion? What does this really mean for what we do?
>
> From that position we can then step back to really question if the things we are currently doing really make any sense. I think of our job, of course, in research, as opening up new frontiers. Then asking, "Is the frontier we are currently exploring basically a closed frontier?" Have the wars been won? Has the game been defined? We have no role to play in that game any longer because we can't change its rules. It is not where we get our high leverage.

Postmodern Management

Postmodern management emerged at the same time as postindustrialism, and is a way to question the assumptions that guided business thinking during the earlier Industrial Age, but that were no longer relevant in a postindustrial society. Complexity then became the description for the overall changes, from the mechanical thinking of industrial society to the nonlinear/organic thinking of postindustrial society, providing an understanding of both the nature of how we create what we know—our epistemology—and of practical conduct

This suggests, in historical context, that both postindustrial business and postmodern social changes were tied to a shift in our scientific knowledge away from physics and toward biology and the behaviors of organisms. In other words, according to science, our organizations could be based not on mechanistic models but on organic ones. In those organizations aware of this powerful shift, it initiated the questioning of their past beliefs and methodologies as they attempted to understand the behavior of social structures, individuals, and organizations. This was being done against the background of changing ideas and theoretical structures relating to the processes of organisms, which was in fact an attempt to create a new model of evolution—establishing, in effect, a whole new framework and foundation for the organization's behavior.

A process for organizations to utilize this postmodern method to question the assumptions and beliefs that mark the difference between mechanistic and organic characteristics of its business thinking can be found in Appendix 1. This is extremely important for business, because innovation can take place only when we challenge our static ideas.

Innovation doesn't simply appear because we will it to do so. It emerges out of our understanding of the way we know and learn—our epistemology. David Deutsch, in his book, the *Fabric of Reality*, says that epistemology is one of the four strands of explanation that make up what has come to be called the theory of everything. Why should business care? Because without a precise explanation of a problem, we can't solve it. Albert Einstein said, "The reciprocal relationship of epistemology and science is of a noteworthy kind. They are dependent upon each other. Epistemology without contact with science becomes an empty scheme. Science without epistemology is—insofar as it is thinkable at all—primitive and muddled."[9] This same statement could be rephrased for the business world: "Business without epistemology is—insofar as it is thinkable at all—primitive and muddled."

Challenging what an organization holds as sacrosanct—what its founding stories about itself (its *metanarratives*), what management thinks drives its business, and what it knows about the way it learns—must be a continual process. When an idea is obsolete, the organization must have the courage to discard it, even if it has been successful in the past. Closing a system to protect ideas because "they're what we've always done," is speeding down the Autobahn to cognitive failure.

Learning to Assess Current Conditions

Apple Computer made certain assumptions about its industry and marketplace, deciding to keep its operating system, which they believed was the best operating system on the market, proprietary. The decision was wrong. Closing the system and holding their better idea sacred, meant the company spent the next twenty years trying to make those early decisions come out right, or tried to find ways of compensating for them. The result: After twenty years, they're struggling because a wrong decision was made on the basis of flawed thinking, even though the decision was based on "knowledge" that had been successful in the past—maintaining a propietary system—and on an idea that really was better.

The lesson to be learned is that *past success does not account for current conditions.* It's the same in any industry or business. Knowledge is always promoted because in past experience it worked. Unfortunately, this rarely takes into account that conditions have changed.

In *The Guns of August,* Barbara Tuchman points out how the French generals planned to defeat Germany in the Franco Prussian War. They figured that there was not much difference between the two armies. Both were well trained, had the same equipment and the same tactics. The French would win because they had the greater *élan,* or spirit. Tuchman explained: "Her [France's] will to win, her élan would enable France to defeat her enemy. Her genius was in her spirit, the spirit of *la gloire* of 1792." It was not competence in battle, but *élan.* "How do we know that?" they might ask. "Because when we went into battle and won the revolution, we had the spirit to win. We've looked back over our past victories and we can see spirit is what makes the difference." Unfortunately, spirit did not carry the day. While the French charged off toward Berlin, following the shortest route possible, the Germans came around the back way through Flanders and took Paris.

In 1914, the French go to war again. Again the French assume both sides know the same things. But Germany says, "We know something they don't know." Germany invades France with artillery, firing against France's cavalry. The French soldiers are killed, élan and all, and the Germans aren't. Within a few months, the French discover that warfare has changed. It's not predictable or stable. They decide to modify their strategy because their old knowledge no longer works.

The French learn their lesson and change. France has learned something about the marketplace. In the 1930s, they think everyone fights the same: The secret is the concentration of firepower. They have the answer and create the Maginot Line in time for World War II. They place firepower on their entire German border. It's impenetrable. The next war starts and airplanes fly over the Maginot Line and around it. Warfare has changed again. Mobility is the key. Once again, the lesson is learned too slowly.

Sometimes, however, the lessons are not learned. When that happens, the natural process steps forward and systems die. The Soviet Union is an excellent example of a closed system locked into an outmoded vision of the world in which it functioned. It came into the Industrial Age late, and by the time the world was fully ensconced in the Postindustrial Age, it was too late for the Soviets in their closed system to make the adaptation. Why does this happen?

Complexity makes us continually aware of the answer to this question: We have failed to realize that conditions change, that the models we create don't necessarily hold up everywhere, in every instance, and—most important—that nothing is stable. One of the first things we learn in complexity thinking is that all complex adaptive systems are part of a situation in which everything is changing. Stability is only a brief transition.

Complex adaptive systems can remain competitive within this complex environment only if they develop the capacity to learn. Learning is nothing more than seeing and responding to changes and finding ways of leveraging those things that make a difference. If we can make minor adjustments at the leverage points, the changes can produce major impacts out there in the marketplace.

How do we determine these leverage points? We first have to get unstuck from our old ways of thinking. To do this requires an ability to adapt, innovate, and remain flexible, not only in what we do and how we do it, but in how we think, learn, teach, conceptualize, and formulate.

This is true of large organizations and small businesses alike. Unlike the Industrial Age corporate giants, the most successful Postindustrial/ Information Age businesses are often considerably smaller in staff and infrastructure. One reason for this development is that a smaller company has the ability to change direction rapidly. Bellcore's executive director, William Barr, likens this to the difference between large deep-sea creatures and the smaller life forms that live on a coral reef. The large deep-sea creatures take a great deal more effort and a much larger turning radius to change direction. They cannot react as swiftly to possibilities unless they come face to face with them. Coral-reef creatures are in a constant food chain cycle in which, if they cannot change direction quickly and adapt to a new situation, they're lunch.

However, when it comes to competitive innovation or the fact that business failures are cognitive, it makes no difference whether a company is of the deep-sea variety or the coral-reef. That 50 percent of all small businesses fail within the first year says more about the ideas or lack of ideas that foster those businesses than about competition, location, or their ability to move rapidly. It invariably goes back to the abstractions out of which they operate their business. Opening another dry cleaner just like the dry cleaner down the block, which is just like the dry cleaner next to it, "dooms them," as Whitehead's quote implied, "to sterility after a short burst of progress."

Questioning the ideas and being willing to change them when they no longer support the business strategy can create havoc in the most innovative companies. Hatim Tyabji, the CEO of Hewlett-Packard VeriFone, believes he is continually questioning conventional wisdom. "I expect to be challenged constantly," he says, "and I challenge people constantly." Does this create havoc in an organization? "I absolutely believe that it creates havoc. I think what it does, in fact, is, it creates a sense of tremendous excitement. It also creates, by the way, a sense of imbalance, because what works today, I just automatically say, will not work tomorrow. And so we will change. But I think that ability to change, that willingness to change, has really created the kind of people we are."

This process of change is obviously not without its risks or its resistances. Curt Lindberg, a senior consultant in complexity management for VHA, an organization of fifteen hundred nonprofit hospitals, believes that resistance is positive. "I view resistance as a good sign, like a barometer, that there are problems here. If there was no resistance to new ideas, my gut would tell me there is probably nothing new here, because it wasn't being challenged."

The Myth of Profit

One place in which resistance is always encountered is when the fundamental meanings of concepts change at times of major transition. The transitions from Agrarian Age to Industrial Age to Postindustrial Age thinking are hazy at best. In each of these transitions, fundamental business concepts like profit have undergone radical transformation, analogous to the changes that have occurred in the meanings of the fundamental concepts of science such as space, time, matter and energy. The same words continue to be used, but they have different meanings.

Agrarian society antedated preindustrial society and agrarian productivity preceded industrial productivity. Farms were replaced by factories. There is also little question that Agrarian and Industrial Age thinking still persists at the same time as Postindustrial/Information Age thinking and will continue into the Postinformation Age. The fact that these old ways of thinking continue to exist does not suggest that business can afford to organize around these outdated ideas as generative models. The answer is that business cannot. The world has become a very different place. There are different phenomena at work. That doesn't mean Agrarian and Industrial Age thinking will go away. Nor does it mean that some of those ways of thinking are not useful or relevant in today's business. They are and continue to be. In fact, it is necessary for characteristics of all ages to persist and endure, side by side with emerging new ideas. Historically that has always been the case. Einstein used exisiting language to describe his new ideas on relativity. But we must also recognize the significant change that has taken place, and the development of new ideas that follows.

One way to explain why these differences exist is to imagine the Agrarian, Industrial, and Postindustrial Ages as trajectories in time (see Figure 1). Visualizing this concept makes it evident that as one age moves off on its own trajectory from the others, the distance between them grows significantly. This doesn't mean that the ideas that led an age in a particular direction are less valid, only that if a new way of thinking prevails and we continue to follow older ideas, we could be led far afield very quickly.

One area in which Postindustrial Age thought is taking a radically different trajectory from Industrial Age precepts is the role of profit. The entire conceptual framework for profit in the market comes out of the Industrial Age. Unfortunately, it no longer provides an adequate theoretical basis for understanding postindustrial business.

Henry Ford commented in 1916, "I don't believe we should make such an awful profit on our cars. A reasonable profit is right but not too much. I hold that it is better to sell a large number of cars at a reasonable, small profit. I hold this because it enables a large number of people to buy and enjoy the use of a car and because it gives a large number of men employment at good wages."[10] In spite of his understanding of its limita-

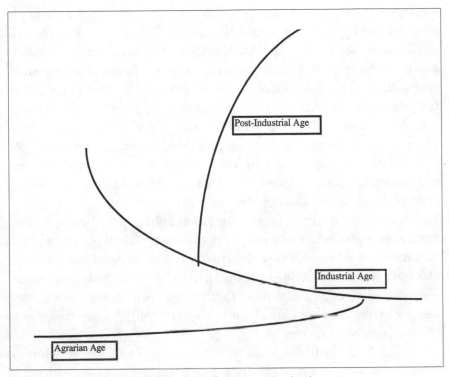

Figure 1. Epoch trajectories in time

tions, Ford was still driven by the concept of profit and had to make certain decisions that were profit-related to sales.

Why is profit no longer an adequate model for postindustrial business? Industrial Age thinking is a linear cause-and-effect model. Profit is a valuation of what the mechanism can grind out if it follows certain cause-and-effect activities. One can clearly delineate such things as the cost of production, the cost of distribution, the cost of marketing, and the cost of record keeping. A formula can be built from these out of which pricing structures can be calculated. The result is a mechanical model in which a business can predict and organize its activities around a differential that occurs. It labels this profit. There isn't any mystery to it. Within certain ranges a business can control its profit because it knows that if it can reduce this cost or increase that revenue, it can create mathematical models that will tell it the effect on profit. The investors can make certain profit-related decisions. The stock market reflects those decisions, and you have an Industrial Age economy and an Industrial Age thinking about business.

What has happened in today's market is that none of these linear segments can be formulated or related to each other with any kind of mechanistic type of assurance. Means do not fit ends. Certain actions can be taken that are causes of certain definable effects—they may not be predictable, but they are at least definable. Today, however, so many variables enter into any stage in a mechanistic process that a business can no longer deal with them fundamentally as a linear process. This doesn't mean that the process has no linear characteristics, but that a company has to disengage from them because the Industrial Age model doesn't always work. Colin Crook, Citicorp's former senior technology officer, has said, "We can't function that way any longer at Citicorp. We can't even make five-day models, let alone five-year plans." The Industrial Age way of thinking, by itself, is not pragmatically useful anymore.

Profit, in today's business climate, needs to be approached as nothing more than one of many different ways to measure a company's progress. This notion would have made no sense to Industrial Age thinkers. Profit was not a way of measuring something; it was the source of measuring. It was what all of the measurements that go into the planning and strategy-making process were aiming toward. It was the only meaningful way to assess a company's success.

In the Postindustrial Age, however, this vision needs to be reformulated. Jay Keyworth, President Reagan's science adviser and a member of the board of directors of Hewlett-Packard, was one of David Packard's closest advisers. Keyworth recalled a pivotal conversation he had with Packard that influenced Keyworth greatly. Packard said, "We measure the excellence of business by profit. Profit is the privilege the customer lets you take away for providing your service—high privilege/high service. *Profit is the measure, not the reason, for business.* The reason you do business with a customer is to give the customer something he doesn't have."

However, as the uncertainty principle of German physicist, Werner Heisenberg (1901–1976) has shown us, in order for anything to be measured, the system has to be stopped. When we ascertain position or velocity in space/time, position and velocity become frozen points that cannot be measured simultaneously. We can know either an object's position or its velocity, but only at a specific point. From this perspective, profit isn't about taking a look at an emerging system, it's about a frozen system that is no longer pragmatically efficacious. As we will see in the chapter "Demystifying Complexity," new diagnostic tools are required within complex systems, because the precision of those used in mechanistic systems are not adequate to address an organization that is not driven by traditional measurements.

The major problem with closed, frozen systems, exemplified by companies driven only by profit, is that they are incapable of changing and adapting. They can accommodate themselves to the lack of adaptation within their own system by adjusting operations to deliver profit despite other failings. However, as soon as unanticipated changes enter the picture, the system is put in grave danger because the frozen company cannot react.

In Industrial Age, closed-system thinking, the answer to the question Why do we start a business? is simple. It's to make a profit. But why start a postindustrial business? Here the thinking becomes blurred and muddied. Business still has more than 50 percent of its energy and experience rooted in Industrial Age thought. It cannot give up the fundamental notion of profit any more than it can give up a lot of other behaviors and rules that lock it into the Industrial Age. We can only point to where the formulation might be found. In postindustrial society, business can no longer be treated as an isolated system that does not coevolve and interact with all of the other ongoing systems of the society. The meaningful question—it may be the only question that can be asked of any business in terms of the possible existence of that business in society—is, What does that business contribute, and what is the form of the contribution to the social system as a whole? The function of business is to contribute goods and services to society and to find ways of constantly improving the value of those goods and services. The frame of reference is not the customer or profit. The theoretical model for Industrial Age business was to find out what the customer wanted. In the Postindustrial Age, a business frequently designs products and services without initial concern as to whether this is what people want or whether there is even a market for those things.

Jay Keyworth's company, Encanto, is producing an add-on module for personal computers that will provide users with a personal web site, a direct connection, not one provided by a server. Why do I need a personal web site? Keyworth says it could serve anyone from grandmothers with grandchildren living at both ends of the country, and SOHOs (small offices/home offices). No one asked for this add-on, but Encanto's business is creating quite a stir without the aid of a focus group to divine customer desires.

The professionals who run focus groups may not like the sound of this, but their statistical approach to what a customer may want is not appropriate for today's market. Everything that is rooted in that way of thinking is tied to the status quo, to producing orthodox novelty. It makes no sense to ask customers, "What do you think about a fax machine?" if they don't have the vaguest idea what a fax machine is. Even when a description is provided, a customer can't see the use. This was evident with the introduction of Sony's Walkman and with personal computers, too. It was probably also true for many of the items on the list of ideas made possible by Einstein's ideas. The notion is very subtle, but in today's business market ideas don't develop because of customer demand.

Is this deemphasis on profit some kind of communist plot to undermine the capitalist system? Hardly. It may come as good news to the reader that socialism and Marxism also represent the kind of dead-end thinking of industrial society that has little pragmatic relevance to postindustrial society. As mentioned earlier, this is the ultimate reason the Soviet system broke down. All of its thinking was modeled on the Industrial Age. By the time it was able to wake up and recognize the world had changed and entered the postindustrial period, all the theories and models it had held on to had broken down. Though this breakdown was never alluded to in the media, the Soviet collapse was ultimately a dissolution at the level of theory. The ratio of the country's information to its infrastructure was completely off.

Within its closed society, the Soviet Union did everything it could to keep information out. Ironically, the ultimate result was that Communist walls came tumbling down all over Eastern Europe. And in a dramatic example of a frozen system that could no longer remain closed, even the mother source, the Soviet Union, dissolved.

We see evidence of other crumbling walls in an article in the *Washington Post* called, "Franchisees Unite to Fight for Their Lives—Judgments Against Parent Companies Tip Balance of Power."[11] This article refers to franchise companies like Little Caesar Enterprises, Seven Eleven stores, American Corp., Dairy Queen, and Meineke Discount Muffler Shops, Inc. Franchise business accounts for over 40 percent of the American economy. The article gives a great deal of attention to Mail Boxes Etc., which had just paid $5 million in cash, and an undisclosed amount of stock, in an out-of-court settlement with thirty-three ex-franchisees. These disgruntled ex-owners alleged that the company had vastly overstated their chances of success. Overstating the probabilities of a franchisee's success is a pretty vague crime for a $5 million settlement. How does a company even quantify success?

The judgment against Mail Boxes Etc. is within the framework of what we call information. The franchisees weren't saying to the courts, " Mail Boxes Etc. failed us because they didn't have a large enough organization. They didn't have the right stores or locations." There was nothing wrong with Mail Boxes Etc.'s infrastructure. They suffered a failure of information. They didn't succeed in providing the franchisees the information necessary for them to understand the business possibilities they were getting into, nor did the company engage in the processes that would enable some continuity of franchisee success. This was, ultimately, an information indictment.

The courts said the franchisees were victims of a system that was outmoded and that they had been damaged by that system. They couldn't place their finger on why it was outmoded, but the courts awarded the judgment because the franchisor didn't understand its system well enough to know that it had been reversing the ratio of information to infrastructure. That reversal did damage to the franchisees, and Mail Boxes Etc. paid for their information failure.

Had Mail Boxes Etc. questioned the assumptions of its business with formulations like: "On the basis of everything we know to date . . . What do we think we can accomplish? What are the directions of the industry? What can we reasonably expect our franchisees to earn?" They might have averted the settlement situation. Unfortunately, they were not thinking of their business on the deeper level of abstraction out of which their organization needed to operate. The shallowness of their ideas directly shaped the behavior of the business. Since they were concerned only with questions of profit, focusing on what they could do to increase revenues, profit, and market share, the real value questions were obscured and lost. The result was a frozen system in which there was little or no information flow and innovation, and consequently, little or no growth.

In the chapter that follows we develop the organizational core strategies that drive postindustrial business and that are the source of emergent ideas and novelty: the interactions between principles, models, rules, and behaviors. Prior to that, however, we will offer an example of what we are calling "a nonlinear investigation." A different question-based nonlinear investigation will follow each chapter. Nonlinear Investigations are designed to provide a starting point for the recognition of nonlinear patterns within an organization. They offer a frame of reference for an individual or organization as a prelude to the formulation and analysis of any proposed strategy in relation to its potential applications. They are meant to open the inquiry in both continuity and novelty, to take account of both the necessary and the possible, and to allow for emergence of successful adaptive behaviors.

NONLINEAR INVESTIGATION NO. 1:
BARRIERS TO INNOVATION

*I am not of the opinion that there exists an essential difference between
concepts and methods in the fields of "common sense" and science. . . . The
whole of science is nothing more than a refinement
of everyday thinking.*   •   Albert Einstein

If, to use Champy's language, businesses are made of ideas—ideas
expressed as words—then the critical barrier to innovation is
stuckness in inadequate ideas and/or formulations. This investigation is simply a process of asking critical questions about your
company's ideas and their formulations.

The process will reveal the source of many of your ideas and
will enable you to discard those that are no longer useful and
have become barriers to innovation. Here are some questions.
You may think of others.

1. To what extent are our practices tied to conditions or circumstances that have altered? To what extent are they taken for
   granted as habits? How would our company know if conditions or circumstances had changed, if the changes had been
   gradual over time?

2. To what extent do our ideas and formulations reflect prevailing fads in business thinking? How can we distinguish such
   fads from authentic ideas?

3. What beliefs in our company are not open to question? How
   has this happened?

4. What do words like *purpose, vision,* and *paradigm* mean in our
   organization?

5. To what extent does our company look for someone to blame
   when something goes wrong? How is this blame expressed?

6. To what extent does our company have to be certain of outcomes before making changes? What are the tests of such certainty?

7. To what extent do we honor an idea according to who in the company has the idea?

Principles, Models,
Rules, and Behaviors

You cannot think without abstractions; accordingly, it is of the utmost importance to be vigilant in critically revising your modes of abstraction. It is here that philosophy finds its healthy niche as essential to the healthy progress of society. It is the critique of abstractions. A civilization which cannot burst through its current abstractions is doomed to sterility after a very limited burst of progress. • Alfred North Whitehead

In order to assess the cognitive framework of an organization, we need to understand the interactions of four fundamental elements contained in every business: its principles, models, rules, and behaviors. Looking at these dynamic structures can give us a clear picture of the way our organizations are structured and the ways they interact. We can then take the steps necessary to sustain change and break the cycle of persistence that is a constant restraint to real innovation.

S outhwest Airlines takes off and flies as one of the most successful air-lines in the skies. They do so by operating under a simple principle: Run a low-cost, low-price airline where the savings are passed on to the customer. This principle is the source of ideas that allow the formation of the models necessary to run Southwest's business. The models that emerge are a reservation system that is simple, no seat assignments, air-port check-in with a reusable boarding pass that facilitates the airline's unreserved seating policy; a no-frills approach to food; maximum utiliza-tion of crews and equipment that emphasizes quick gate turnaround. These models, in turn, influence the behavior of both the employee and the customer. Lacking seat assignments, customers realize that if they have a seat preference they have to show up early to be one of the first 30 passengers on board. Rules are then established that Southwest will pass out seat groupings one hour before boarding. Baggage transfers to other airlines are limited. In order to have a quick gate turnaround employee behaviors are such that they all work together, cleaning the planes, check-ing people in, and getting passengers seated. By not having frills, flight attendant efforts are directed toward seeing to the customers in a way that relaxes the perception of strict aviation rules. They wear shorts and polo shirts in warm weather; the model influencing this behavior is that mak-ing travel fun encourages humor and puts the flying public at ease. Relaxed passengers means fewer human behavioral problems with only nature's turbulence rocking the flight.

Volkswagen is an example of a company whose principle was sound but that was unable to sustain its success. The principle was "the people's car." Volkswagen had locked themselves into an unchanging "Beetle" look, based on this principle. Their theoretical model was that the people's car was very simple, with low frills, and economical. With the initial suc-cess of the Beetle, they locked things down and closed the system. Along come the Japanese, who figured out simply how to shrink the big car, pro-viding more comfort for less money. Volkswagen couldn't let go of their past success and were quickly and more comfortably being passed by the Toyotas and Hondas on the road.

How we assess and relate to the ideas and abstractions out of which we make the decisions that run our organizations is critical to our success. It is how we build the appropriate logics and communicate ideas so that certain conclusions can be drawn and actions taken that, as Einstein sug-gests, are neither confused nor muddled. If Champy is correct, that busi-nesses are ideas, then we need a way of effectively formulating those ideas and addressing the way people relate to one another. As a vehicle for doing so, this chapter unlocks the distinctions between principles, models, rules, and behaviors. Recognizing the relationships between these distinctions lets an organization open up a very powerful method for questioning what it holds sacrosanct. It also allows itself the opportunity to define, diagnose the source of, and solve problems.

As we will demonstrate, whenever we misunderstand the proper relationships among principles, models, rules, and behaviors, mistaken directions that inevitably fail can emerge.

Before we can describe those relationships, however, we must first define our concepts. Once we understand the nature of these fundamental ideas, we can describe their pragmatic relationships.

What follows, then, is a discussion of ideas, not things. We will attempt to ground these ideas whenever possible in examples. By their nature, however, abstractions are essences, nuggets of ore that are not easily seen by those untrained to locate them. When we view them individually, we can usually identify them. The difficulty in distinguishing them arises when they begin to interact with each other. Why is it important to understand these often challenging ideas? Because they drive the ways our organizations fundamentally operate. They are the basis for *everything* that takes place within our organizations. And when accessed properly, they provide the only source of innovation available to sustain our organizations' very existence.

In *If Aristotle Ran General Motors,* Tom Morris describes how the keys to sustainable corporate excellence follow from four foundations or dimensions that are based on Greek thought of twenty-five hundred years ago: truth, beauty, goodness, and unity which correlate with intellectual, aesthetic, moral, and spiritual virtues. Aristotle contended that existence was possible only when all four of these were part of the mix. The word *cosmos,* which for us refers to the universe as a whole, originally meant "beautiful order." We feel, however, that Morris may have misjudged Aristotle. If Aristotle were alive today, he would probably take these four notions out of their ancient context and reword them as principles, models, rules, and behaviors.

Principles

Principles refer to the most abstract level at which we can speak about a company and still make sense. Principles are not meant to be descriptions of anything. It is a misuse of this abstract level to expect them to provide scenarios, specificities, or quantities. Principles offer a way of discovering how far back we can meaningfully push our inquiries into what we are doing. Through that activity, we can understand and formulate the ideas that run our business. It is important to realize, too, that if we were to violate the principles upon which our business operates, we would either fail or become something else. Principles are fundamental to the character and nature of what we are doing. They help us recognize that whatever we're doing makes sense to us in a certain way.

A fundamental example of a principle that would hold for most of today's postindustrial businesses is that they must be able to maintain a high ratio of information to infrastructure. As we will explain later, in many of today's businesses, when the ratio gets too low there are serious problems, and the businesses can fail.

Reformulations of principles are always tautologies. They are just different ways of repeating the same fundamental idea. It is not very productive for an organization to spend a lot of time thinking about its principles, because they don't change. They are simply reiterating and reasserting for our common understanding what will enable us to do well. Since they are tautologies, if we try to pick them apart, analyze them, restructure them, we will never get outside the framework of that tautology. One of Hewlett-Packard's principles is to "satisfy our customers." Any way this principle is stated will say the same thing. The place where formulation and change occur is in how H-P is going to be directed by its prinicples—at the level of model. This does not mean that principles can be ignored. To the extent that we lose sight of the principles that drive our ideas, we are in trouble.

Models

Models or theories are what we construct on the basis of principles. When we say that ideas drive our models, we are describing a situation in which we build things in the likeness of our principles. Humans were created in the likeness of God. Southwest Airlines was created in the likeness of a low-cost, low-price airline. Models are the structures and concepts undergirding the complex adaptive system we call a business. Because they provide form to our ideas, they continually intersect the range of adjacent possibilities. If principles are ultimate abstractions, models are abstractions in action. And, as we will demonstrate, it is in relationship to models and theories that behaviors are defined and all innovation takes place.

This is why ideas are so critical to doing business. If our ideas generated by our principles are wrong, the models we build based on them will be faulty, too. In addition, we must also understand that our models, since they are only likenesses, are ultimately flawed. Models are only as good, effective, or accurate as the available feedback and the feedback generated. For example, in a traditional command and control operation in which a CEO is making all the decisions, he might surround himself with yes-men who merely echo his ideas. In this situation, the accuracy of the organization's models would be suspect because the available feedback would not be very good. In this or in other less controlling atmospheres, we might improve available feedback with a new computer system that provides a higher level of feedback that was not previously available. Or improving the efficiency of some of our models may have to wait, because the level of feedback necessary to improve them has yet to be conceived.

Rules

Rules are temporary, approximate ways of adapting to very local conditions. They do not define the system. Their only function is to guide how the system behaves or operates in relation to certain kinds of changing conditions and circumstances. They are the ways we operate models. The sole reason for a rule's existence is pragmatic. If rules work, keep them. If they don't work, drop them. Work usually has a very precise definition that underlies why we formulate that rule at all, so rules need to be designed to provide an initial level of comfort and structure while someone is becoming familiar with a way of doing things. We have very specific rules regarding the operation of machinery so that people are not injured. We don't want people running machines when their senses are impaired. Less specific rules govern how we behave in our homes. The important factor about rules is that they are not fixed and unchanging. As will become evident, locking into rules as a method of operation freezes the possible and eliminates real innovation.

Behaviors

Behaviors are what the people in the organization actually do in the performance of their activities and work, in the execution of their models. The question is, How is that behavior generated? It appears to be generated by a person's simply learning the rules, but in reality, paradoxically, it does not. To understand behaviors, we must return to models. The relationship of each individual agent within an organization to every other agent within that organization is influenced by the models that make up the business. What makes a model or theory work is that it is constantly being modified in relationship to the behaviors it informs. It is what we call a recursive relationship, feeding back and forth between the two aspects. If we want to make the likeness of the principle of a low-cost, low-price airline work, to approach the ideal, we must be continually adjusting that likeness, modifying and shaping it in relationship with our behaviors. This is what we call productive behavior. We cannot reduce that adjusting process to the domain of rules, because rules are in place to tell us how to make the *previous* likeness of our ideal work, not to develop a new likeness. If our behaviors are to construct a new and better likeness, they cannot be limited by old rules that no longer relate to the new likeness. Models have a core of intelligibility, but only when that intelligibility is expanded and understood through our behaviors is productivity possible. To complete the recursive circle, behaviors then provide feedback, informing and reforming the model. The implication is that through their actions, everyone in the organization is ultimately responsible for the appearance of the organization.

Abstractions in Interaction

As we have suggested, in complexity thinking understanding each individual aspect of a complex adaptive system does not provide an awareness of the possibilities and innovation that arise through their interaction. To make the principle-model-rule-behavior process work, an organization must first understand what it holds sacred, then fling open the doors of the altar that holds it, and free what is presumed sacred to interact with the pragmatic world. Whitehead said, "A civilization which cannot burst through its current abstractions is doomed to sterility after a very limited burst of progress." If the word *business* is substitued for *civilization*, this statement takes on more immediate significance.

Whitehead is saying that we must recognize that our sacred truths, the essences of our businesses, are temporal. They bear fruit, wither, and die. They are not perennials or recyclable. They must be constantly replaced. In addition, there are different levels of abstraction within our organizations, and these call for radically different kinds of formulations.

As previously mentioned, Einstein said that we can't solve a problem within the frame of reference that created it. If the problem lies within the frame of reference of rules, no matter how much we juggle the rules, we are not going to understand the problem, much less solve it. But if we were able to step outside those rules and look at the model they support, then perhaps from that perspective we could deal with the problem in a different way that was not previously accessible.

A Context for Assessing Principles, Models, Rules, and Behaviors

Within the context of the organization, these four elements determine how the organization is structured and how it acts. The smallest event (an interaction between two people) that takes place in an organization does so in reference to some models, rules, and principles. This interaction must be consistent with the larger organization and its relationship to the other elements. This is demonstrated in Figure 2A.

In this example, the company's models have dual functions. They provide a means to structure and organize the business, and a method for decision making and prediction. The models are consistent with the principles of the company, and support the framework for the rules and behaviors of its employees. By understanding these relationships, an organization can begin to explain why things happen the way they do. Once this takes place, an organization can better align its fundamental principles with its operations.

Like the embedded structures found in all complex adaptive systems, principles, models, rules and behaviors are mirrored and embedded at each level of the organization as shown in Figure 2B.

Problems in operations, at the lowest level or smallest scale, can always be traced to a misalignment among some of these elements. Some interactions among principles, models, rules, and behaviors work well together, and some don't. *Rule-generated behavior doesn't work.* The test is purely pragmatic. Rules are designed to limit behaviors. When behaviors are limited, they cannot interact freely with models to produce new likenesses of the organization's ideal, and sterility ensues. The only behaviors

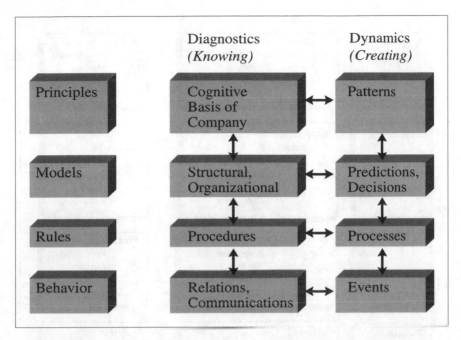

	Diagnostics *(Knowing)*	Dynamics *(Creating)*
Principles	Cognitive Basis of Company	Patterns
Models	Structural, Organizational	Predictions, Decisions
Rules	Procedures	Processes
Behavior	Relations, Communications	Events

Figure 2A.   Strategic diagnostics and dynamics (© 1998 by Santa Fe
Center for Emergent Strategies)

that produce pragmatically acceptable results are those that are generated out of theories or models, not those generated by rules. This concept is critical to an organization's ability to adapt and change.

Rules bind us to old models. This is why within many organizations we find that informal organizations do most of the innovative work. These organizations, sometimes referred to as "shadow" organizations, exist as a way of circumventing the outmoded rules of the formal organization.

Behaviors directly generated by principles don't work either. Principles are simply the source of ideas to formulate models. Principle-generated behaviors don't work because behaviors are people-based and therefore rely on relationships. Principles are not things or descriptions of things. We cannot interact with them. Models, on the other hand, provide the structure for relationships and the feedback they require to remain viable. Thus rules must be model-based.

How do models and theories generate meaningful changes and behaviors? The answer is counterintuitive and consequently it is one of

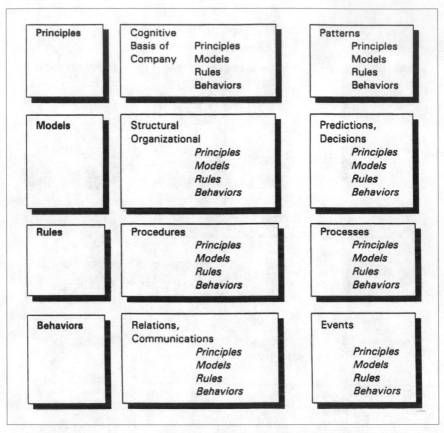

Figure 2B.   The next level of diagnostics and dynamics (© 1998 by
Santa Fe Center for Emergent Strategies)

the most challenging ideas we will present in this book. It is also one of
the most important to the successful operation of a business. Einstein said,
"A theory can be tested by experience, but there is no way from experience to the setting up of a theory." In other words, *experience never results
in theories.* This idea is one that businesses will resist most. But even leaders of countries are beginning to understand this. Vaclav Havel, the president of the Czech Republic, made a similar point in a speech to the U.S.
Congress. He said, "Consciousness precedes being, and not the other way
around, as Marxists claim. . . . Without a global revolution in the sphere
of human consciousness, nothing will change for the better in the sphere
of our Being."[1]

We constantly attempt to build models of the way things are on the basis of what we have done previously. We forget the message stated in the previous chapter: Past success does not take into account current conditions. While behaviors are based in part on experience, theories and models exist outside experience. Their creation requires in us an ability to conceptualize the adjacent possibilities, which by their very nature have yet to be experienced. We will discuss this extremely important concept in greater detail in the chapter "Real-World Applications for Coevolving Metaphors." For now, understanding the significance of the relationship between models or theories and behaviors will suffice.

How do these distinctions and interactions among principles, models, rules, and behaviors relate to how we run our organizations? In his 1958 book, *Personal Knowledge: Toward a Post-Critical Philosophy,* Michael Polanyi states, "Evolution, like life itself . . . originated by the action of an ordering principle, an action released by random fluctuations and sustained by fortunate environmental conditions. . . . Once a flame has been started, its shape and chemical composition can vary without extinguishing it. To this extent, its identity is not defined by its physical or chemical topography, but by the operational principles which sustain it."[2]

When principles go out of existence, the system that is a derivative of them also goes out of existence. It may cease to be what it is and become something else, but this is *not* the system changing, it is the old system going away and a new system coming into existence. That is a major difference. The business implications are very great.

Michael Dertouzos said in his 1997 book, *What Will Be,* "The AT&T divestiture caused it to get out of the computer business, which in turn prompted IBM to exit the communications business. At a deeper level, the reason the early ventures, and similar ones in Europe, failed was because they jumped into areas where they had no core business experience and aspired to offer everything. . . . Companies in the 1990s stand to waste a great deal of money pursuing the same folly."

Implicit in what he is saying is that AT&T should stick with adjacent possibilities and not forsake its principles. It cannot be successful at something other than its core business, and to the extent that it tries to do so, it is going to destroy itself. Collins and Porras in their book, *Built to Last,* also believe this to be true. They found that in the companies that lasted, "Executives did not set new core values and purpose; they discovered a core that they already had in common, but that had been obscured by misalignments and lack of dialogue." AT&T might decide they don't want to be AT&T anymore, that they want to be something else—which is fine, but if they try to be that something else as AT&T, it is just not going to work. This can be demonstrated in one industry after another, as when Eastman Kodak ventured into the pharmaceutical industry with catostrophic results. It just doesn't succeed.

When it comes to mergers and acquisitions, a company can buy a business outside its core strategy, if the company understands that the acquired business must continue to be that business. It may become a profit center within the larger entity, but the acquirer is not going to make it into something other than what it is.

Midas International Corporation, known primarily for its muffler shops, acquired a number of travel trailer companies in the 1960s. They allowed each one to operate autonomously within its own existing management structure, rather than attemptimg to integrate them into the existing Midas franchise culture, and they did so successfully. To this day, many people have no idea that Midas was ever in this business.

Once an organization is taken out of its principle base, the models and the theories don't hold up because there are no longer any core ideas upon which to base them.

Understanding the Impact of Information and Infrastructure

A critical factor in organizing and understanding the ideas that drive a business—the interactions among its principles, models, rules, and behaviors—is establishing the proper ratio of information to infrastructure. We discuss how an organization can establish this ratio in the chapter "Ideas Are the Geometries of Behaviors," for now the knowledge of the existence of this relationship is all that is required. As mentioned earlier, information does not refer solely to the transfer of facts. It is also tied to an understanding of *how* we know. It has always been assumed that information was not about something such as purpose, values, or usage. Information conveyed what was presumed to be matters of fact about something other than itself: "The ball is red," not "The information about the ball is red." The framework for this way of thinking was that there is a subject and an object, or the observer and the observed. In this view, information could be true or false or accurate or inaccurate. The focus was on the content of the information not on its formulation.

The shift that has occurred in complexity thinking moves us outside the subject-and-object domain. The frame of reference is not the relationship of the presumed facts, but the formulation itself. Now the assumption is that we are not so much communicating facts as *informing*. We are communicating *interpretations*. Our formulation is our way of putting it together.

Today, information has more the character of a pattern, conveying a whole picture, rather than the components of a pattern. The assumption is that only from the pattern can we infer or interpret or formulate what we call facts or the discrete data relating to a situation. This process eliminates the distinction between the subject and the object. The presumption has been that anything that may be referred to has some independent, objectively verifiable status apart from the way it is formulated. According to Einstein and others, it does not. This represents a radical shift from a linear way of thinking to a nonlinear one.

When we eliminate the distinction between subject and object, we return to something akin to the dialectical model mentioned earlier, which joins, for example, thesis and antithesis, in which being and non-being synthesize into becoming. It's not one or the other. It's both.

That doesn't mean that we can't make a distinction and focus attention on one part or the other. When we come up with a principle for business, the ratio of information to infrastructure is critical. This means that if we block or limit the process of patterning and formulation (innovation) by closing our systems with an increase in unnecessary infrastructure, we get stuck repeating the same patterns and formulations over again. The pragmatic consequence of that is stagnation and/or dissolution.

Infrastructure is not only physical, but can also be mental. We see this when we construct interior walls based on such things as preconceived ideas. For example, an idea in relation to a rule can take the form of infrastructure when the rule drives the idea. There is no opportunity for change. The behaviors simply repeat themselves since they cannot get beyond the mental construct. Rules, here, are the counterpart of physical infrastructures. Unless they can be continually informed by way of a new model or theory, there is no basis for change. The rules don't change in and of themselves. They change when there is an expansion of a model or a theory that generates other rules.

For innovation and emergence to be fully realized, the infrastructure mustn't get in the way of the emergence. We need to look at those places where we are stuck, whether we are locked in by the walls we build, by the roads that lead to our businesses, or by the sacredness of our ideas that we can't get beyond.

Neither rules nor physical infrastructure has any inclination or capacity to change themselves. When we drive to work, we go the same route as if in a groove. We keep repeating the route over and over again. That road will also remain there forever, until some idea that represents a different way is brought into play. We close that road or build a new road or design a new system. Left to its own devices, that road is always going to be the path one takes to work. In the same way, rules do not change themselves. They simply define the ways operations occur. Those rules will remain the same unless informed by that which is not itself a rule or certainly not wholly a rule.

It takes a tremendous amount of effort to change the infrastructure. For example, to build a new road we must start with a new idea, which initiates planning and design. Once approval has been gained, there is the application of the physical aspects, the people, machines, and the asphalt. There is also the residual mental infrastructure that remains in the people who now must take a new route to work and forsake the old. We see this very clearly when we attempt to change our organizations. *Changing mental and physical infrastructure, once it has been rutted and frozen, is extremely difficult.*

Innovative Interactions

As stated earlier, the source of innovation and change does not exist in the rules or principles, but rather in the models, which includes the theories, formulations, and metaphors we create. Principles and rules are locked in place, and no innovation can occur from interactions with them. The cycling that occurs between rules and behaviors is simply repetitive. Behaviors can't change the rules, and the rules can't change the behaviors. The only source of change is an expanded formulation or theory or model or metaphor which then calls for different rules.

We see evidence of getting stuck in rules in the conflicts that have continued to exist throughout the world for hundreds of years. This "stuckness" is so pervasive that an American sees what is happening in

Yugoslavia and wonders how these behaviors can be so mechanical. The behaviors have become ingrained by the rules they have imposed on themselves in relation to their adversaries. Why don't they change? They can't get out of the cycling between rules and behaviors.

That does not mean that people cannot change their personal infrastructures, but it does take a willingness to break through those frozen preconceptions. It also takes a powerful new model that can transcend the cycling relationship of rules and behaviors. If that transcendence doesn't occur, people become locked in, and coevolution—the interactive, developmental effects that entities in relationship have on one another—cannot occur. This reinforces the idea that the generative source of emergence is in the domain of model, theory, metaphor, and formulation. Models are the source of the success or failure of every enterprise, because models are ideas in action.

To get outside the repetitive cycling between rules and behaviors, which resist change and hinder new possibilities, we have to reach an understanding generated by principles and formed within model and theory that does not exist anywhere else. Our ability to model and model again, not simply renewing the old model but creating something anew, is that point where emergence and innovation happen.

That emergence happens is one of the principles of our universe. Can we prod emergence and innovation? Can we do anything to help bring them about? Does the capacity for innovation almost presuppose actual innovation in some way? We may not be able to force innovation and emergence, but we may as complex adaptive systems be able to prepare the environment for their arrival. Then, when it does happen we are able to respond and integrate the emergence into our systems so that we can either flourish because of it or adapt to it in a way that doesn't destroy us.

A Sustainable Model for Inconceivable Development

From our principle of emergence, which states that what is possible at this moment is possible only because of the last level of possibilities that have emerged (the adjacent possible), we can build a model that prepares the ground for both sustainable and inconceivable development. Like all successful models, it is simple, with three basic components; with practice they become almost automatic.

When emergence happens, it changes our understanding of our system and the models we have devised for it. We must respond as follows:

1. Step 1 is to adjust our models on the basis of a new understanding, that has been initiated by the emergence or innovation of a new possibility.

2. Step 2 is to adjust our relationships, our behavior and rules, according to our new understanding of our model.

3. Step 3 is that something new emerges, because something always occurs whenever there is an interaction between model and behavior, once we have taken the first two steps.

4. Step 4 is to go back and readjust our models on the basis of this new emergence.

5. Step 5 is to adjust our relationships on the basis of our new model.

6. Step 6 is that emergence happens within the interaction.

7. Step 7 is that we return to our models, adjusting them according to our new understanding.

8. Step 8 is that we adjust our relationships again.

9. Step 9 is that emergence happens.

10. Step 10 is that the process continues.

    Here is an example.

- Step 1, The Apollo Corporation is a ficticious manufacturing company that has operated successfully in an Industrial Age mode for the past 50 years, but has recently seen markets and manufacturing practices passing them by. The new CEO, brought in to turn things around, comes to the understanding that Apollo has closed its systems and needs to open them.

- Step 2, In a meeting with his direct reports, the CEO lets it be known in order to open their systems the organization must adjust its relationships to its employees according to this new understanding. The

CEO realizes that building trust requires first taking a small step: Management will seek written feedback from their employees on a new vision for the company. This requires them to break certain rules about employees' time away from their operations.

- Step 3, in addition to the written feedback on the new vision, something unexpected emerges, an opportunity to build respect between management and employees. Management had never considered that their employees had ever given the operations of the company much thought.

- Step 4, management realizes they've opened the door successfully, and they decide to open it further. They seek the help of their workforce to craft a new distribution strategy.

- Step 5, they present their request for input to the employees in a series of open forums. The hierarchy of job levels is ignored and everyone has equal input.

- Step 6, the exchange in the forums is lively, and a completely unanticipated strategy emerges, one based on just-in-time deliveries. Management agrees to redesign factory operations into more of a flow. In addition, an employee-management council is established.

- Step 7, in light of the new council meeting, the organization decides to realign its departments cross-functionally to improve communication and efficiency.

- Step 8, cross-functional meetings take place to redesign compensation and work responsibilities and to eliminate job designations. All employees are now operation associates.

- Step 9, the new alignment increases throughput operations and quality of product and quality of life in the organization. Increased satisfaction with jobs and job performance give rise to an innovative product development coming from the factory floor.

- Step 10, the process continues, as does continued development.

When adjustments are made after each emergent possibility arises, what we see after the second or third emergence is a development that would have been absolutely inconceivable from the perspective of our

standing. Our tendency, however, is to stop the process after
second emergence and close the system back down to protect
the fabulous innovation that has come about. The key to sustaining the
development process is the continual adjustment of model and behaviors
and rules—of relationships. As soon as we freeze the model, and, subsequently, our relationship to behaviors, we return to orthodox novelty.
Emergent novelty is possible only when the system is open to the adjacent possible. Here, what was once inconceivable becomes actualized.
Organizations that fear there isn't time to sit with the complex interactions and allow emergence to happen need to address more closely the
work unleashed by the previous emergence. That work fertilizes the
ground for the next emergence.

Sustaining Sustainability

In some organizations the mere act of sustaining any activity beyond an
initial level of introduction would be a major accomplishment. Many people, it seems, would rather persist in their tried and true experiences than
venture continually into the new or inconceivable. Performing the same
old same old is what we call the cycle of persistence. This persistence
should not be confused with perseverance. Persistence is getting stuck.
Perseverance is continually moving forward. How can an organization
break this cycle of persistence and create real sustainability?

Multiple Strategies and the Sustainable Model

Motivating and sustaining inconceivable development is a matter of
encouraging growth, not fostering extinction. The jungle grows when a
multitude of species drop their seeds and spores and they are provided an
opportunity to grow. Because of these environmental conditions, some
seedlings succeed, some do not. By giving what Mike Simmons refers to
as "multiple strategies" the chance to germinate and take root or naturally
die on their own in our organizations, we eliminate the need for sugges-
tion committees—and suggestion-rejection committees.

One avenue an organization might use to encourage growth could be
to start a so-called "seedling fund," a concept based on the notions of Dr.
Charles Smith, whereby individuals/groups acquire value by participating
in the growth, development, and success of other individuals'/groups'

organizational ideas. Successful idea implementations provide greater return to the individual's own seedling account. Unsuccessful ideas generate bankable value for the participants, though not as great as if the idea succeeded. The intrapreneur of an unsuccessful idea implementation does not lose, get fired, etc. He or she simply goes to work for others to regain value before being able to implement an idea again.

Participants can either invest their seedling fund returns into ideas of their own, or if a person/group does not have an idea of his/her/its own that they wish to grow, they can invest their funds in another's project. They can also participate in the project in which they invest, thereby gaining more value for their account and reaping the benefits that may come from their partner's seedling operation. In addition, an intrapreneur can seek seedling funds from coworkers to invest in his/her idea. The sustaining motivation is that these funds grow and benefit organization and individual alike. The details and coevolution of such a fund and its variety of payoffs would need to be customized to each individual organization.

By establishing a seedling fund, we set up a system in which we succeed by supporting the success of others. We also create multiple strategies that provide for sustainable operations. In recognizing the power of these semiautonomous units, an enfranchising system is created that provides fertile ground for growth and reward for sustaining sustainability.

Allowing for Emergence

How is the ground initially prepared so that companies can learn to sit with the complexity and allow possibilities to emerge? Is it possible in environments where people are locked into contentious ways of doing business to allow for unhindered emergence? Adjacent possibilities abound. As demonstrated above, what might be inconceivable can be realized by taking very small and deliberate steps.

To open our organizations, we have to expand our capacity to examine the fundamental ideas that are guiding our decisions and influencing the formulation of rules and the resultant behaviors. We have to be able to get at those ideas, or we will be stuck forever in abstractions that may be rooted in orthodox novelty. The insidious aspect of this is that our ideas may be so invisible to us that they function like unconscious assumptions. Having made ourselves conscious of principles, we can apply them toward building effective models, which in turn directly affect the relationships that produce the necessary work.

NONLINEAR INVESTIGATION NO. 2: SUSTAINING DEVELOPMENT

The wrong conception which I want to object to ... is the following, that we can hit upon something that we today cannot yet see, that we can discover something wholly new. That is a mistake. The truth of the matter is that we have already got everything, and we have got it actually present; we need not wait for anything. We make our moves in the realm of the grammar of our ordinary language, and this grammar is already there. Thus we have already got everything and need not wait for the future. • Ludwig Wittgenstein, from a conversation recorded by Friedrich Wasimann, ed.

An organization today is an information phenomenon. This is a way of saying that it exists in an informational network and cannot function or even continue to exist apart from that network. This investigation was designed to assess the potential of the system for robust (or successful) adaptation from one specific perspective. This is done by way of leverage points.

Leverage Points: Places where small inputs produce major results.

1. Locate activities in our company where substantial effort produces small results. Why do we continue these activities?

2. Are there any activities in our company where small inputs produce major results?
   - If so, what are they?
   - How does our organization account for this?
   - What can we learn from this?

3. How can this anomaly—small inputs producing large results—be understood in terms of the ratio of information to infrastructure in our company?
   - Do small changes in infrastructure produce large changes in productivity?
   - Do large changes in infrastructure produce equally large or smaller changes in productivity?

- Do small changes in information (including reformulations, new metaphors, new theories) produce large changes in infrastructure?
- Do large changes in information produce equally large or smaller changes in infrastructure?

4. How does our organization go about looking for or creating leverage points?

Demystifying Complexity

"Edges are important because they define a limitation in order to deliver us from it. When we come to an edge we come to a frontier that tells us that we are now about to become more than we have been before. As long as one operates in the middle of things, one can never really know the nature of the medium in which one moves." • William Irwin Thomspon, The Time Falling Bodies Take to Light

Modern science has always transformed the way modern business is conducted. It has provided the theory by means of which we explain and predict what takes place in the world. In the past few years, science has entered into a radically new arena of understanding. In order to keep pace with this change, and to comprehend how to implement its dynamics, business has to understand how science defines the world in which it operates. The new sciences of complexity are providing explanations that are changing the way businesses succeed. This chapter will provide an overview of this new understanding as it relates directly to business organizations.

Complexity Unveiled

Science is the process of comprehending the confounding. It's a method of measuring the confusion of the universe in such a way as to find order. The only scientifically acceptable means for accomplishing this feat is through experience guided by theory.

Contrary to common thought, science is not a natural process. It may study natural processes, how nature organizes and reveals itself, but the pursuit of scientific knowledge is not an inherently human way of expressing oneself, like language or sexual desire. According to the Austrian physicist and Nobel laureate Erwin Schrödinger, who is also a Greek scholar, science is simply "thinking in a Greek way." Schrödinger believes that if it hadn't been for the thinkers of ancient Greece, scientific thought might never have appeared on Earth. Nowhere else in the history of human development, in no other culture or society, did such a system of thinking evolve. Some may profess science to be Greece's monumental gift to the world, surpassing all else.

The word *science* comes from the Greek roots *techne* and *episteme*. *Techne*, the familiar and more universal term, meant any skill in doing, professional, learned competence as opposed to instinctive ability or mere chance. *Techne* is geared toward production (*poietke*) rather than action (*praktike*). Though arising from particular experiences, *techne* refers to the generalization of a knowledge of causes. It is, therefore, a type of knowledge and can be taught.

In Aristotle's era, *episteme* referred to a demonstrative, syllogistic, or logical knowledge. Though sense knowledge is a necessary condition of epistemic thought, these experiences must be viewed within a logical context. Experience alone does not yield causes or principles—the objects of science. The Greeks believed that causes or principles could be reached only through structured, logical mental activity.

For the past twenty-five hundred years, science has been equated with breakthrough thinking, the continual knocking down of the old walls that represent what has been previously thought. With the emergence of complexity thinking and its reliance on high-speed advanced computation, the scientific community appears to have come to a new demolition party. The business community, attracted by new possibilities filtering through the crumbling walls, wants complexity thinking to be immediately manifested in practical applications. Unfortunately, the practical applications of the new sciences of complexity are not as apparent as the surface image that is projected. They exist, but they may not exist in those places shining brightest.

Over the last hundred years, science was incorporated into business because Newton's mechanistic model fit so well into the machine-based Industrial Age structures. Now, complexity science's influence is actually shaping the information of Postindustrial/Information Age businesses, and contemporary structures that are stuck in mechanistic ways of thinking are crumbling under their own inability to adapt. Unfortunately, business cannot simply rebuild on the same foundation of these dismantled structures. It must grow something entirely new.

The Emergence of the New Science

One aspect of this new science of complexity is the arrival of biology developing outside of mechanistic and linear thinking. What we are seeing because of this is the *emergence of the organic*. The models of science are not only mechanistic. They are rapidly emerging into the organic. What we call complexity thinking reflects the impact of the organic, with a renewed focus on biological processes of evolution.

This shift from the mechanistic to the organic is also having a major impact on business. Unfortunately, businesses are still locked into the Newtonian mechanistic linear ways of operation. As John Holland states, "The task of formulating a theory of complex adaptive systems is more than usually difficult because the behavior of the whole Complex adaptive system is more than a simple sum of the behaviors of its parts. Complex adaptive systems abound in non-linearity (which is another way of saying that organic systems as opposed to mechanistic systems abound in non-linearities) and non-linearities mean that our most useful tools for generating observations into theory—trend analysis, determination of equilibrium, sample means, and so on are badly blunted."[1]

If our traditional, conventional tools, derived from the assumptions of the Industrial Age, are badly blunted in today's world, what alternative tools do we look for? The clues as to what those tools might be are being developed within complexity. One such tool would be a nonlinear approach that doesn't look for simple cause-and-effect elements but identifies leverage points. At leverage points, very small inputs can make major differences. It is critical to look at the consequences of both the positive and negative aspects of these leverage points. Negative results would mean that a little mistake in the beginning could have catastrophic effects as it expands out. Positive effects could mean that a small adjustment could have major implications as things develop.

How quickly can we create these tools to deal with the problems confronting today's businesses? There is a problem. The inquiries made in complexity are still in their infancy. All business can do is enlarge its thinking and follow where these new ideas lead. When we speak about emergent strategies, we are not trying to impose conclusions but rather to allow for their emergence. Emergent strategies as defined by the Santa Fe Center for Emergent Strategies are very particular. As discussed earlier, emergence means literally a "diving out of the depths." *Strategies*, from the same Indo-European root as *cognitive*, means "to weigh in the mind." Strategies, unlike plans, which are linear, are also multidimensional. Emergent strategies, then, are ideas that come from the depths of our complex understanding and have been weighed in the mind. They allow for possibilities to arise from a variety of deep levels of thinking. It is very hard for business to let go of its mechanistic and very linear cause-and-effect models and adopt an evolutionary model in which we sit back to see what can happen from any direction without knowing what will come of it. To do so is to relinquish control, direction, role, and intentionality. Businesses get very nervous just at the idea of this process.

Of course, one of the complicating factors in this evolutionary approach is the question of time. By its nature, evolution is a long process. Businesses in today's "gotta-go" environment feel they have to do everything right now. They can't wait to see what process adaptation is going to look like. They have to choose how they react and respond to a certain situation or certain changes in the environment/marketplace. Decisions must be made today on what will be produced next year. Raw materials must be ordered. Manufactured materials must be produced. Software must be developed. People must be trained. How does a company anticipate these things? Holland is advising companies to take a closer look before they speed ahead to try and outpace time. If a postindustrial company makes the faulty assumption that the world it lives in is mechanistic and attempts to use tools designed for mechanisms, Holland says their tools will be too dull to provide the precision demanded to do the job. What is a company to do?

Science and Business

For business, science is a tool—a way to locate and identify the patterns, models, and types of behavior that characterize and measure an organization and its operations, from its most fundamental procedures to its most complex processes.

In business as in science, measurement is a way of stopping time, of taking a snapshot. Anyone can aim and press the shutter, but taking a photo of value requires composition and perspective. But how does one gain a proper perspective on the illusive and confounding? The Nobel Prize–winning physicist Murray Gell-Mann recommends we take what he calls a "coarse-grained approach." The fine-grained portrait looks at each individual grain of sand on the beach in an effort to understand its dynamics. To obtain the coarse-grained view, one steps back from that up-close and personal approach and obtains a viewpoint in which the individual grains may blur, but the whole beach, with its meandering shoreline, seabirds, and bronzed sunbathers becomes distinct and clear. The coarse-grained approach is the way we will look at how complexity intersects with the world of business.

Understanding the Complicated, Order, Complexity, and Chaos

Beth comes into Jerry's office and finds him shaking hands with her best friend, Cathy, who has just been given the promotion Beth was expecting. Bill, Jerry's direct report, had assured Beth the promotion would be hers. At this precise moment Marian, Bill's assistant, comes running in to say that she, Marian, is the one that has received the promotion and that the contracts have already been signed. It seems Marian had placed her own name on Beth's report, which Cathy had simultaneously delivered as hers to Jerry.

This may sound like the stuff of daytime TV drama, and it's probably not a bad plot line, but in our context it's actually an example of a complicated pattern of behavior. The potential may seem chaotic and the situation complex, but since we can clearly see the pattern and understand that the behavior goes no further than the surface, the circumstance is merely complicated.

Fortunately, the distinctions among the complicated, the ordered, the complex, and the chaotic are neither complicated nor complex. However, distinguishing among them is essential to defining an organization's ability to compete.

Let us begin with the most concrete. Few people have trouble understanding the concept of order, except perhaps those of us who are helplessly and irrevocably organizationally challenged. For most people, however, order is simple. It's solid. It's neatly packed. It's never out of place, in fact that's pretty much what order is, an exact place—which in the world of physics means, dead in its tracks. As soon as you know something's place, you've stopped it. The German physicist Werner Karl Heisenberg made this clear with his uncertainty principle which states that when you measure a subatomic particle's momentum you can't tell its location and conversely if you determine its location you can't measure its momentum. When we measure place to maintain order, we stop momentum and can stifle progress. As we will see, the perceived safety of order, of knowing one's exact place and making every attempt to maintain it, is wall building at its most pervasive. This is not to imply that a certain amount of order is not absolutely necessary within an organization. The essential factor, as we will demonstrate, is finding the proper mix between order and complexity, between infrastructure and information, a mix that provides support while at the same time allowing forward momentum to continue. Identifying the proper balance is key to business planning—establishing how an organization wants to run its business and defining what kind of business a company is in. But before we look into that identification, it is important to define what we mean by complexity and chaos.

The Santa Fe Institute's Stuart Kauffman believes that there is continuum from order to complexity to chaos—that objects evolve from order to chaos through complexity. This passage is often explained by using the concept of phase transition as a metaphor. If you take an ice cube, a solid, and you place the ice cube on a table top, it starts to melt into a liquid. Once it has completely melted, it will eventually begin to evaporate into a gas. Each of those transformations, from solid to liquid and from liquid to gas, is a phase transition. In our context, order would be represented by the solid phase, complexity by the liquid, and chaos by the gas. Let us now use Kauffman's imagery and make our own phase transition from this solid ground of order, and slip into the liquid realm of the complex.

Oozing and swirling in its fluid tide, flirting with the intricate edge of chaotic dissipation, complexity thinking describes how memory and information, once trapped within the solid confines of order, can flow from one area to the next. Information in this context is not just data, but patterns, models, and types of behavior. Within this *liquid* realm, the patterns of the complex mix and swell in seemingly unpredictable fashion, bursting forward with constant surprises. The reason these patterns seem unpredictable is that their level of complexity is so deep that we can't always see the combining that takes place to create the new combination. Murray Gell-Mann's coarse-grained perspective becomes imperative if we are to comprehend things that are complex. It's like looking at Georges Seurat's pointillist paintings: If we try to view each individual dot of paint on the canvas, we miss the larger, more beautiful picture of the bathers on the beach.

It is also important to take into account, as Murray Gell-Mann points out, that "no definition of complexity is intrinsic. It is always context-dependent." In this case, our context is business, and the perspective we seek is one that can be characterized as seeing the forest, not the trees.

Another example from a visual context that demonstrates that the whole is greater than its parts comes from the world of abstract expressionist art. To some, abstract art is totally impenetrable. When they view the rampaging swirls of a Jackson Pollack painting, the details seem incomprehensible, order seems absent. But to those who see from a more coarse-grained perspective, the object as a whole can be one of tremendous power and beauty. It appears chaotic, but it is only the *appearance* of chaos, and not chaos itself. But what is chaos?

Chaos is where order maintains no barrier and no wall is strong enough to hold chaos's evaporative essence. Mike McMaster defines chaos as "a state where patterns cannot be made nor details understood." On the other hand, per McMaster, complex situations "can be maintained by paying attention to principles and patterns and leaving the details alone. Chaos distinguishes those situations where no projections, plans, or analysis will make sense, and the way forward is to 'clear an island of certainty,' to make small efforts and observe, or to get rid of the situation."[2]

One problem in understanding chaos is that there is more than one definition of it. *Webster's Dictionary* defines it as "A condition of utter disorder and confusion." Mathematically, chaos is defined as a demonstration as to how a slight variation at one end of an equation can produce profound, unpredictable, and ultimately uncontrollable consequences at the other. Fractals, those beautiful swirling patterns, are examples of such a chaotic demonstration. Within the sciences of complexity, chaos is also viewed, according to McMaster, as a description of a state without pattern or comprehensible detail. The chaos surrounding chaos is understandable . . . even though chaos itself may not be.

Many also believe that situations that seem chaotic may only appear to be so because we do not yet understand their underlying patterns. The chaotic marketplace is a common reference to global commerce. However, if these markets were truly chaotic, the only successes we'd see would be those governed wholly by happenstance. If that were true, organizations could save billions by firing their marketing departments, focus groups would be relegated to the same annals of history as the Inquisition and witch trials. The reality seems to be that we may not understand the details of how the market works, but if we take a more coarse-grained view, we can find patterns, models, and various types of behavior that will lead to greater comprehension. Are global markets chaotic? No, they are complex. In the last chapter we described learning where to find the patterns in the complexity and developing models based on those patterns in order to motivate successful types of behavior. Without models we cannot ask the right questions, and thus we cannot motivate successful types of behavior.

But to truly utilize the vast potential of complex environments, we must be willing to let go of our quest for complete control and order. As information-gathering and -utilizing systems, we humans need to realize that coherent information flows most easily within the fluid context of the complex, not in the solid walls of controlled order. The most powerful and innovative location within that realm is at the edge of chaos. At this critical juncture, just this side of the phase transition into chaos, the greatest possibilities for innovation exist. Mining along this outpost on the edge of confusion may seem dangerous, may go against every wall-building, safety-seeking instinct we have, but it is here that information thrives and the surprise of innovation is commonplace. Organizations must learn to operate along this precipice so that they neither fall into the total disorder of chaos nor are inundated by the overburdened infrastructure they have built to protect themselves.

Complexity in Action

The Santa Fe Institute (SFI) has been exploring complexity's edges since 1985 and has become one of the foremost research environments in the

United States dedicated to nonlinear and adaptive systems, the sciences of complexity, and the useful tools that apply to solving problems. Over the last few years, the institute formed the SFI Business Network, composed of over forty companies, all interested in putting complexity to work. These companies gravitated to SFI on their own, without any solicitation. They wanted to see if what was emerging from the edgewise explorations in these research walls had real applications for business. The interest of these businesses helped SFI to identify five areas in which the computer simulations developed through SFI's research could be applied to business. These simulations were originally developed to explore the process of evolving agents, to facilitate pattern recognition and data mining. Because these computer programs were so good at learning and pattern recognition, SFI realized, in conjunction with its Business Network, that these simulations opened up powerful new possibilities for business in five areas. (1) manufacturing and supply-chain management; (2) adaptive organizations; (3) evolutionary computation; (4) time series and economic dynamics; and (5) general use of simulation.

1. Manufacture and Supply-Chain Management

Within the manufacturing environment, the problems of manufacturing and supply-chain management seem endless. These problems relate to the flow of materials or product from one place to another and the information that has to come through the system to guide and change it as the material progresses. Anyone who has worked in manufacturing can testify to the complex interactions required to get product out the shipping bays. The important factor in understanding these complex and interactive flow issues is not to try and focus on the blurring details, but on the whole system. Most manufacturing operations managers will tell you the biggest problems they face usually center around bottlenecks in the system. Computer simulations show that these bottlenecks in the flow often occur from the full-tilt utilization of local resources and capacities—what is referred to as "localized optimization."

DuPont ran into just such a problem. Les Shipman's primary job is to smooth out the process by which DuPont sells and installs nylon carpeting. The process starts in Asia with the pumping of oil. The oil is refined into various materials and eventually goes into nylon as a bulk product. The nylon is textured, colored, and spun; woven into carpeting; distributed around the world; and ultimately ends up on someone's floor. The whole process from oil well to floor takes about a year, and a lot of people control various parts of it. The manager of a chemical plant knows that he has to produce a given amount of chemical X based on the input of chemicals Y and Z, but the amount of X is somewhat decoupled from the amount of carpet DuPont is actually laying at the time.

The manager of the chemical plant doesn't believe the forecasts coming in from the people in sales. He decides these guys don't know anything. "I know how to run this operation," he thinks, "and I am not going to let myself run out of product. I'm in trouble then. I'm going to deal with the guy upstream who needs my output because he is my buddy. I am going to deal with the guys downstream, who need my product. Since I don't know the rest of them, and don't trust them, I am going to optimize my part. If it means I have too much inventory on hand, that is the penalty the company has to pay. At least my operation runs smoothly." This is localized optimization.

If everyone operates in this fashion along the line, there's a good flow of material, but an enormous amount of money tied up in process. The complexity in such operations increases when one considers unexpected problems such as the floods in the spring of 1997 that took place in North Dakota. A lot of new carpet was needed to replace ruined carpet in homes and businesses, and there was a sudden surge in demand. How is that information fed back into the system? Are looms suddenly weaving at a fevered pace? Are oil wells pumping more, faster? Where is the system impacted, and how does DuPont begin to work it through? Then, once the need has been met and all the homes in Fargo, North Dakota, have new, dry carpet, how does DuPont adjust for the fact that they won't be selling any new carpet there for the next ten years?

This is an example of the kind of complex problems encountered within manufacturing supply chains that are often difficult to address. Software that can simulate the many and various interactions and their possible outcomes can be a powerful and valuable tool. All the linkages in the supply chain can be inputted into a program, and as further information that affects the system is added, it becomes evident where blockages will occur and where local optimization will weaken the system. By simulating what could happen along these nonlinear paths, organizations can see in advance what takes place when they adjust certain local optimizations. They learn how bottlenecks can be avoided, how to adapt to unexpected catastrophes, how to redirect flow when a resource has not arrived because of a strike or a delay at sea. After studying these simulations, an organization can go back to its plant managers and suggest a course of action that would allow the organization to model the system better, improve productivity, and avoid possible just-in-time shortages—which would undoubtedly result in better bonuses. This is the complexity of human behaviors driven by models, not rules.

Complexity provides a number of simulation tools for these manufacture and supply-chain businesses. One kind is agent-based simulation, where the agents can be either components or work stations. (An agent is an entity interacting within the system.) The simulations can also build in elements like demand and unexpected occurrences like floods in North Dakota.

A second kind of simulation is general adaptive computation. This includes such powerful breakthroughs as genetic algorithms, which can vastly improve such areas as scheduling. Genetic algorithms "are programs in which strings of computer code are randomly mutated and made to compete against one another until a winner emerges: the program best able to perform the task."[3]

The third kind of simulation is probably the most difficult. Though an organization may have computer simulations at its fingertips, it still has to figure out what it is trying to simulate in a model. According to the Santa Fe Center for Emergent Strategy's Bruce Abell, "Knowing what to model is still an art, just as is knowing how to structure an organization. How to abstract the salient elements is of critical importance. The danger with computer simulation is that if the simulation is too slick, too easy to use, you can get it running, with results that will look great but which, ultimately, are meaningless."

Another example of a supply-chain problem that has benefited from simulation can be found at J. Sainsbury's in England, a large grocery-store chain. Part of their company policy, their model, is to have whatever the customer wants when the customer wants it. Accommodating this model requires very large stores and inventories. It is a real problem when products don't move as they should. They may have products they sell only once a week, but that once-a-week sale brings in a customer who buys lots of other things. That person could come in every other day, because she knows she can always get that product when she wants it.

This is not a problem faced by Citicorp when it gets stuck with excess money because of a supply-chain problem. They simply use the money the next day. If a market gets stuck with a more spoilable kind of lettuce, it's waste.

Sainsbury's grocery stores carry twenty-five thousand products coming in from different places on a regular basis. They have a group of ten people in what they call their innovation department, five of whom are mathematicians. By applying computer simulations to the complexity Sainsbury's faces on a daily basis, from aubergines to zucchini, they have been able to work with vendors, distributors, and customers to make sure the morels are fresh.

The MITRE Center for Advanced Aviation Systems, in McClean, Virginia, runs a think tank for the Federal Aviation Administration whose mission is to look at future air traffic control issues and systems, which look very much like supply-chain problems. In this case, the resource is air space: In a system that is very hierarchical, in nature, air space schedules are prepared well in advance, and planned with safety uppermost in mind. An enormous amount of air space is reserved for each airplane—seemingly far more than what is actually needed for safety. This system causes some real economic problems and losses for the airlines, because at critical times they can't get enough planes into the air.

MITRE is experimenting with simulations to see what would happen if they started decentralizing some of those air space decisions. What impact would there be if commercial pilots were allowed to have control over the air space surrounding their own planes—called "free flight." They are also looking at the possibility of allowing airlines themselves to be involved in real-time decisions about rescheduling. As the situation currently stands, airlines don't have that option, and situations can arise where, for example, due to weather they have to send an empty plane instead of a full one, because everything is scheduled in advance, and the schedules are locked in.

Companies like Coca-Cola also have supply-chain problems. Coca-Cola bottles about 250 different drinks in a single bottling plant. They might have a dozen different drinks, and a dozen different packages for each of the drinks. This is the kind of process in which a company doesn't want to make any unnecessary changeovers, say, from Diet Coke to Minute Maid lemonade. Once the switch is turned on, Coke wants to be sure the real thing comes out. If it has to be turned off, a week's supply may already have sluiced its way through the process.

The real problem for Coca-Cola is to match demand with what they are going to put through. As with Sainsbury, the problem is the freshness of products that don't sell sitting on shelves, and making sure you have products when people want to buy them. Again, these are problems arising from all kinds of uncertainties. Coke knows they are likely to sell more product in July than in December, but if there were a particularly hot Fourth of July, their projections could be off. They also have to take into account the kinds of promotions being offered. McDonald's failed to do this properly when they underestimated the demand for one of their much sought-after Happy Meal giveaways. The disgruntled children and their beleaguered parents will not forget this misjudgment. With simulations, companies like Coke can adapt faster to their environments and improve the way they run their plants.

Manufacture and supply-chain management is characterized by nonlinear interactions of local optimization and the way these impact a whole system. The result can be loss of earnings because capital is tied up. In some instances, the problems are so endemic to these systems that the organizations haven't even identified the problem, and wrong decisions can create losses that will never be recovered. There are certain points at which the product—whether it is rotten cabbage, pink and chartreuse sweaters, or orange carpeting that doesn't sell—can't be recovered.

2. Adaptive Organizations—Metaphors and Simulation

As might be expected, the nature of adaptive organizations has created a broad interest within the organizational consulting communities. In looking at these simulations, SFI identified three primary areas that affect adaptive organizations. The first is that over the past ten to twenty years, incredibly rapid changes in the business environment have resulted in many of today's markets becoming more highly distributed—spread across the whole from periphery to periphery. This means that successful international companies have to sell their products in a lot of different markets and countries. They also are producing those products in a lot of different countries with supplies that come from even more locations. Instead of the localized businesses characteristic of the Industrial Age, things have gotten very spread out. In some cases they have become virtual—companies are having their products made by other companies and delivered to still other companies. These products never go through a main plant. This distributed climate has profound implications for organizational structure.

The second area is technology. Technology has had a major impact on both the tools used to make products and the kinds of products being made. This area has also altered the speed with which innovation is disseminated and information gathered. It has allowed for the collection of information on consumer interests and preferences and on how a product is sold and delivered.

The third element affecting adaptive organizations is the broad arena of competition. This is due in part to internationalization, but not always. Products are being produced by companies in places that traditional suppliers never imagined would be their competitors. The advent of Netscape is one example. Microsoft didn't see how quickly things could change. Suddenly, the most powerful and profitable company in the United States can, in less than a year, go from being on top of the hill to worrying deeply about what's happening under them—only to be followed a short time later by a major anti-trust lawsuit which threatens the very nature of the way it does business. That's how volatile the business world has become.

These three factors share one common feature: They are all time-based. As has become quite evident, everyone is in a hurry. When looking at adaptive organizations, we find that deliberate top-down management structures are very time-consuming. They also don't take advantage of the opportunities for innovation that come from a distributive organization.

There is a lot to be learned from natural systems. The operations of the human immune system, with its ability to process tremendous amounts of information and recognize and react to problems without a central processor, is awe-inspiring. Of course, when an organization tries to apply this metaphor directly to its system, it often forgets that such things as human cognition in large groups, and the constraints of business need to be included as well.

Still, there are powerful lessons to be learned from natural complex adaptive systems, particularly with regard to innovation. For example, the ability to coevolve quickly with other colleagues or even markets within a business environment often marks the difference between survival and dissolution. Organizations don't have time to adapt slowly anymore. If a business is not ready to innovate and act on a new idea, someone else will.

The value in studying adaptive organizations comes first in the application of metaphors from natural systems, as in how natural ecological communities process resources and energy. Or how biological distributive problem solving is utilized by the immune system. Or the generation of very complex behavior from very simple models if the right models are chosen. Or problem solving by examining fitness landscapes in which a better solution might be found in another location that is also changing. In these situations, no single solution is possible, only metaphors for ongoing adaptation.

Other tools besides metaphors can be found in the processes of evolution and coevolution. Businesses in supply, transportation, and power utilities are interested in analytical research being done in network dynamics—the interactions of linkages and pathways—because they are so multidimensional. What these industries find particularly interesting are the networks that are not written down, such as unofficial shortcuts that bypass major highway bottlenecks, which are used daily by those truckers who know. We also see these informal dynamics in the unofficial means for handling and dumping surges of electric power. The unpredictable connecting linkage in this network is the individual with the ability to find alternatives and solutions without prescription and without central approval.

Other natural-system occurrences that have demonstrated themselves to be useful tools in organizations are scaling phenomena—the degree to which a certain size of an organism may be more efficient than others. In some cases, it could be that a company should be broken into smaller pieces, because theoretically and practically it can be seen that certain levels of self-optimization will work better at a certain size.

3. Evolutionary Computation

Scientists have also been working on evolutionary computation. This has been a very promising tool for business, enabling the user to build processes of evolution, change, and adaptation into computer programs. This form of computation has powerful applications in scheduling, simulation, data mining, and recognition or self-writing programs. These self-writing programs have the ability to learn built into them. This means the user doesn't have to have solved the problem before writing a program to it.

Evolutionary computation can also be used for design purposes. One characteristic of evolutionary computational techniques is that they are unprejudiced. They don't say, "That is a dumb idea and it will never work." They'll try anything. They may be inefficient in many ways, because they don't have intuition. On the other hand, they do have an extraordinary discovery capability that is decoupled from the thinking that says, "That won't work," or, "I already solved that problem once; I don't want to compete with my own solution." This is a very powerful tool for distributive problem solving, in which the problem is not collected in one place, but is a problem of the whole system.

4. Time Series and Economic Dynamics

Time series is a process of pattern recognition from diffuse but representative data in which scientists and businesspeople are hoping to find a kind of mechanistic behavior that is embedded within it. This behavior is unrecognizable except to very powerful computers. As we will see from people like Doyne Farmer and his stock market prediction company, aptly called the Prediction Company, businesses are finding fertile applications in this area. In addition, insurance businesses are using time series studies to understand the frequency of natural disaster phenomena, something DuPont could probably use as well.

5. General Use of Simulation

This area of simulation looks at markets and systems and asks, "What if?" These simulations allow companies to perform experiments on their systems, by means of a computer that could not be done safely otherwise. The Monterey-based company, Thinking Tools, has been excelling in this area. Originally the business simulation division of Maxis company, the maker of the computer game SimCity™, were spun off as a separate company at the end of 1993. Out of their experience in computer game development, they've designed simulations in which project managers can explore the impact of a variety of disasters that could befall a project. Coopers & Lybrand is using general simulations for city planning to make choices that might play out in simulation over a long period of time. These simulations are useful to see what happens when markets of various kinds are deregulated, and to understand network behaviors that affect transportation, communication, and financial networks.

The Marine Corps is using general simulations to produce computer-generated forces for simulations of war-gaming. Defense organizations face similar kinds of spread-out environments as businesses. These organizations used to have only one focus; now it's the whole world. They are as dependent upon changes in technology as anyone else. However, now they no longer control them. There are also a lot more competitors to deal with now than previously.

Like their commercial brethren, defense organizations are becoming more distributed. When you are the only big fish left, and all the rest are little fish, you'd better not lose your coral-reef nature so that you can still effectively deal with the little fish. This becomes patently evident in trying to battle an urban guerilla force whose mobility is one of its greatest assets.

This is what Lt. General Paul K. Van Riper and his director of the Commandant's Marine Warfighting Unit, Colonel Anthony Woods, are currently engaged in: finding out how the Marines can become more distributed, flexible, and adaptive. They know it's a necessity both in the field and in their communications, because the battles of the future will be waged in urban settings rather than on more traditional battlegrounds. In urban battlegrounds, smaller units will need to be sent out to disperse guerilla forces. We've seen these issues arising in places like Bosnia and Somalia. These small semi-autonomous units will be able to respond and adapt more quickly than larger divisions.

Defense organizations are also looking toward complexity for a better understanding of the new arena of information warfare—what they can reap from computer science. Just as the scientists at SFI are concerned about how much reliance to place on simulation, the military has expressed its concern about the actual scientific basis for simulation. They feel they have done a great deal of pragmatic work, but they don't have the theoretical backup to understand simulation's usefulness. In this era of government cutbacks, the military also has an issue with the affordability of information systems. The Office of Naval Research is using complexity thinking to help design systems that are affordable, have the qualities that they require, and will be usable for a long period of time.

Complexity in the Workplace

In addition to its computer simulation explorations, complexity thinking in the business community is fueling a great deal more than "What if?"

simulated effects. The emergence of organic systems has provided power-ful metaphors that have fueled innovative ideas that many companies are just learning to integrate into their slowly opening operations. The SFI sci-entist David Lane refers to these organic metaphors as models of "worlds of experience." Flowing out of these "worlds of experience" are emergent strategies that are shattering the preconceived and revealing the possibil-ities for the inconceivable.

As noted, allowing innovative ideas and the possibilities that flow from them to emerge naturally at best is difficult for any organization. When managers are pressed by the quarterly report bottom line and the hot breath of shareholders, patience is not often a word that's heard within the lexicon of today's industries. One company that has not fallen into those traps and exemplifies the success that can come from allowing the possible to emerge is the outdoor sportswear manufacturer and wholesaler Patagonia.

Allowing Emergence

When the founder of Patagonia, Yvon Chouinard, opened his business, he had one idea in mind, and, surprisingly, it was not profit. Not too surpris-ingly, as he explained from his Ventura, California, office, "In almost every case where we've decided to do the right thing, it's turned out to make us more money."[4]

Patagonia is a privately owned company and therefore is not subject to shareholder pressure. Its bottom line is driven by Chouinard's interest in supporting environmental causes. Ten percent of Patagonia's pretax profits go to environmental organizations. In 1995, Patagonia posted over $150 million in sales, allowing Chouinard to disperse over $1.5 million to a variety of nonprofit environmental organizations throughout the world.

The key to understanding Patagonia's success is that its growth is due to demand, not leverage. The company was founded on the idea of pro-ducing high-quality climbing equipment; eventually apparel and chil-dren's clothing were added. Chouinard set up the company to be run by a group management approach, and then allowed the direction of his operations to emerge. He calls the company's growth "the natural way for companies to expand." It is a lesson he says he learned from his outdoor activities: "Never exceed your limit. You strive, you push the 'envelope,' but you live for those moments when you're right on the edge, but you never go over."

In complexity thinking, what Chouinard described is placing a company at the edge of chaos, and waiting for the possibilities to emerge. What his "experiment" in business has shown is that there's an excellent model for success within that way of thinking. It also proved to be a successful model for one of Chouinard's early retail customers.

Aspen Mountaineering, a small storefront company in Aspen, Colorado, started out with a single idea: to offer the finest-quality mountaineering equipment. The company hired only mountaineers as salespeople, who were instructed to be absolutely honest with the customer about the products being sold. They were to tell the customer if they thought the price for something was too high; they were to tell the customer if they thought what the customer required was less than what the customer thought.

In this Rocky Mountains town there were lots of other mountaineering shops that had been opened for quite some time. Aspen Mountaineering opened for business in the off-season. Commerical rents being what they are in Aspen, the store's location was outside the main shopping area. The immediate impression one might get was one of certain disaster: The market was already saturated; start-up in the off-season was misguided at best; and they were starting in a mediocre location, to boot.

All of these factors are traditional elements that have long been blamed for business failure. Aspen Mountaineering, based on the simple idea of offering the best quality and being absolutely honest about it, became the number one mountaineering store in Aspen from the day it opened its doors. The company recognized the adjacent possibilities of offering the best in customer service and quality products, and allowed the rest to emerge. As with Patagonia (Aspen Mountaineering was one of Patagonia's earliest customers), the primary concern wasn't with profit, so they didn't have to force the market. They were simply concerned with providing the finest quality available. They had the right idea, the right approach to that idea, and from an entrepreneurial startup, success emerged.

As mentioned previously, complexity thinking is inherent in every living system, no matter how large or small, no matter if it is an individual, a group of ten, or a corporation of tens of thousands. Complexity will operate differently at each level of organization, but it must be reckoned with in all organizations. As the Nobel laureate physicist Philip Anderson explains, "At each level of complexity entirely new properties appear."

Similarly, the computer executive James Bailey, formerly of Machines, has said, "Out of individual behavior emerges a group behavior that cannot be understood or predicted by looking at the behavior of the individuals alone. Out of the behavior of many groups come still higher levels of behavior, again inexplicable in terms of the individual groups looked at in isolation."

Putting complexity thinking's multileveled emergence into operation while remaining mobile enough to adapt and innovate as the possibilities emerge spells sustainable survival from big to small. The complex path may not be linear or as predictable as those who would like to control every aspect in a situation would prefer, but it is the natural process of success. To fight it is to fight an inherent aspect of nature. And has been evident in every aspect of life, nature always wins.

The Power of Generative Relationships

The process Bailey and Anderson were describing is actually one of complexity's most useful business tools, generative relationships. Generative relationships are created when two or more people or groups of people with diverse objectives and independent and autonomous responsibilities work together on a common project to improve the performance of all the participants involved. A scientist, David Lane, and a businessman, Robert Maxfield, in their paper "Foresight, Complexity, and Strategy" presented a story of a small California computer company, ROLM, and how it changed the way business was done in the telecommunications industry.

In the 1970s, ROLM developed a new PBX telephone switching system. As Lane and Maxfield explain, "PBX buyers had no incentive to ask for a system that could do anything other than what existing PBX models already did." And yet they did. ROLM went up against AT&T, ITT, IBM, and Stromberg Carlson, and ROLM came out on top by developing generative relationships between their sales representatives and the telecommunications managers of their potential clients.

ROLM was facing an uphill battle. They were asking potential clients to take a chance on a small company with a "fancy" new technology and give up their safer relationship with corporate giants. Those initial few who took ROLM up were not disappointed. ROLM's claims of dramatic savings and productivity enhancements were true. Needless to say, the telecommunications managers (TMs) became heroes in their companies.

The relationships built by the sales representatives and the TMs went beyond the sale. Acting as a conduit, the representatives began carrying requests from the TMs back to the ROLM engineers, who incorporated the requests into the design. The improved products were released to even greater acclaim.

This process continued over the next few years. New requests for improved functions expanded the product, the company's reputation, and ROLM's client base. The generative relationships between sales reps and TMs, working together to fill the needs of the other, turned ROLM into a market leader. Their original business plan forecast was for a best-case scenario of making $12 million in the first three years. The actual figure was $50 million. Two years after that, it was $200 million. ITT, Stromberg Carlson, and other companies that had been in the PBX business before 1973 were out of the business by 1980.

Lane and Maxfield write:

> It is important to realize why the ROLM account representative–TM relationships became generative, and those between, say, ATT salesmen and the TMs were not. In terms of their attributions about the role of PBX systems and their administration, the ATT salesmen and TMs saw everything eye-to-eye, at least before the changes unleashed by the ROLM PBX after 1975. This attributional homogeneity meant that the ATT salesmen and the TMs had nothing to learn from each other—and certainly no basis on which to establish a relationship around conversations that could challenge how each viewed what a PBX was and what it meant to administer a PBX system. The problem was not that ROLM listened to its customers and ATT did not: it was that the customers had nothing to say to ATT that could change how either ATT or the customers thought or acted. In fact, the interactions between ATT and the TMs were channeled into recurrent patterns in which their underlying shared attributions played no explicit role and so could never be up for negotiation.[5]

Lane and Maxfield state that there are minimum requirements for generative relationships to work, including an essential diversity and distance between the participants and simultaneously a shared directedness that motivates the participants to bridge the distances that exist.

One group that exemplifies these requirements is the Smart Card Forum (SCF). SCF was founded to help introduce "smart cards"—basically, credit cards with integrated computer chips inside them—into the North American market. These chip cards have been flourishing in Europe, Asia, and South America for years, but because of some reluctance from MasterCard and VISA, this new technology had not previously been introduced in the United States or Canada. Under the guiding hand of Catherine Allen, then a vice president of Citibank, and William Barr of Bellcore, the Smart Card Forum was assembled. From its initial membership, the Forum has grown to over 230 corporate and government entities, representing the financial services; telecommunications; health-care, travel and entertainment, and transportation industries; the legal, regulatory, and education sectors; and government.

What is so unique about this organization is that its members are essentially competitors who have been brought together to solve a major problem: introducing a new technology that will one day be ubiquitous. In complexity, a generative group is one that joins together and by the generation of their joint input furthers the group individually and as a whole. It is the embodiment of the complexity notion that the whole is greater than the sum of its parts.

SCF was faced with the task of introducing a new consumer technology that would require the cooperation of merchants, manufacturers, financial institutions, and legal and regulatory organizations. Billions of dollars were at stake, both in necessary outlay to bring this new technology online and in the potential revenue that would be drawn from the technology's use. Realizing that in order to make this transition work competitors would have to become partners, the SCF rapidly formed its work groups to solve the problems that everyone would face bringing this product to market. These industry players could never have accomplished this task individually. It took the collective thinking of the entire group not only to address problems but also to come up with highly innovative possibilities that never existed before. Working together, they established standards of use and design, developed applications and shared them among competitors, formed partnerships for multiapplication cards, and launched a new industry. To board the MARTA (Metropolitan Atlanta Rapid Transit Authority) train in Atlanta, many riders are already using smart cards.

Had the founders not had the insight, awareness, and knowledge of the complexity of their task or of complexity thinking and the power of generative relationships, this new technology—which is going to revolutionize the way business is conducted—might have withered and died a death similar to that of beta home VCRs.

Flocking: Swarming Resources

Along the southwestern edge of San Francisco Bay, in the shadow of the San Mateo Bridge, is Perkin-Elmer's subsidiary Applied Biosystems. The company's mainstay product is strands of DNA linked together in customer-requested sequences, and their innovative approach to research and development has enabled this unit of Perkin-Elmer to produce fifty percent of the corporation's $1.2 billion revenues—and the highest profit margins in the organization. Their success is due to their ability to apply the liquidity of complexity in a very powerful manner.

Applied Biosystems' fluid nature allowed it to move information from research and development through production with incredible speed. They use a technique called "flocking," what birds do, which is based on complexity's notion of *swarming*. In this company of 1,200, there are 200 chemist-researchers who are all empowered with the simple mission to create innovative products. Their work is primarily done through teams consisting of marketing, research, development, manufacturing, and all of the allied services, such as materials and marketing communications.

When a concept that is recognized to have excellent potential surfaces, Applied Biosystems "flocks" its creative research and development resources to that idea. Descending en masse on the new product, they temporarily leave their current projects aside. This collective intelligent body of knowledge focuses itself on the immediate task before them. The result: What once took Applied Biosystems a year to get to market now takes three to four months. Their new products to market has increased from six per quarter to nearly one per day. By providing an environment in which the whole is greater than the parts, they have been able to flow information without hesitation and gain a competitive edge. The chemist-researchers love it, because they know their ideas will receive the same treatment if they can be seen to be valuable.

There has been an unanticipated result from this behavior, however. According to Applied Biosystem's Ken Prokuski, "The environment we're in is generating ideas and opportunities that are far greater than we can address. The idea-generating machine here has gone nonlinear, which will fundamentally change what we do. For example, we started a major project in our plant in our UK plant. Initially, this was a twelve-month project. Once we started working on it, we discovered we could do it in under six months. The more we worked on it, the more we sped up the time line. There are some very unusual things happening here," Prokuski said with an air of understatement. "We're trying to figure out why. There are some things within Complexity that give the glimmer of hope for understanding. Nothing in conventional wisdom explains what we see."

Self-Organization—Letting Go of Control

When the new owner of a Supercuts franchise in Corpus Christi, Texas, took over operations, he had learned that the previous owner blamed his lack of growth in part on a questionable location and market. Within three years, after growing at the rate of 35 percent per year, the franchise set new records for the number of haircuts in a single day and broke their own record on two separate occasions, performing close to one thousand cuts in twelve hours. How did it happen? It was all a matter of what in complexity thinking is called *self-organization*, which has been defined by Peter Coveney and Roger Highfield as "the spontaneous emergence of non-equilibrium structural organization due to collective interactions between a large number of objects."[6]

The new owners were not novices. They had been the franchise owner of a number of other Supercuts locations in New Mexico, Texas, and Florida. But they approached this operation differently. One of the tenets of Supercuts is that they offer low-cost haircuts, performed by hair-cutters trained by Supercuts. The stylists are employees, not independent contractors. The shops are open seven days a week, twelve hours a day on weekdays, on a first come, first served basis. If a client wishes to request a particular haircutter there is an additional charge. The conceptual emergent thinking of the Supercuts Corporation epitomizes innovation.

In this particular Supercuts location, the new owners brought in a new way of thinking. They worked closely with the shop manager so that she would incorporate their ideas. First, at very busy times, instead of the manager setting a fixed schedule, the schedule evolved by itself. Without external control, the process of self-organization occurred, and the shop always had the proper amount of cutters to meet customer demand. The haircutters knew which shifts during the day were busy and which were slow. Since a good part of the cutters' recompense came in the form of tips, more of them were willing to work during the busy hours than the slow. Some preferred less pressure and competition and took times when traffic was slower. The employees figured it out themselves, with the manager stepping in when necessary. Was this approach planned? Actually, it came about because the shop was becoming so busy that the manager could not devote much time to scheduling and asked her employees to be responsible for themselves.

Another area of responsibility that was to be shared by all employees was called "super duties," regular cleanup and maintenance jobs. Again, rather than schedule each cutter to perform different tasks, every employee in the shop knew what needed to be taken care of. When they had a moment between cuts, they automatically swept the floor or routinely checked bathrooms for cleanliness, and the manager assumed the same responsibilities. Her job was to make sure the shop was running properly, and when the others saw her cleaning toilets and washing basins, the self-organization had its attractor. (In complexity thinking, an attractor does exactly what the word describes, it attracts behavior—either to a fixed point under steady-state condititions, or to a strange attractor during chaotic conditions.)

But flexible scheduling and sharing chores don't bring customers in the door in droves. One factor in the business's success was that employees were encouraged to establish their own promotions with customers. For example, a cutter might be cutting a man's hair and asks his name. "Richard" comes the reply. The cutter would then shout out to the people waiting. "Today's special: Anyone named Richard gets two dollars off his haircut, all day." Birthday specials were also a favorite, as were free haircuts for children on a particular day. Bring in a buddy and get a free cut also worked. These promotions were never planned, advertised, or designated by anyone in management. The employees self-organized, and the system flourished. The customers loved it, too, and their loyalty proved it. People would line up at opening, and the shop was busy all day. Because each franchise unit is basically a business unto itself, no corporate approval was needed, but no one ever abused the system.

Scientists have found that when the control factor is removed and the complexity is allowed to emerge, self-organization takes place. Within the sciences of complexity, this notion is coming to be recognized as a biological fact that is radically changing how we understand the way systems work. It is even radicalizing our notions of natural selection. The question "Which came first, the chicken or the egg?" is getting new attention, and scientists are discovering more and more links to self-organization as the answer. Complexity's new way of thinking has opened up the adjacent possibility to understanding more than just the idea of the survival of the fit; it has begun answering an even more perplexing question about the arrival of the fit. This notion relates to the first life system organizations on earth, the groupings of chemicals that gave birth to proteins and amino acids, which, in their complex combinations, gave birth to life, and then allowed natural selection to take place.

Discoveries like these have led the physicist Mike Simmons, the founding vice president of the Santa Fe Institute, to say, "What is emerging out of our studies of complexity will one day rival the discovery of fire." Prometheus opens the boundaries and the adjacent possibilities emerge.

In its relationship to business, the concept of the arrival of the fit is also apt. When beginning any new business or project, or even birthing an innovative idea, in order for it to survive to reach the natural selection process, its organization must emerge naturally out of the organic system. Cognitive failures in business are usually far from organic. They're often forced and manipulated, with poor design and intention. Instead of marking the arrival of the fit, they generally signal that they are dead on arrival.

The reality is that complexity thinking won't keep people from making cognitive mistakes. It will, however, help them better comprehend the complex systems within which they are trying to operate.

NONLINEAR INVESTIGATION NO. 3:
EMERGENT PHENOMENA

The world is, as Aldous Huxley once put it, like a Neapolitan ice cream cake where the levels—the physical, the biological, the social, and the moral universe—represent the chocolate, strawberry, and vanilla layers. We cannot reduce strawberry to chocolate. . . . The unifying principle is that we find organization at all levels.   •   **Ludwig von Bertalanffy,**
General System Theory

If, as John Holland said, "Non-linearities mean that most of our useful tools for generalizing observations into theory—trend analysis, determination of equilibria, sample means, and so on—are badly blunted,"[7] then the possible implications are enormous. One of those possibilities is that all generalizations may be linear, and that any tool for generalizing, if applied to nonlinearities, is not only badly blunted but also irrelevant. If this is true, what new tools can perform generalizing tools' traditional functions? What would nonlinear tools that deal with interactions or ideas look like?

From one perspective, nonlinear tools must allow for the emergence of unfamiliar patterns: nonlinear geometries, quantum probabilities, expanding space, and nonequilibrium markets. The tools must be sufficiently abstract to allow for a broad range of patterns and perhaps ultimately of all possible adjacent patterns. The following questions will help open the investigation into this exploration.

Emergence: James Bailey, a computer executive, has said, "Out of individual behavior emerges a group behavior that cannot be understood or predicted by looking at the behavior of the individuals alone. Out of the behavior of many groups comes still higher level behavior, again inexplicable in terms of the individual groups looked at in isolation."

1. In our company, do we assume that our group behaviors can be understood or predicted by looking at the behavior of individuals? If so, what do we miss?

2. How does our organization foster the coevolution of ideas?

3. Does our organization tend to restrict planning to the selection of means to achieve desired ends? Or to what extent are ends open possibilities?

4. Do we tend to look upon markets and customers as having a fixed identity which is independent of our interactions with them?

5. Does any unexpected thing happen in our organization? If so, how does our organization deal with the unexpected?
   - Denial
   - Rationalization
   - Blaming it on an accident
   - Faulting incomplete data
   - Claiming sabotage
   - Welcoming the unexpected
   - Incorporating it into the process

Language, Narrative,
and Metaphor

Like a buoyant force, language lifted intelligence to higher levels. Articulate thoughts interlaced facts within a widened expanse of memory, and greater intelligence made possible more elevated forms of linguistic expression. Intelligent minds were naturally selected, for whoever could not find the apposite words, comprehend and obey the voice of command, recall the effective strategy, or respond with the efficient tactic had little chance of surviving. • Edward Harrison, *Masks of the Universe*

Communicating within the organization is never easy, but communicating new ideas and new ways of thinking, "ideas expressed as words," is often inconceivable. In this chapter we look at the importance of language in business, and at how new ideas are being communicated so that innovative resources can be unlocked. We analyze why *what* we say and *how* we say something are critical to its being acted upon. And we unmask the power of corporate stories as a means for transferring information, knowledge, and experience.

No matter the industry, how large the business, or what product or service is being delivered, business is possible only because of language. Whether written, spoken, or psychically inferred, our ability to language our ideas allows our daily human activity to take place. As the Nobel Prize–winning physicist Richard Feynman succinctly expressed it to his officemate and fellow Nobel laureate, Murray Gell-Mann, "Murray, language was invented to communicate." Of course, there is also Lily Tomlin's remark that language was invented to satisfy man's deep need to complain. Whatever the reason for its creation, without this unique ability to express our ideas, feelings, and emotions, we would not be sharing this information now, and business would not be conceivable.

In science and engineering, the most precise language for expressing an idea is mathematics. If we tried to explain human relationships in mathematical form, such as X+Y=Z, we may provide an efficient calculation, but we would never come close to a precise description. Business succeeds solely on the basis of human interaction, and human interactive language requires more than efficiency to communicate understanding and meaning.

In the mechanistic universe, language has been viewed like all other phenomena, atomistically. Instead of being seen as a system, it becomes an object that can be analytically taken apart to find the guiding, heuristic link of each word. The assumption is that language represents *something else*, and we want to find out what this thing is that the expressive interpretive words represent. When we talk about opening systems, freeing our businesses from the constraints of closed boundaries, we're talking about the way language is used and understood, the role it plays in communicating ideas.

In the past, whenever a new way of thinking has emerged, it has brought into existence a new language necessary to describe the new context. What the past has also demonstrated, however, is that in order to explain new ideas and theories, our languaging of them must also be connected to the old language. By way of analogy, Descartes demonstrated this when he ushered in the new world of science by putting ideas into the language of medieval scholasticism, even though the language and the concepts he was overturning were all scholastic in context. To establish what he was doing, he first felt that he had to prove the existence of God, using a traditional medieval method of proof. His new ideas and language could not be complete without being grounded in the methodological system he was overturning. In this same way, the transitional period for any new way of thinking tends to utilize the older forms of language to introduce new ideas. A common mistake in organizations is to introduce new concepts by radically altering the way we speak about things. This abrupt language change can cause mistrust and unease among those expected to implement the new ways. By thoughtfully integrating the new language into the old, lowers resistance, and new messages bearing change are not as threatening.

In the chapter, "Demystifying Complexity," we spoke of leverage points as a means to unlock complexity thinking because at these points a small effort greatly expands the system. This is an example of the mechanical language of Newtonian physics being used to describe the new thinking of complexity. The process continues.

Language arises from our frame of reference, how we position what we want to communicate. If our frame of reference is to become more efficient, our language needs to reflect that. The frame of reference in previous centuries was that of a presumed, objective, preexistent reality. The observer could observe without altering the observed. The function of language was to represent or imitate that reality. The twentieth century, however, has been characterized by a major emphasis on rethinking the nature, role, and function of language.

Recently, Fernando Flores has been expanding the philosophy of "speech acts," which refers not to the formal meaning of language, but to its usage. Flores's consulting firm, Business Design Associates, is a $30 million–a-year company with clients like IBM and Boston Consolidated. He was quoted in an article in *San Francisco* magazine as saying, "Philosophy is indispensable for generating the innovation we bring to clients." From the German philosopher Martin Heidegger, Flores learned that existence evolved from interaction. In studying the theory of speech acts, Flores realized that language conveyed not only information but also commitment. For Heidegger, language was not about describing a separate world that existed out there. He believed that the world existed only *through* language. It is Flores's contention that if we were to eliminate language, the computer a worker assembled would be reduced to a meaningless object. If, however, computers exist only through language, then it follows that so do the offices that hold them.[1]

According to Flores, "A human society operates through the expression of requests and promises." In a *Wall Street Journal* article, Thomas Petzinger contends that for Flores a business is such a collection of simultaneous commitments. "In this 'network of commitments,' everyone is a customer, a provider, or both at once."[2] Not only is language important to business, it creates business.

How Language Is Used

Within the context of complexity thinking, many organizations use language as metaphor in the description of narrative, or storytelling. These language-based ways of communicating and feeding back information are very much in line with pragmatic philosophy. This narrative approach is a critical aspect of self-organization. Thinking Tools' founder, John Hiles, believes "Organizations and stories are very close to one another, because they are both holders of knowledge."

In his book *The Gates of the Forest*, Elie Wiesel tells this story:

When the great Rabbi Israel Baal Shem-Tov saw misfortune threatening the Jews it was his custom to go into a certain part of the forest to meditate. There he would light a fire, say a special prayer, and the miracle would be accomplished and the misfortune averted. Later, when his disciple, the celebrated Magid of Mezritch, had occasion, for the same reason, to intercede with heaven, he would go to the same place in the forest and say: "Master of the Universe, listen! I do not know how to light the fire, but I am still able to say the prayer," and again the miracle would be accomplished. Still later, Rabbi Moshe-Leib of Sasov, in order to save his people once more, would go into the forest and say: "I do not know how to light the fire, I do not know the prayer, but I know the place and this must be sufficient." It was sufficient and the miracle was accomplished. Then it fell to Rabbi Israel of Rizhyn to overcome misfortune. Sitting in his armchair, his head in his hands, he spoke to God: "I am unable to light the fire and I do not know the prayer; I cannot even find the place in the forest. All I can do is to tell the story, and this must be sufficient." And it was sufficient.

God made man because he loves stories.[3]

Unfortunately, business historically has not loved stories. Management in business organizations has often gone out of its way, often in the name of productivity and efficiency, to eliminate the sharing of stories in companies. Gathering around the watercooler or coffee machine to chat, or lunches out with colleagues has been replaced by the equivalent of cubicle lock-downs. As we will point out, this goes against the very grain of what we, as a society, know and yet is tied to a lineage of thought that has allowed this devaluation of story to persist. Paradoxically, as the following brief history points out, it may be because of science's attempt to reduce language to its simplest form—an equation—that we discovered what we have about the world and are now rediscovering the power of story to convey it.

In Western civilization, our initial exposure to one another and the way in which language is used are almost entirely metaphorical, mythological, and evocative. We told stories. The early works of philosophy and science were all written in that way, too. Plato doesn't write treatises, he writes dialogues. Each dialogue is a kind of story containing many myths.

As the language and its use matured, there was a very deliberate effort to disengage language from the mythological and the metaphorical. In the generation after Plato's, Aristotle produced his treatises on each individual science. Out of these treatises, now void of myth, it was possible to formalize the language and disengage it from the person who used it. Aristotle looked instead at what the language was conveying in its own terms, independent of the feeling and emotions that occurred; he desubjectified them. This was done by way of constructing grammar, or codifying how language was being used. It was also done by creating logic, which formalized processes of analysis and conditions of intelligibility for all discourse.

By reducing language to its essences, Aristotle created a whole new possibility for the power of language. This focus on language as a formal system led in a direct line to natural science, which attempted to remove not only all feelings and emotions, but all sensual content whatsoever. Mathematics did not deal with quality, but with quantity. This was paradoxical because Aristotle was not a mathematician. Plato, who was, did not divorce geometry from expression. He wanted to integrate them. Aristotle did not.

For the next couple of thousand years after Plato, there was a steady removal of the subjective, sensual, and qualitative elements of language, resulting in science. This disengaging of the subjective and the sensual was necessary to the development of science and became part of its essential meaning. Galileo wrote at the very beginnings of modern science:

I feel myself impelled by the necessity, as soon as I conceive a piece of matter or corporeal substance, of conceiving that in its own nature it is bounded and figured in such and such a figure, that in relation to others it is large or small, that it is in this or that place, in this or that time, that it is in motion or remains at rest. . . . In short by no imagination can a body be separated from such conditions: but that it must be white or red, bitter or sweet, sounding or mute, of a pleasant or unpleasant odour, I do not perceive my mind forced to acknowledge it necessarily accompanied by such conditions. . . . Hence I think that these tastes, odours, colours, etc., on the side of the object in which they seem to exist, are nothing else than mere names.[4]

In the two-thousand-year development we are describing, leading up to our own new way of thinking in science and business, the ideal communication would have been one that disengaged any utterance from extraneous things like the sound of the voice, or facial expressions. It was an attempt to totally rule out mental language as having anything to do with validity, truthfulness, or accuracy or even meaning. Everything else was extraneous. Galileo made the distinction between primary and secondary qualities. Primary qualities had geometric properties. Secondary properties did not. Within science, the only meaningful utterances were those that had to do with geometric properties. Anything else was an illusion.

Within a mechanistic efficiency, this made perfect sense. Within an industrial marketplace, this may also have made sense. All of modern science rests upon these distinctions. Colors, taste, and sound are simply what happens to the observer and have nothing to do with the object observed. By being able to screen out the subjective, people like Galileo, Descartes, and Newton were able to do incredible things, compared to what had previously been done in this civilization and to what any other civilization has been able to do.

That perspective remained essentially unchanged until the late nineteenth or early twentieth century. Then a radical change started to occur in Western civilization. There is a sense in which twentieth-century thought is returning to early sources.

Complexity has to be understood not only as a major change within science, but also as part of a process of similar changes taking place in the whole culture. This is why Einstein's dispelling of the distinction between primary and secondary qualities, as mentioned in the chapter *"A New Way of Thinking,"* was so significant.

Instead of reducing language, stripping it of all things deemed unessential to developing scientific thought, we find that in today's open-system organizations language is about including everything, scientific or not. There is a wonderful analogy between Einstein and Descartes. Each saw what he was doing as a development from and within what was classical, as the working out of certain implications and possibilities within that way of thinking. They did not reject the language or the theoretical constructs that preceded them. They were taking them where they led—which by the way is what we're doing with complexity thinking and its application to business. No matter how revolutionary a new idea may be, we are all working within an inescapable position, seeking to understand more deeply and more profoundly what came before in the context of what is presently possible.

No better example of this exists than Einstein and his subsequent impact on business. Einstein discovered that the problem with the physics of his day was the provinciality of its understanding of knowledge and how it is generated—its *epistemology*. Einstein came up with the powerful recognition that our use of linguistic forms was rooted in what he called the "free play of creative imagination." He explained, "All our thinking is of this nature of free play with concepts; the justification for this play lies in the measure of survey over the experiences of the senses which we are able to achieve with its aid. The concept of 'truth' cannot yet be applied to such a structure."[5] This one concept is one of the most powerful ideas a business can incorporate into its way of doing business. Not understanding its implications has been the source of countless business failures. There is no necessary way of understanding the universe that is imposed by some presumed rational structure of the language. *We can never reason or theorize from our experience to our concepts.* That is not where rationality lies. Einstein called the relationship of experience to concepts intuition. He put forth the revolutionary view that language was rooted in something nonlinguistic, to which we cannot ascribe the "characteristics of language," which is essentially and primarily a formal structure. For example, it always has a grammar and an implicit logic.

The full implication of this is that we can talk about experience and all share experiences, but experience has a different status in relation to our theory of existence than concepts. When we are talking about theories, we are talking about concepts. We are talking about ideas. When we are talking about experiences we are talking about behaviors, sensations, intentions, feelings, and willings. We communicate ideas through our experiences, our stories. But we do not conceptualize them through experience. This idea is critical to every businessperson attempting to do business.

There is a very peculiar dualism at work here. When we talk about theories, we are talking about the way ideas relate to each other. We determine the relative value of a theory through a conceptual formulation and analysis of that theory. There is a sense in which, if our experience doesn't bear it out, so what? Take, for instance, the creation of non-Euclidean geometries, which could never have been derived from experience. They describe a world that no one ever experiences, and yet it is a valid and powerful geometry. Those non-Euclidean geometries did not care what the world was like. They didn't know what the world was like. Yet through the implications of certain concepts and conceptual systems, they become something whose value enables us to deal with our experience. Without the new language of non-Euclidean geometry, the theory of relativity would not have been possible. Einstein was talking about curved spaces, not flat spaces. Euclidean geometry was inadequate within this new way of thinking. Einstein needed a new language to explain it.

For Einstein, it made sense that the physicists of his day were having the problems they were experiencing. They were unwilling to be open in their thinking and entertain possibilities other than those they had already decided worked. The same can be said for those in business. The problem Einstein's contemporaries faced wasn't scientific. It was conceptual. They didn't understand how concepts and experience relate to each other. Therefore, they held on to concepts as if they came from and were proved by experience. They are not.

Einstein had the audacity to suggest that if the way we define space or time or matter or energy does not produce satisfying results, then change the definition. That's all. No definition is privileged. The only test is pragmatic. Does it work?

Once Einstein changed the definitions, he found more powerful ways of saying what he wanted to say. So powerful, in fact, that today, the general theory of relativity is no longer called a theory by most physicists but rather is taken to be a description of the way the world is.

For businesspeople who have made the mistake of basing theory on experience, it should be mentioned that Einstein was not above making the same mistake. There is a famous story that when he was developing his general theory of relativity, his calculations implied a universe that was either expanding or contracting. But like his colleagues, Einstein assumed a static universe. Experience had not yet shown that stars collected into larger collections of galaxies or that those galaxies were expanding away from one another. As Timothy Ferris describes in his book, *The Whole Shebang*, "Einstein regarded the implication as a flaw. His response was to modify the equations by introducing a new term—the *cosmological constant*—to make his theoretical universe stand still."[6]

It was soon discovered that what Einstein's theory had originally predicted, which he discounted because it was counter to experience, was in fact the case. Later he would consider the creation of the cosmological constant the greatest blunder of his career.

A story about Galileo also supports this notion that theory leads experience. It has been said that when Galileo had stepped out onto the Leaning Tower of Pisa and famously dropped two unequal weights to the ground, he immediately turned and began walking down. When an assistant asked if he didn't want to watch the result, he replied that he already knew what the result would be. Galileo gives credibility to this story in a dialogue he wrote on the speed of falling bodies from *Two New Sciences*, "But even without further experiment, it is possible to prove clearly, by means of a short and conclusive argument, that a heavier body does not move more rapidly than a lighter one provided both bodies are of the same material."[7]

Let us make the implications of this discussion perfectly clear for business: If theory is led by experience it delivers nothing more than orthodox novelty—more of the same. It is only when theory anticipates experience that emergent novelty, true innovation, can come forward. We will discuss this often controversial notion in greater detail in the chapter "Real-World Applications for Coevolving Metaphors."

Theories in Transition

From Newtonian physics to Darwinian biology to hermeneutics to Einstein to quantum theory to complexity, all have been moving in the direction from closed systems to open systems. With theories in transition, we get caught in both worlds. In fact, most of the world we live in is still a very closed system, with the methodologies that are appropriate to those closed systems firmly in place.

Postindustrial business is caught right in the middle. It has inherited as a matter of course and habit, not as a matter of deliberate choice, the assumptions and methodologies that develop in closed systems. These assumptions and methodologies for the most part no longer exist in their original form. In spite of this, business still tries to deal with them as if they did. The language for those linear systems and all the other vocabularies associated with that system are also describing a world whose form has changed.

Take, for instance, the word *boss*. The very nature of a boss implies a linear command and control system based on a progression of superiority and inferiority relationships. Rarely would someone introduce her manager as an associate or a person with whom she works, but rather as a superior, a boss. We may find, however, that as our language changes to more closely resemble the interactive nature of our organizations, the word *boss* may be replaced by something like colleague. We may have different roles within the organization as colleagues, and my colleague's responsibility may include some of what I do, but we are both embedded in a larger system. The world has changed. The traditional linear hierarchy of a command-and-control *boss* is reflected in the vocabulary of the past. It also signifies a very closed system in which the boss is in charge, in total control.

This command and control approach is one reason why many in business feel they don't have any other choice but to continue operating out of the old way of thinking. They ask what would happen if they truly operated in an open system in which they had to anticipate where the new thinking was headed. This is especially true of bosses. Their concern is that while acting as an open system, they would still have to do everything in a world organized and structured within an industrial context, with its limited thinking and methodologies. Their own people would probably think they were crazy, especially since this new way of thinking means a loss of predictability and stability. The questions and fear would mount. What does it mean that we are not concerned with making a profit? How are we going to survive if we just sit back and see what emerges or allow our organization to occur? Our stockholders will kill us. We won't know how to relate to our customers. We won't know how to relate to our vendors. We won't know how to relate to our bankers or to our attorneys or to the government.

The fact is, we are not operating in this world as a compromise. We are working within the system in which everything that goes on around us is also working. We are all within the same system. If our people were asked to break with that system in some fundamental way simply because we could get things done with less effort and could be more effective and more productive, the price to pay and the risk of doing so would be great. They might ask, Why should we do it anyway? Our profits are up 20 percent this year. The dollars of net profit are great. The dividends for stockholders are good. We have no motivation to change. We might be able to do something better, but there is no urgency, no felt need. Another example: The stock market experienced unprecedented growth in 1997, establishing new records, so why jeopardize anything?

The answer is simple. We are going to change whether we want to or not, because the world and our ideas are changing. This was particularly evident at the beginning of 1998 with the plummet of Asian stocks. All the people we are doing business with are also in the process of changing. There is a choice. We can go along with it, anticipate it, have an awareness of what our processes are and not lie back and wait until it turns out to be too late. Or we can construct our fishbowl and have the sense of protection from the world outside, only to become extinct.

Let us return to the turn of the century and imagine ourselves to be a manufacturer of horse-drawn buggies. A reporter comes to us and asks if we are aware that the internal combustion engine has been invented and there would be a radical change in transportation. Some of our competitors might say, "We'll wait until that change occurs. We are not going to do anything about it in our company, now." As history has shown, those who waited until that change occurred were too late and went out of business. In the language of complex systems, they didn't adapt soon enough and the species died.

The same could be said for those unable to give up vacuum tubes for transistors or analogue recording for digital. Many companies have made catastrophic decisions to close their systems and they have paid the price: bankruptcy and ruin. The American steel and railroad industries are examples of systems that have chosen to close their systems and suffered the consequences.

It has become evident that we can no longer deal with customers or employees the way we once did. We can't deal with the economy or banks the way we once did. The nature of economic behavior and money has changed. And the arrow of time points in one direction. If a company is trying to stop it by persisting and holding on to ways that have been learned and resists learning new things, the message is clear.

Telling the Story

So how is this new way of thinking being communicated? By a return to stories and narratives that communicate emergence. Stories are one of the best methods for "pointing" to new ideas. Stories are a way of distributing knowledge to bring people up to speed. And, as John Hiles reminds us, both organizations and stories are containers of knowledge. Few organizations have developed this notion as far as Xerox's Palo Alto Research Center, known as Xerox PARC, and few storytellers are as accomplished as its research director, John Seely Brown. What follows is one of his stories.

Brown has overseen many of the computer breakthroughs that have changed the computer industry. For one, computer multitasking emerged from the walls of PARC. Brown is often asked, "Is your research center engaged in technology push or market push?" He doesn't see things quite so dualistically. "What is really interesting" he says, "is the fact that technology obviously influences the market, as an evolved market obviously influences the kind of technology we use. What we really have is a coevolutionary system, neither market pull nor technology push, but a coevolution between these two conflicts."

Getting to this understanding of the market ahead of the competition is the key. How is that done? According to Brown, it's simple: Any organization has on its periphery all kinds of naturally occurring experiments. The periphery is where the renegades live, and of course it is on the periphery that the rubber hits the road. That is where learning organizations happen. But do we see them? Do we capture them? Do we learn from them? The answer for most of us is, no. Part of the reason is that we don't even see it. We have to learn to see the learning and see the residual effect that's happening.

For example, Brown has a dedicated self-interest in proving that large corporations have a life after Netscape. "Many people say large corporations are dinosaurs. I obviously don't believe that and don't want to, because only large corporations can afford research centers." He also believes that the larger the corporation, the larger the periphery. The greater the periphery, the more naturally occurring experiments take place there. "There's almost nothing we can do about it," he says. "In fact, large corporations have more chances to learn to improve on the periphery, where the renegades are, than the small corporations." These are also the direct contact points to an organization's adjacent possibilities.

The key factor for Brown is to figure out how to really tap in to the emergence that takes place along the edges and honor it. Along those edges, he feels, new kinds of sustainable competitiveness exist. As he says, "Let's face it, there's only one sustainable competitiveness in corporations, and that is to learn faster."

Xerox PARC, in order to access the periphery and learn faster, has created a set of new analytic constructs called "a community of practice." Brown describes this as a team that basically has been working together for a long period of time, but that has no obvious beginning or end. Within this community, they come together and work and through time they begin to construct their own language. They have their own short cuts. They have a real sense of membership: When somebody new joins them, that person initially feels like an outsider. There's a strong sense of belonging in the community. In fact, if you are an outsider you have to learn to become a member. Brown points out, "Most executives fail to differentiate between learning about and learning. There are all kinds of ways to learn about business. But what about the learning to *be* business. A businessman instantly, in five minutes of conversation, knows, in talking to someone, if that person is practicing business or is just someone who knows about the business." Direct involvement is different from being an observer.

This same differentiation happens down in the distributed constellations of communities of practice in the workplace. They are not just high ideals. In fact, what Brown sees is that real work requires a confluence of people climbing over authorized structures to get the work done, "which gives us new opportunities to rethink how we can create a work environment that actually supports the construction of meaning in the workplace. Meaning actually comes from your membership in the authorized communities, but it also comes from your membership in the emergent communities of practice."

According to Brown, the story of these communities of practice starts around a very fundamental technology: the copier.

Many years ago, Brown was called in to look at building an artificial intelligence system as a learning tool for Xerox's tech reps. At that time they had about seventeen thousand tech reps repairing office equipment around the world.

His first step was to go to Xerox's training center in Leesburg, Virginia, to meet the master sergeant of the tech rep force. According to Brown, this guy had little interest in meeting some Ph.D. in computer science, and some kid, just out of grad school, who would be coming to teach him how to improve his seventeen thousand–strong tech rep force.

Brown recalls that he walked in the room and the fellow was sitting at his desk. He looked up at Brown and said, "Okay, Brown, you're so smart, think about the following. I have a copier sitting here with intermittent copier quality faults. If you pick up the manual, here is the authorized practice and procedure it says to use. You take one of these great test patterns that you've created in your laboratory, and put it on the electronic platen of the copier, and dial in five thousand, push start, and go get some coffee, because five thousand copies take some time. You come back here and pick up the stack of copies, and go through them until you find a bad copy. When you finally find this bad copy, you compare it with the diagnostic chart and go to the next step.

"That is the way we have been trained to troubleshoot intermittent faults. But of course, you, Brown, with a Ph.D. wouldn't possibly think of doing it that way. How would you do it?"

Brown, immediately put on the spot, did what any overtrained Ph.D. would do: He hemmed and hawed. When he finally realized that his differential equations would be of little help to him, he quickly gave up. The rep sergeant smiled. "You just don't understand reality, do you, Brown. You know how I do it?" He walked over and picked up the wastebasket. He walked back to his desk, and turned it upside down. "Now, I sort through it. And I find one bad copy after another bad copy after another. Because, where do you put the bad copies that come off the copier? The wastebasket. I've got a natural filtering device that sits here all day, whose sole purpose is to collect bad copies."

Brown immediately recognized he was speaking with a genius. "The important point," according to Brown, "is that not only was this a radical improvisation on his part, but if I'm working in the world, let the world do some of the work. You don't have to do it all by yourself. For a computer scientist," he adds sarcastically, "there's no sense in letting the world be allowed to work its course."

It was from this encounter that Brown built an idea he calls "organizational judo." Like regular judo, organizational judo allows someone to use the forces naturally occurring against a situation, to read those forces, work those forces, and turn it to an advantage.

As he left that first meeting he realized that it pays to take a more serious look at what is happening on the periphery of the organization. He then did something quite unusual. He hired a group of anthropologists. "We told them to hop in the jungles and live and work, day in and day out, with the tech reps. Eat with them. Travel with them. And discover what planet they were on, because we didn't know, and, more interesting, the tech reps would also find out that they themselves didn't know, because they were engaged in practices that were basically inarticulate relative to their own theory among themselves."

The anthropologists went and they discovered some surprising things. The first was that whenever the going got tough, the tech reps would call in someone else. They'd sit together trying to diagnose what was wrong. These machines are very complicated, some with thirty microprocessors.

"What do these guys do?" Brown asks with obvious joy. "Do they carry their heavy procedure manuals with them. No way. They leave them in the car. Instead, they come in, quickly find some of the symptoms, and a wonderful process takes place: They start to construct and weave a narrative from the fragments they acquire."

When they returned to their home base, they would swap stories. The stories that were the most interesting were those that had a surprise outcome. They were the trickiest problems because they would mislead the troubleshooters. But they also misled those listening to the story. The most important experiences ended up matching the most interesting kinds of stories to tell.

They sat around telling their stories and listening to each other, passing on their experiences, instructing, adding refinements to the stories, which eventually circulated around the world to the corps of tech reps. As a corporation, however, Xerox was more interested in optimizing their tech reps' time in the field than having them telling stories at home base. They were involved in quality movements and optimization movements. They decided that sitting around and telling stories was a waste. According to Brown, they created great big signs saying NO WAR STORIES.

"The consequence," says Brown, "was that we did a brilliant but unexpected job of stopping them. The naturally occurring learning went off—which forced us to send these people back to our training facilities in Leesburg to spend more time being trained in how to repair this equipment. When they got back to the field, they'd sit around and tell stories about how stupid the training was. In our processing, we actually destroyed much of the natural learning."

Xerox eventually learned its lesson, and built some very simple and collaborative technologies to enable these communities of practice to be constantly linked to each other, even if the reps were traveling or on customer sites. At any time during the day, each was linked to another tech rep through a two-way radio system. This system not only supported and created a problem-solving network but actually provided a new learning medium. New tech reps joining the community of practice could simply listen and learn, almost as they might on the Internet today. As Brown explains, "When they thought they had the right idea, they would move from the periphery to the center, offer their idea, and move back again. We had unconsciously built a learning process that had a distributive apprenticeship for learning. We also built better communities of practice at the same time."

The next step was to build a system that implemented the social processes of science. When the tech reps discovered something useful in the field, they would write it up and submit it to a peer review of other tech reps. The ideas would be refined, and if any disagreements surfaced they would be referred to an editing panel, also chosen by the tech reps. Once it was accepted, it was posted on an internal Web site, accessible only to the tech reps.

Xerox is currently getting approximately 25,000 calls a day into the process. They incorporate these new insights happening on the periphery, post them, and in so doing create a self-generated new process.

Some of these insights were so substantial that the reaction of the corporation was to reward them. This idea was carried back to the reps who had started the program. Without exception, every one of them said no. They didn't want a bonus. Why? As the tech reps came up with their ideas, they attached their names to them. If their name survived the process it was posted with the idea. Other tech reps around the world would use it, and these tech reps with name recognition would become more essential members of the community of practice. They were building a social mechanism. Their identity was being constructed by becoming a more central member of this community of practice.

VeriFone, whose products include such things as the ATM readers in supermarkets, has built a similar process to handle problems similar to Xerox's. Recently purchased by Hewlett-Packard, with thirty locations scattered around the world, VeriFone has been called a company where work follows the sun. When the office in Dallas is wrapping up its day, Bombay is just starting and picks up where Dallas left off.[8] Like Xerox's Brown, VeriFone's CEO Hatim Tyabji is a storyteller. He speaks very proudly of the distributed qualities of his company, in which authority is totally decentralized. He makes a point to stress the fact that VeriFone has no central headquarters. As he explains, "When you challenge conventional wisdom to that level, you end up creating a climate within the company where you accept nothing. It makes the company very positive."

That distributive quality goes beyond the lack of a headquarters. By spreading authority, Tyabji has created an environment he likens to a blueberry pancake: Within a blueberry pancake, "all blueberries are free and equal."

With a company as spread out as VeriFone, shared communications might seem to be impossible. But with e-mail and the advance of technology, VeriFone remains tightly knit. By way of e-mail, Tyabji and his senior management send out regular memorandums, called "Excellence in Thought," to all employees. These memos are VeriFone's way of continually connecting their three thousand employees to the company's philosophy. "Excellence in Action" is e-mails from employees back into the system. They are the stories from the various fields that are shared within the company.

"I think openness affects the workforce in a very positive way," Tyabji says. "Because of this openness, fifty percent of our people work outside of the United States. We have people that are in different countries, ethnic backgrounds, cultural values, and they all have come together to a common set of values and a common VeriFone culture that transcends their national cultures. We continually reinforce that value system to our people. That's the important element, continual reinforcement. There's no magic to it. I put out an e-mail, but I assume nobody reads it. You have to have the openness of your message being in print, in e-mail, and then constantly reinforced by the spoken word." Tyabji's personal approach has grown VeriFone in ten years from a dozen employees and $31.2 million in revenue to three thousand and $472.5 million in revenue with a 10 percent net income. The company was so well run, that Hewlett-Packard bought them rather than compete with them.

The Real Message of the Story

The telling of stories is a way for individuals to relate to each other in a fashion that transcends the story's specific content. Something greater emerges in the telling. This is why myth is so powerful as a bearer of our cultural archetypes. It is also why the most important teachings of Buddhist doctrine can be transmitted only person to person. The paradox is that the story itself is not always the message. Telling a story implies a listener, and that speaker-listener relationship immediately creates interaction. Out of this shared interaction something new, innovation, emerges. The greatest concern about this process is that we get locked into the stories we tell: "If I've got to hear that story about the founding of the company one more time . . ." Unlike the mythological stories repeated around the campfires of our ancestors, the stories we tell in business need to be experiential. They need to be a means of sharing information. As soon as they become part of the infrastructure and stop informing, they've lost their meaning. How can we live in the new and the now, and still not get stuck in memory or anticipation?

Often the most difficult assignment to give employees is to ask them to think, to have them ask meaningful questions, engage in dialogue, and be willing to follow the logic that unfolds, wherever it may lead. As members of a TV society, many of us have become lazy, preferring our ideas be fed to us. "Let me do my job, but don't ask me to think what that job should be or accomplish." The opportunity to share stories is a way to break this cycle of persistence, because when people are encouraged to listen, it opens them to adjacent possibilities they might never have known existed.

Unfortunately, there are no shortcuts to the adjacent possible. The critical factor becomes how quickly in this process of evolution the possible can be recognized. Our ability to adapt quickly to an adjacent opportunity is what separates us from species that have died out and members of our own species who have been left behind. Individuals who recognize this and act on it are those who are able to free themselves from the present long enough to form a perspective, and are then capable of some transcendence relative to the present state of affairs.

This transcendence is greater than adaptation. Like spoken and written language itself, it is peculiar to humans. It is our ability to be new and now, to generate something beyond the normal adjustments of daily life. Unlike the complex adaptive systems that proliferate throughout the biological chain, we are capable of being something more. We are capable of purposeful action. Consequently, by creatively participating in our existence in a manner no other species does, we have created what Applied Biosystems' Ken Prokuski has called purposeful complex adaptive systems. These are man-made organizations, not found anywhere else in nature, and designed with purpose.

Operating Businesses as Purposeful Complex Adaptive Systems

The way things happen and the way behaviors occur are always through an ongoing opposition between differing requirements, desires, demands, interests, or values. There are always things to be reconciled. What one has to recognize is that there is an ongoing process in which these things tend to merge into something that works, and the dualism drops away.

Resolution takes place in the ordinary course of two people coming together with differences, at whatever level they may occur, no matter how abstract or concrete or intensely felt. To the extent these differences occur, they are going to get resolved. They may not get resolved until after the business dies, but resolution is certain. How does this happen? As purposeful complex adaptive systems, we cannot ignore what is possible. This is why the organizations that learn how to open themselves to greater possibilities have a big edge over those that don't. Fortunately, this is something that can be learned. As Einstein said about the nature of knowledge and how we create it, if we don't ask questions at a certain level of theory we will continue on with no dialectical process occurring.

We must learn to ask good questions of each other with every problem that arises. It's something that must take place in every single interaction among the agents of an organization. Storytelling is one mode for providing a context for our questions. Our stories state ideas that link to something already known to the listener.

But stories are relevant only when real meeting takes place. Psychologist and author Irene Claremont de Castelejo describes this meeting "as the capacity to meet and be met." At this juncture we as individuals are able to coevolve and open to the adjacent possible. Our ability to language what emerges from that meeting allows us to apply a new way of thinking within our organizations, and to assume our place as purposeful complex adaptive systems.

NONLINEAR INVESTIGATIONS NO. 4: ORGANIZATIONAL INNOVATION

Abstract ideas are the patterns two or more memories have in common. They are born whenever someone realizes that similarity. . . . Creative thinking may mean simply the realization that there's no particular virtue in doing things the way they have always been done.   • Rudolf Flesch

In order for a nonlinear tool to be useful, it must be sufficiently abstract to be used to make sense of a broad range of nonlinear strategies, while at the same time leaving open the relationship of such strategies to their "intended results." Nonlinearity means, in one sense, that strict means-end relationships are neither possible nor workable and that they can be understood only in relation to each other. Ends precede means fully as much as means precede ends. Any "intended result" is itself called into question.

Formulate a major problem of your organization. In relation to this problem:

1. What are the most fundamental assumptions, beliefs, models, and metaphors relating to this problem in our organization? How have they been derived? How have they influenced efforts to be innovative?

2. To what extent are these approaches linear? How could they be reformulated in nonlinear terms so that they enlarge the range of possibilities for innovative behaviors?

3. To what extent have we limited or encouraged the sharing of narratives, anecdotes, and metaphors within our organization? Is there a formal or informal process for doing so?

4. To what extent are the thinking and behaviors of our organization tied to and limited by a linear world view? Discuss in terms of the following:

   • The way ideas are generated and disseminated within the organization

   • The systems in place for coevolving thinking

5. How do organizational values limit what is accepted as knowledge ? How does what people think they know limit what they consider to be important? Investigate the following:
   - Priorities
   - Source of priorities
   - Sacrosanct values

6. What is the relationship between new ideas and new practices? Discuss the following:
   - Ease of implementation
   - Resistances
   - Response and adaptation

7. How does an organization facilitate a different level of thinking from the one that "created" its problem?

Real-World Applications for Coevolving Metaphors

Everything factual is already theory. • Goethe

It is one thing to undertake a new way of thinking, and another thing entirely to incorporate and activate the ideas that arise out of our thinking into the world at large. In this chapter we will discuss how these ideas become represented metaphorically and how they directly influence and inform our behaviors and interactions. We will explore such areas as feedback and simplicity. We will also examine the idea of continuity, which exists in a nonlinear world but is evident only in hindsight. What we will find, however, is that businesses that attempt to generalize from that hindsight perspective in an effort to predict what is to come inevitably fail.

In this Postindustrial Age, the spring running the clockwork universe has come unwound. Time still exists, but the mechanistic model devised to compartmentalize it, to build walls and maintain it, can no longer contain the flow. Does this mean the business world is now running amok? No. It means that our metaphors and the ideas they describe must support an accurate depiction of the world in which we work. Within an emergent universe, the metaphors and models that affect our business behaviors become more fluid, coevolving with the full landscape of the business environment. Within this contextual flow our interactions must feed back and inform our business performance.

The tools John Holland described as blunted in this new environment all operate within a framework of induction. We can generalize from the past to determine what the future will be. There isn't any mystery in the relationship between parts A and B. It's a mechanical relationship. And within that understanding there's a stability, a safety within a vastness that would seem too much to comprehend without the mechanism. The world of the future will be like the world of the past, not necessarily identical nor containing the same details, but similar in kind. There is a linear progression from A to B.

Nonlinearity does not provide the same degree of safety. It bursts forth with the discovery that today is not at all what we expected and it really looks nothing like yesterday. With this understanding of the world, the stability between past, present, and future slips away. We can no longer be sure about what will happen tomorrow and the kind of continuity it will have with yesterday.

The model and the metaphors of organic and evolutionary processes are quite different from those of mechanistic processes. There are continuities, but they can be recognized only in retrospect. Within every new organizational level in the process, within the myriad of possible agent interactions, the unexpected occurs.

The nonlinear investigations provided throughout this book have been designed to aid in the pragmatic summarizing of an organization's ideas and metanarratives. These are the concepts that have driven operations and through which a business creates its metaphors to define and communicate its goals and objectives. These tools offer a way to look back to see the continuity, and to take a snapshot of today. But so doing makes it patently evident that there would be no way to know while operating from the past what that future would be. By taking the time to identify and comprehend what those past assumptions and beliefs have been, what they supported, and what they no longer define, we free our organizations to transition from the metaphors of the previous age into a new world of emergence and complexity.

Delineating the Linear and the Non

The inevitability is that the infrastructualized stability of the linear world will become the ruins of the next age. Just as we admire the castles and museums dotting the European countryside, we will continue to marvel at our linear bastions that still demonstrate their elegance and grace, their majesty that demarcated a very different world. But the nonlinear model is not as perilous as it may seem at first glance. The difference is that it is about movement, not stasis. It is about flowing forward, being aware of the interactions between experience and our interpretation or conceptualization of that experience—being aware of how we represent that experience and then of the metaphorical course that governs our behaviors and relates back to the experience and defines the outcome. When we look back on that process, we do not see a straight line.

Of the early Darwinists, the anthropologist and author Loren Eiseley wrote:

> The nineteenth-century evolutionists, and many philosophers still today, are obsessed by struggle. They try to define natural selection in one sense only—something that Darwin himself avoided. They ignore all man's finer qualities—generosity, self-sacrifice, universe-searching wisdom—in the attempt to enclose him in the small capsule that contained the brain of proto-man. Such writers often fail to explore man's growing sense of beauty, the language that has opened and defined his world, the little gifts he came to lay beside his dead.
>
> None of these acts could have been prophesied before man came. They reveal something other than what the pure materialist would be able to draw out of the dark concourse of matter before the genuine emergence of these novel human phenomena into time.[1]

Objects and Behaviors

The mechanistic, linear viewpoint operates on the assumption that the objective world is the same for all observers. We have certain experiences of an object, and there is an interpretation of them by means of which those experiences are reported back. Newtonian science would say that if one reported back an objective experience, someone else should be able to duplicate it. And if the same conditions and controls were in place, our experiment would have the same outcome as the previous experience. We make the assumption, of course, that we are talking about the same object, the same kind of experience with it, the same way of representing that experience, and ultimately the predicable behaviors that follow. Through this process, astronomers can predict the precise location of a star millions of light years away, at a specific time.

In an organic, nonlinear world this process needs to be re-understood and restated. When we are speaking of an organic, nonlinear world, we are talking about complex adaptive systems. This is true whether we are looking at organic systems that grow, learn, adapt, and coevolve, or man-made organizations, which, owing to different degrees of interaction, have a life of their own but can still be modeled in relation to the organic. The first difference between the mechanistic linear and the organic is that within the organic we are looking at our relationship to behaviors, not objects.

As we mentioned earlier, objects arc things *out there* with their own *objective* nature. They are something to be known. When we focus on behaviors, the pragmatic view is that there is little relevance in speaking about what is true or false, real or not real, or even objective. *Within the complex adaptive system of behaviors, everything is relational.* What we find is that when we experience an object nonlinearly and begin the representation of that experience, a radical shift occurs. There is a much more intimate and symbiotic relationship between the experience and the representation than there is between the experience and the object experienced. In this fashion, what conditions the experience is not just what is received from some presumably unchanging *out there*, but the interpretations that we bring to bear on the experience. How we represent the experience, symbolize it, and metaphorize it has as much influence on the experience as the experience has on the representation, symbols, and metaphors. In essence, a recursive relationship occurs between the experience and representation that cannot be disengaged. Within this context, the causal flow from object to experience to interpretation breaks down. In an experiential sense, the object becomes no more relevant than anything else within that context. We cannot separate the experience from the representation nor the representation from the experience. Experience can be historical, cultural, or genetic, or can even emanate from what the psychoanalyst Carl Jung called the *collective unconscious*, which Jung defined as bearing the archetypes that we all share.

For example, before we experience something we have expectations. Experience occurs within a framework of expectation. If we are predisposed to disliking something, such as a particular movie actor, this predisposition would influence our experience of that actor's films. We make a judgment based on our expectations. We cannot just focus on the experience without the influence of expectation.

What emerges out of this symbiotic relationship between experience and representation is behaviors that in turn are determined by their relationship to the process—what we are engaging in and why we are engaging in it.

Einstein said that he sees no difference between the world of science and the world of ordinary common sense. Because of this recursive cycling between experience and interpretation, every encounter that includes a complex adaptive system is subjective. Complete objectivity is a limiting concept. As individuals experiencing the world, we can only relate to things or each other through our perspective or point of view. In this sense, objectivity is a mechanistic and vain attempt to distance ourselves from the experience, our interpretations, and the coevolving effects that are inevitable in a complex, nonlinear world.

The economist Brian Arthur tells a story about an old mathematician riding in a railroad train that is crossing the border from England to Scotland. In the compartment with him is a small boy who stares out the window, and just as the train goes into Scotland, he sees a black sheep and says, "Oh, look, sheep in Scotland are black." Also sitting with the mathematician and the boy is a minister, who also happens to be an amateur logician and mathematician. He says to the boy, "Don't be silly, that is not true. All we know is that there is at least one black sheep in Scotland." Then the old mathematician spoke to the minister: "That is not strictly true either. All we know is that there is at least one sheep in Scotland, at least one side of which is black."

Relating to Things

A distinction must also be made here in relating to objects. The object does not relate to the individual the way the individual relates to the object. For the most part, *things* are incapable of providing feedback. To relate to things better, we apply feedback mechanisms and devices: gas gauges on cars, thermometers in turkeys, spell-checkers in computers. But they are simply that: mechanisms and devices, linear feedback processes. Coevolution in relation to things is very different from the coevolution that takes place when individual experiences individual. In each case our predisposition may affect our relationship toward the other, but the interactions and resulting complexity are far greater in the experiences that take place between living systems than those between individuals and things.

In either case, when we recognize the recursive relationship between experience and representation we are operating in the domain of nonlinearity. By doing so we set up an environment that is constantly expanding and open. We now have not only the possibility of an open system but its necessity. It also means that we can no longer presume to contain or control the relationship between all the various elements of our world, even though many organizations still, vainly, make the attempt.

It follows then that there is also an openness between experience and concept. Neither determines the other. This is the point Einstein was making when he said that there is no rational or demonstrable concept or metaphor for experience. Metaphor is nothing more than what he called "the free play of imagination." Within imagination, there is openness, creativity, and novelty. Once we have formulated a conceptual system out of that free imaginative play, the reasoning takes place in which the symbols, metaphors, and experience relate to each other. Rules get established and logics emerge, as do geometries and grammars.

The Metaphoric Analogy

The role of metaphor in this process is extremely important. George Lakoff and Mark Johnson make clear that, "our ordinary conceptual system, in terms of which we both think and act, is fundamentally metaphoric in nature. . . . Metaphors as linguistic expressions are possible precisely because there are metaphors in a person's conceptual system."[2] Thus models and metaphors play a similar role in providing a context for behavior.

What is important, however, is the relationships that have been altered between an object, the experience of the object, the interpretation of that experience, and the action that results. When we move from the mechanistic linear to the organic nonlinear, what changes is the flow of information. We do not move from object to experience, but rather in a recursive two-way flow in which each aspect is influencing the other. There is no unique atomic experience that is totally independent or free from the conceptions and relations within which that experience occurs. *Out of this relationship between interpretation and experience innovation occurs.*

We should reiterate, however, that in spite of this recursive relationship between experience and/or metaphors, there is no such thing as experience without theory or theory independent of experience. However, theory is always implicit in experience. It's only theory that allows experience to be intelligible. Theory shapes, and influences experience much more deeply than experience shapes theory. In a mechanistic linear process, we have the sensation and then we can say what we saw. In an organic nonlinear approach, we have the metaphor or theory in relation to which it is now possible to have sensations that were not possible otherwise. In human experience, there is no independent and predictable atomic sensation. As complex adaptive systems, we do not simply behave as things.

For example, McDonald's has already made up its mind about how it operates. Whenever its franshisees try to tell them about their business, McDonald's sees it as hostile and unreasonable. They have taken a stand that is a situational response to the market rather than taking an innovative one. From this perspective, the experience at McDonald's will always be what the patterns already are—they will repeat and reconfirm the prevailing view.

Since McDonald's has already made up its mind about not trusting its franchisees, it can't hear the franchisees except within that framework and pattern of expectation. The same is proving to be true for McDonald's at other levels of activities whether they are expectations of customers or its market. How does a company break outside that process to free itself from ideas and interpretations it has already formed and experience has confirmed? How does an organization free itself to listen without expectations? It's a difficult answer that no one really wants to hear. The answer lies in developing the capacity to project a transcendent position, as Einstein suggested, stepping outside the issues to a higher level of abstraction. This higher level enables the organization to view what is occurring without being restricted to the inital level of understanding. In other words, the company has to learn how to "think." It has to learn how to ask relevant questions about what it thinks it knows. It's a healthy process of adaptation that does not resist but welcomes change. McDonald's is not doing this and so anything they do will only reinforce their deteriorating situation.

In her book *The Metaphoric Process,* Gemma Corradi Fiumara states: "Theories of knowledge might be regarded as ideas about the structure of the interactions that are operative in the 'mind' of those who create theories. These internal structures may be referred to as 'implicit theories' because they exist in some sense in our worldview without being explicitly formalized." Fiumara then hypothesizes that explicit theories originally arise from implicit ones, even those that are empirically derived. She goes on to suggest that if Aristotle were correct, that "metaphor is a sign of genius," then "the generation of implicit theories is highly to be valued."[3]

William Irwin Thompson stated this same idea differently: "In a world in which humans write thousands of books and one million scientific papers a year, the mythic bricoleur is the person who plays with all the information and hears a music inside the noise."[4]

Metaphor and the Nonlinear Experience

By way of an organic, nonlinear example of metaphor's human quality, Loren Eiseley, in his essay "The Star Thrower," describes a scene in which he was walking down a craggy shoreline in Costabel.[5] He spied a person in the distance bending down, grasping something, and throwing it into the roaring ocean beyond the surf. When Eiseley reached this lone figure, he found him freeing starfish stranded in the sand by the low tide and flinging them back into the oceans so they could live. Eiseley's first impression was that this "star thrower is a man, and death is running more fleet than he along every seabeach in the world." But then something changed for Eiseley. Upon further reflection, he returned to the site and joined the star thrower, heaving the struggling starfish back into the ocean, and in essence, renewing their life.

> I picked up a star whose tube feet ventured timidly among my fingers while, like a true star, it cried soundlessly for life. I saw it with an unaccustomed clarity and cast far out. With it, I flung myself as forfeit, for the first time, into some unknown dimension of existence. From Darwin's tangled bank of unceasing struggle, selfishness, and death, had arisen, incomprehensively, the thrower who loved not man, but life. It was the subtle cleft in nature before which biological thinking had faltered. . . . Tomorrow I would walk in the storm. . . . I would walk with the knowledge of the discontinuities of the unexpected universe. I would walk knowing of the rift revealed by the thrower, a hint that there looms, inexplicable, in nature something above the role men give her.

From the point of view of complexity, if we operate a business within a mechanistic, linear model, we are going to confuse the way in which what we know and what we experience relate to each other. The mechanistic model presumes a fixity of what passes for knowledge as if it were embedded in the process and unchanging. In making this presumption, we can come up with conclusions that are only pragmatically inadequate. Only by stepping outside the mechanistic linear context of thinking, outside the business itself, can we open the system to new possibilities. This requires a continual questioning of what we assume to be true. This is why in the mid-eighties quality circles were so effective. They brought workers together daily to question the process. One of the main tenets of just-in-time was continuous improvement—a continual questioning about how to make the process better.

Thinking Tools' John Hiles likens keeping the system open to the way in which Laplanders handle their herds of reindeer. They don't steer the herds—as a shepherd or cow wrangler would do—they follow the herds, yet remain linked to them. They are tuned into them, though not necessarily knowing which way they will go. From these herds they make an exceptional living. Sometimes an opportunity presents itself that may resemble a large herd with great possibilities for reward. The only action, as Hiles says "is to become Laplander to that herd. We don't know which way it is going to go, but we stay in tune."

Generalization Lock-in

When we become locked into a closed system in which we generalize from the past to come to conclusions about the future, we cannot break out of the systems about which we are generalizing. Nor can we break out of the interpretations that we bring to bear on our experiences. Since our environment is constantly changing, if we remain stuck, coevolution cannot take place. The result is that our business rapidly becomes out of phase with the changing environment. No adaptation occurs, and the species dies out.

This is evident in the continual demise of companies. When Thomas J. Peters and Robert H. Waterman, Jr. went out in search of excellence, they looked at forty-three companies they thought were on the right path. Within less than five years, two thirds of them were in decline.[6]

So how do we protect the species from extinction? What steps do we need to take to help ensure a healthy and prosperous corporate life cycle? We do so by continually questioning the ideas that drive the complex interactions of our businesses.

As mentioned previously, the nonlinear investigations offered in this book are a means to pragmatically summarize all the ideas a business has put together. If practiced diligently, they facilitate the transition to the world of behaviors, action, and applications, a world in which emergent novelty is a matter of course, not a novel occurrence.

Emergence Happens

It may seem contradictory to describe an environment in which we allow emergence to happen, while simultaneously outlining how to utilize complexity in real-world applications. This paradox can be dispelled by understanding that allowing strategies to emerge does not mean doing nothing. Emergence and innovation take place in the interaction between our models and behaviors. The key words here are "in the interaction between." Emergence happens, but not without an interaction. Once that has taken place and a new metaphor, model, or theory emerges, we have to identify the change, then adjust our understanding of the system it affects to reflect that new understanding. We then adjust our behaviors and their subsequent interactions according to that new understanding. Within these interactions, emergence and innovation take place again.

A simple illustration demonstrates the complex nature of this task and the variety of interactions that are possible (see Figure 4).

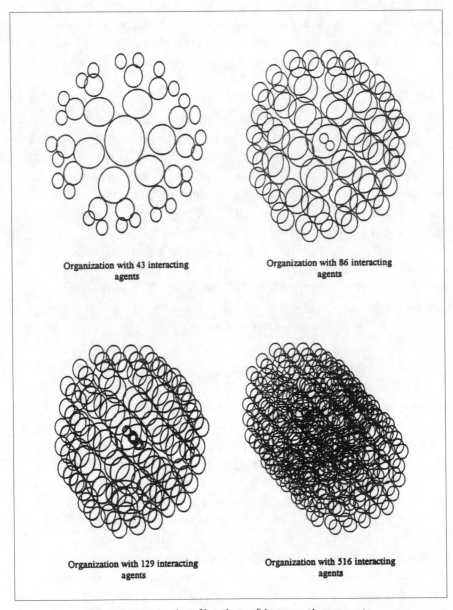

Organization with 43 interacting agents

Organization with 86 interacting agents

Organization with 129 interacting agents

Organization with 516 interacting agents

Figure 4.   A visualization of interactive agents

Applied Biosystems' Ken Prokuski emphasized that when they opened their research and development process to this way of thinking, more innovative ideas emerged than they had time or money to implement. That is intuitively understandable if one simply looks at the complex interactions possible in an organization of less than six hundred people.

The Fuel of Emergence: Feedback

When we talk about the process of emergence, of evolution, we are ultimately describing a process that occurs in the domain of information. Ideas emerge, metaphors emerge, forms of intelligibility, logics, and concepts emerge. Only through the emergence of these new ways of organizing data, through the representation and interpretation of the experiences, can change occur in the organization.

Any change in ideas will be reflected as a change in the infrastructure. It will affect the way certain things are done and the facilities for doing them. Similarly, the feedback that consequently comes from the infrastructure has been made more complete and sophisticated, by adapting these more pragmatic and effective ideas. These ideas allow for a deeper kind of feedback because we have better ways of formulating their application, which enables the continuation of the emergence of new ideas and metaphors. By "better" we mean more pragmatically applicable and better able to yield the kinds of behavior changes that the business values. As we mentioned when we discussed principles, models, rules, and behaviors, our models are only as good, effective, or accurate as our available feedback. The better the feedback the more precisely we can model our organization's principles.

Only through an understanding of a system as emerging, self-organizing, and nonlinear can we locate where these processes of feedback become possible, namely, between our models/metaphors and our behaviors. It does not take place between rules and behaviors. This form of feedback is sterile, as is that between principles and behaviors. All that these interactions create is more of the same, a further retrenchment into old ways of doing.

By both locating where feedback occurs, and how we think about our models and behaviors we now make it possible for authentic and relevant ideas to emerge on a continuing basis. They are relevant because they speak directly to the essence or core of the nature of a business entity.

They cut right to the heart of it. By freeing up the flow of ideas and feedback, we free up the flow of the business. This again relates back to the notion of quality circles.

Ever since the 1970s, even before quality circles, many manufacturing companies have employed a system called Manufacturing Resource Planning as a way to provide feedback and maintain their complicated operations. This linear computerized approach to managing planning, scheduling, material requirements, capacity, and execution relied heavily on the feedback of those involved in each step of the system. With all the complex operations required to manufacture products, this was one of the most successful computer-driven approaches available. The system, however, could not and did not function successfully without diligent feedback (see Figure 5).

We should make a distinction here between mechanistic linear and organic nonlinear feedback. Mechanistic linear feedback does work, but where and how it works must be understood. It works very well in relationship with things. We want the pilot of our plane to receive accurate linear feedback from his altimeters and radar. We expect process gauges to reflect the proper pressures in our manufacturing processes. There are, however, some areas in which linear feedback is not adequate.

If we use computers as a metaphor, there is a difference between serial and parallel dynamics. For complex calculation, serial computation would take years to produce the same result that parallel processing could perform in a fraction of the time. The model is that feedback involving nonlinear behaviors cannot be adequately dealt with sequentially, but only in parallel.

The Failure of Sequence

In her book *The Resurgence of the Real*, Charlene Spretnak talked about the rational use of medical models that are based on sequential processes.[7] In this model, doctors move from a simple cause to a simple effect. They treat the effect in isolation from everything else going on in the body and look for the cause of that effect. A patient comes into a doctor's office having experienced occasional fainting spells. The doctor approaches the problem sequentially. The fainting is the effect of something; what are the probable causes? Nothing is found. In reality, there may be more than one "cause," and it may not be a thing, but the

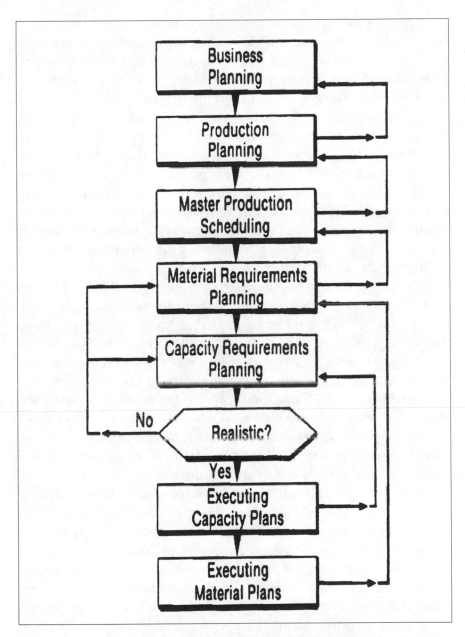

Figure 5. **Manufacturing Resource Planning feedback loops (© 1980 by Oliver Wright Companies)**

patient's own living complex adaptive system interacting within itself. There is no simple linear explanation—operation on a variety of interacting levels simultaneously.

A parallel process might look at the fainting as something that is occurring to the total organism. How can this be understood in relation to other behaviors in the organism with which there may be some congruence, rather than in relation to one particular cause. Many interactions going on within the system could affect the fainting.

It may not be caused by the blood pressure medicine or by recurrent, almost undetectable strokes, or a tumor that the scans have missed, or even low blood sugar. It may be the interactions that are occurring and passing through the filter we put in place while looking at the specifics. Maybe low blood sugar, when combined with a certain kind of air pollution, when combined with the way in which a blood pressure medicine functions, is causing the problem. This might explain in part why an effective *combination* of medicines has been having such a profound impact on maintaining the health of HIV patients.

Another example has recently surfaced which probably would never have been understood in terms of a system of mechanistic/linear feedback. In his book *And the Waters Turned to Blood*, Rodney Barker documents the story of the emergence of a new and deadly species of animal, *Pfiesteria piscicida*, that arose in the estuaries and rivers of North Carolina. This ravaging menace, having lain dormant in the coastal shallows for millions of years, was brought to life as a complex process unfurled. Following a line of linear feedback, scientists were unable to understand why all of a sudden this microscopic killer would devastate fish populations and threaten human populations as well. When they looked at it from a nonlinear perspective, the process was at least understandable.

North Carolina, anticipating the decline of tobacco farming, decided to diversify its economy. Pig farming was encouraged as an alternative. Flushing the effluent of the pigs into the waterways changed the complex ecological interrelationships in the rivers, and awoke a microscopic monster that became a biological threat to both humans and fish. This unicellular animal was capable of mutating into at least twenty-four different forms and could even masquerade as a plant. When human patients began arriving at their doctors' offices with strange symptoms, the conventional linear medical tests showed nothing. Only after the full picture of *Pfiesteria piscicida* had emerged, and the complex interactions that had awakened it were understood, did doctors believe their patients' symptoms were genuine and did the authorities take steps toward limiting the bacterium's spread.

Intuitive Processing

How do we go about identifying and finding nonlinear interactions? First, we become more attuned to nonlinear forms of feedback. Parallel computer processing is one such model, but another is one decision makers are involved in every day. They receive informational feedback from many different sources, synthesize it, and from a very nonlinear progression of mental processing, they intuitively respond with a decision. Intuition is an unconscious synthesis of experience and knowledge combined with an openness to what the decision maker does not yet know.

There is a dynamic at work in intuition. As we move back and forth between the interactions of various aspects of a business, we are constantly formulating a global metaphor, or a metaphor that applies to the total system. In this fashion, the interactions of the elements are fully involved, including the metaphor/model that arises from the interactions of the elements. In this instance, we are constantly moving as much from wholes to parts as we are from parts to whole.

Within this realm of feedback and coevolving metaphors, an emergent decision-making process may also be taking place. In this model, no one agent makes the decision, but all agents interacting and feeding back make the decision without anyone's orchestrating it. By incorporating and assessing nonlinear feedback, whether it is collective, individual, or computational, we can in turn feed it back as new models or metaphors. We receive feedback from the infrastructure, which we then return as information to adjust the infrastructure, which provides further feedback, in a process that continues.

Nonsustainable Success

Unfortunately, many businesses that have achieved a level of cognitive success tend to stop their cognitive process there. They think their past success will allow them to be successful in the future. However, businesses are discovering again and again that they can't rely on their old models, that past success does not take into account current conditions.

Supercuts' Christina Campbell, a franchisee with many of her own outlets, described unexpected decline in her newly opened shops in biological terms: There is a virus out there and we don't know the nature of it or how to deal with it. "I don't even know what the virus is," she said.

"I can't even put my finger on it. I can't define it, but it is spreading. Something is different. For fifteen years I knew how to; now, I do not."

Comparing her business to other, more established shops, she sees that her volume is being maintained, but her profit is also steadily declining. The established shops may have developed a much stronger immune system and can withstand the onslaught of the virus longer than a new shop. Campbell feels that unless a cure is found, eventually the established shops will die, too. The problem should be visible. What Campbell is doing is the equivalent of taking the shop's white blood cell count and temperature and then watching it decline. "The virus is taking over and unless I can come up with the right kind of cure, I can almost predict that within X number of months they are going to die. That shop will die unless I can find a way of saving it."

All of the answers that present themselves are linear kinds of answers—the traditional mechanistic approach to cure. Her old ways of formulating ideas about her operations and making them intelligible don't make sense anymore.

In postmodern language, there is something different about the relationship of these shop owners with their environments. The ways they once related to their environments made it possible for them to plan, calculate, and predict how their businesses would operate. They were influencing that environment just as it was influencing them. And something about the way they were coevolving within it gave them confidence that they knew how to deal with the issues they were interacting with. Now the dynamics of those interactions have altered, and there is no linear answer to their problems.

If they limit themselves to traditional ways of understanding and get locked into old metaphors, they limit their capacity to make sense out of the changes in that interaction. What is missing is a way of understanding the changing interactions differently. Supercuts is not alone: CNN reported a plethora of problems being faced by McDonald's, and the "McBlunders" they have made trying to solve them.

McDonald's market share is steadily going down. The people who spend money on fast food are spending a lower percentage of that money at McDonald's. The average volume for a McDonald's outlet is going down, and naturally, the average profit for a McDonald's franchise is also going down. To use our earlier medical model, the system is sick in some way. How do McDonald's managers diagnose it? They have followed one linear answer with another. They decided first that "they needed to become more upscale"—CNN's words. They introduced the Arch Deluxe, which was a disaster. Then they decided they were too expensive and rolled back their prices to 1955 levels. They failed again, but this time they generated something unexpected: great unrest within the McDonald's franchise system. The franchisees were seeing both their profits and revenues dropping. McDonald's had gotten stuck in the idea that they operated in a two-dimensional universe in which their price was either not high enough or too high. They figured that all they had to do to solve their problem was fine-tune the price. It didn't work. They decided to return to their old ad agency, which had created the slogan "You deserve a break today." Brad Ball, McDonald's marketing chief, said in a *USA Today* article that the company hopes to return to feel-good ads, following efforts that have "been out of balance of late."[8]

How can companies like McDonald's and Supercuts start thinking about their problems in a different way, to discover new behaviors that have not yet occurred to them? How can they properly formulate the issues so that they present themselves with new possibilities without the old system dying? Einstein said the same level of thinking that causes a problem can't be used to solve it. Long before Einstein, Aristotle established a separate science to question the axioms of each science. He called it metaphysics.

The Kyle Principle

Kyle Radaker, a small business owner, offered one reason for aging businesses' inability to maintain their competitive edge against upstarts. The Kyle Principle states that if a business is, say, three years old, and a similar business opens up nearby, the new business is actually starting three years ahead of the first organization. The reason for this is that an aging company finds itself locked into upgrading a model on the basis of what it already knows. The company looks at its experience and tries to build a theory as opposed to looking at how it can use theory to change its experience. A new business doesn't carry that same idea baggage. They start with the benefit of their competitor's experience, but without the lock-in to the ideas.

The Prediction Company's Doyne Farmer has found this to be true in their operations developing stock market predictions software. "We have really benefited relative to our economist counterparts, by not having been brainwashed in a whole system of thinking that is stifling right from the start and contains a lot of fundamentally wrong assumptions."

Introducing another hamburger model when there are plenty of them, doesn't do much of anything. Lowering the price when it is already reasonably low, doesn't do anything but apply a Band-Aid. Wendy's saw a trend toward healthy eating and added pitas to their menu. They're basically using the same ingredients that they have been using in their other products, but the impression is of a new and healthier eating experience. They haven't essentially changed what people are already buying from them, but they have changed the way the basic ingredients are served—created a new model. Instead of putting the ingredients between two buns, it's in a pita pocket. It's still fast food, and can be held in the hands and eaten while the customer walks out the door. Whether it works or not is still to be seen, but it is an example of lifestyle changes McDonald's has yet to understand.

Models get worn out. We become attached and get locked into what our model has always been because it has been successful, and we can't break out of it. Can we radicalize the model, or do we need a new one?

Change at the Level of the Model

The only place a business can effectively change is at the level of the model. What we essentially mean by a model is the way we have organized and structured our thinking about an issue, which gets reflected on down the line in infrastructural kinds of behaviors—in what we actually do.

Ford's principle is manufacturing and selling cars to a mass market. In the 1950s Ford was operating from a model that says they have to have cars that are low-priced, medium-priced, medium-high-priced, and high-priced. They realized they had a void in the medium-high-priced range. Ford put out the Edsel. Ford's way of thinking was very linear and mechanistic, and the Edsel fell on its face. The problem wasn't the principle—the Ford Motor Company is doing today what it was doing at its inception and what it was doing at the time of the Edsel. What was wrong was the way they were choosing to think about the structure of their business, which made them think that what they needed was an Edsel. Interestingly, Ford followed that disaster by offering in 1955 the most successful automobile model that had ever been produced up to that point, the

Thunderbird, followed in 1965 with a car that was even more popular, the Mustang.

If we compare Ford and McDonald's, what Ford was trying to do with the Edsel was produce the Arch Deluxe; both products turned out to be wrong and failed. However, Ford learned something from the ordeal and did something radically different. The T-bird was a totally different kind of car. It was a car for a different *lifestyle*. Peter Drucker makes the point that Ford learned the hard way that they could not let their models—in this case, automobile models—be determined, as they had always assumed they must, by demographics. Their product must in fact largely be influenced by lifestyles.

Looking at a product demographically is very linear. The number of people in a particular income range is X. We'll produce a model to appeal to the people in that income range, which will sell at a price appropriate to their income. Since there are X people in the country in that income range, we project that we can produce enough to sell Y percent of that market, Z number of automobiles. We tool up for it, invest in production—and the cars don't sell. Peter Drucker was saying that we cannot make a one-to-one linear correlation between the target income range and the price of the car and let that determine the model produced. We have to look at the way lifestyles have been changing and produce a car that is not limited to the one dimension, price, for salability.

Drucker would probably agree that McDonald's is making the same mistake that Ford made with the Edsel. They are assuming that they can make a linear correlation between income levels and price. In doing so, they are not looking at lifestyles and all the complex factors that interact to produce a lifestyle. We make a distinction between trends and lifestyles: Trends are more linear, number-driven, while lifestyles are more complex in nature, reflecting various unpredictable interactions with society (other complex adaptive system agents) that are not always obvious on the surface.

The McDonald's Arch Deluxe was an example of a linear "cure" based on demographics. McDonald's figured they didn't have a product that appealed to adults. The linear tool says look at these demographic levels. How many people are there in each age group and in each income group? Let's tailor something for that age group. It didn't work. In an organic, nonlinear world, from looking at a few basically related lifestyles and at what will appeal to or influence that interactive lifestyle, we come up with a radically different answer: the T-bird, not the Edsel.

Differentiating between the mechanistic-linear qualities of trend analysis and organic-nonlinear lifestyles has nothing to do with numbers and everything to do with learning to evaluate nonlinear feedback. This is often much easier for younger companies to do. Aging companies that have constructed walls to protect what they have or what once was successful have locked out their real-world barometer on current conditions. Lifestyle situations change fast. Oftentimes younger organizations adapt more easily to these changes. The ability of any aging complex living system to adapt may start to slow down with age (though many of us may try to deny it). As the rate of adaptation slows and change accelerates, older organizations can fall further behind. They're also transporting an increasing amount of baggage. The rationalization is that since they are older and more experienced, they have more "knowledge" that will carry the day. Unfortunately, the more data they have, the more locked in they tend to get to what was successful in the past. This relates back to Kyle's Principle: New organizations haven't accumulated the same baggage as their entrenched competition, so they tend to move with greater agility.

Established companies that get stuck in their old models are most susceptible to the unfortunate surprise of finding nothing that works to change a situation. But as pointed out by Xerox's John Seely Brown, because they tend to be bigger they also have the greatest potential for interaction, change, and adaptation at the periphery. The key is to open the doors to the periphery of the organization. Innovation occurs as a result of the interaction between our models/metaphors/theories and our behaviors. Allowing those interactions to take place freely and to inform the system can provide new and positive direction.

Complexity-Generated Simplicity

In today's competitive environment, many of our linear models have reached the end of their life cycles. As complex adaptive systems, business organizations must be prepared and willing to move on rather than remain stuck in a past that is rapidly receding. Learning to incorporate nonlinear feedback is not about unlocking a Pandora's box of confusion and chaos. It is about using ideas more effectively to find patterns and possibilities that did not previously exist in the current complexity of a postindustrial business.

There is another point of reassurance for those still leery about opening their boundaries and operating in a nonlinear world. Within the coevolution of our models is a paradox. New models concurrently and simultaneously enable things to become more complex, that is, to develop higher levels of organization that did not previously exist. They also incorporate innovations that did not previously exist but that were always implicit in the continuity of the processes. The paradox is that while moving toward more complex levels of organization we find a simplicity that was not previously accessible or possible on a lower level of complexity. In the *Fabric of Reality,* David Deutsch called this "emergence: high-level simplicity 'emerges' from low-level complexity."

As an example, let us look at a simple process like transportation. If we want to go from Santa Fe, New Mexico, to Rome, Italy, some very complex organizations, activities, and processes enable us to get there. We fly there in an airplane. In order to fly there, someone had to invent airplanes—figure out how to design and manufacture them, how to put together their millions of components, their engines, fuselages, instrument panels, controls, and monitoring devices.

Someone also had to design and build the airport. Someone had to put together the organizations of people who make reservations and schedules and maintain the system. Someone had to find out how to fly airplanes and train people to fly them. Someone had to develop navigational instruments and methodologies. Radar systems had to be invented and built as well as methods for controlling, tracking, and monitoring flights.

Every time we go to the airport and get on an airplane we take this very complex structure, with all its interacting components, for granted. We go to the airport about a half an hour before departure. The plane leaves roughly on schedule. It takes a certain amount of time to fly to the destination, a time that is predictable to within a matter of minutes. When the plane arrives, the airline is ready to receive it. There is an orderly process of disembarkation, the requisite hassle with customs and luggage—but with relatively little fuss and a high degree of predictability, we have moved from point A to point B. The hidden logistics of our trip have been infinitely complex. They are so complex that if we diagrammed or formalized them, the ensuing document would take volumes. The working of the jet engines alone would take an enormous amount of explanation.

This doesn't take into account the historical possibilities that led to the development of the jet engine in the first place.

Let's compare this to making a journey from Santa Fe to Rome in 1800. This trip also would have been a very complex process. Instead of going to an airport and arriving in Rome twelve hours later, first we must find a way of getting to New York. This trip would take weeks of arduous travel, and we would have no idea how long the trip would take once we left Santa Fe. We wouldn't have a clue as to the weather we would encounter en route. We wouldn't know how to plan ahead for food and water. When we finally arrived in New York, we wouldn't know when the boat was going to depart. The boat line would also be fairly vague and unpredictable about the route it would take, and how long the journey to Rome would be.

By the time we arrive in Rome six months later, we would have gone through a harrowing, complex process of behaviors without much certainty, or even simple predictability. It would be nearly impossible to communicate with someone to tell them when we would be arriving in Rome, because there would be no way of communicating any faster than traveling on the boat and delivering the message ourselves.

The paradox in all of this traveling about is that the more complex a situation becomes, the simpler it becomes. Every step of our Rome trip in 1800 is, itself, a relatively simple process. The construction of the stagecoach we ride to New York is relatively simple, as is the operation of the boat. For today's travel plans, there are organizational entities involved in getting us from point A to B. We are dealing with complex social systems that did not previously exist and that are very difficult to understand. Paradoxically, the system *as a whole* is infinitely simpler than the 1800's system, and everything that occurs is much more predictable. The principle here is that as the organizational structures become more complex, they enable simpler behaviors, including more predictable behaviors.

The reason for this is that the layer below the emergent complexity drops away. We no longer have to worry about how the plane is built, who trains the pilots, who is sitting at the navigation devices. All these operations are required to make our trip possible, but as far as we are concerned, we make a phone call, get to the airport, and walk on the airplane. We know what the range of temperature will be on the plane so we don't have to pack a steamer trunk and prepare for both subzero and tropical weather. We know approximately when we are to arrive. We don't have to understand how the engine works, or even how the reservations system works. All of those things can be put out of our minds. We know that they have been incorporated into a system in which we can have a certain amount of confidence, because it is sufficiently complex to be able to do what it is designed to do.

The Technology Impact

We are left with an odd juxtaposition of simplicity amid complexity, as all of the interacting structures that make this simplicity possible get increasingly more complex. This is, of course, directly related to the advancement of technology. In many cases we have allowed technology to assume responsibility for the knowledge people no longer have the time to think about. Thinking Tools' John Hiles sees this as a paramount reason why today's businesses have unparalleled opportunities for innovation. "When the imagination is freed from the job of duplicating the behavior of the system," he says, "and we don't have to consciously push the relationships into the imaginary system, when we are not juggling all those balls intentionally, then we have freed our imagination." This is the way in which Thinking Tools has designed its simulations. The interactive software maintains the infrastructure to free the individual's imagination from the task. According to Hiles, "It's a release of pressure, and depending on how attuned they are, they begin to assume, in some cases for the first time, a problem-solving stance in relation to the system in which they work."

There is little question that the advance of technology has had profound impacts, both positive and negative, on the interactions among people and organizations and on our process for doing business.

In *The Gutenberg Elegies: The Fate of Reading in an Electronic Age* (1994), Sven Birkerts makes the following observation:

> The gains of electronic postmodernity could be said to include, for individuals, (a) an increased awareness of the "big picture," a global perspective that admits the extraordinary complexity of interrelations; (b) an expanded neural capacity to accommodate a broad range of stimuli simultaneously; (c) a relativistic comprehension of situations that promotes the erosion of old biases and often expresses itself as tolerance; and (d) a matter-of-fact and

unencumbered sort of readiness, a willingness to try new situations and arrangements.

In the loss column, meanwhile, are (a) a fragmented sense of time and a loss of the so-called duration experience, that depth phenomenon we associate with reverie; (b) a reduced attention span and a general impatience with sustained inquiry; (c) a shattered faith in institutions and in the explanatory narratives that formerly gave shape to subjective experience; (d) a divorce from the past, from a vital sense of history as a cumulative or organic process; (e) an estrangement from geographic place and community; and (f) an absence of any strong vision of a personal or collective future.[9]

Whether you consider Birkerts's points to be really gains or losses or simply aspects we have developed or not developed, they are factors in our lives that have been altered by virtue of this new circumstance of things becoming concurrently more complex and more simple. If we look at businesses operating in a postmodern world against the background of the changes that have occurred, Birkerts has provided a fairly accurate observation of the postmodern conditions in relation to which thinking, perception, and action will occur. They are the conditions in which organizations as complex adaptive systems are called upon to coevolve with their tautology. What then does this tell us about organizational behaviors and their strengths and weaknesses?

Questioning Assumptions

To answer this question, let us return to the distinctions we have made among principles, models, rules, and behaviors. In effect, we are saying, let's find a simple way of separating out the different concerns that we have about business so that without having to dwell on them very much, we can immediately change them. For example, we may see that what is currently causing a problem is only a simple rule that's not working anymore. We can change it. We don't have to give much attention to it. We don't need an institutional framework to support it. We don't need to make it a metanarrative. We change it. It is, after all, only a rule.

If, on the other hand, the long history of the organization is working almost covertly in relation to our experience, we may look at a simple rule and forget that it is only a rule. We may perceive that it belongs to that which we cannot change. We probably shouldn't even ask the question about it. This way of thinking has led directly to what Birkerts suggested, that from the top down we are not willing to question the basic assumptions of our organization. How do we get beyond that reticence and ask the questions we must ask?

Part of the problem is that our ideas about business, coming from science, have become increasingly cut off from the world of living experience and from the technologies that develop out of that experience. There was a time when a scientist was simply an educated gentleman. Now, scientists are increasingly living in a remote part of the society called the university. They are operating in languages that are not shared with the world outside the immediate discipline within which they are functional. And they are addressing issues that have little if anything to do with the living processes that we describe when we are talking about change in the world. There is a sense in which a physicist today has much more in common with a fifth-century B.C. Greek philosopher than he does with a 1998 sales clerk in the store who is going to fly from Santa Fe to Rome tomorrow.

More to the point, we need to recognize that our ideas take place within the very large, pervasive, and ubiquitous framework of "Western thinking," according to whose atomistic tradition nothing comes from nothing. We like to think that we are a "today's operation," without ties to history, that we don't need to look back or question the past. This is a dangerous misconception. Throughout all phases of the history of this civilization, nothing has happened that was not rendered possible by the prior occurrences that took place within that process. No one sat down in 1800 and invented and built a jet airplane.

Within the emergent process, new possibilities that were not previously possible occur, because the process had not emerged in a way that rendered that possibility possible. We could not say to someone in A.D. 1300, "Why don't we go to Mexico?" In retrospect, from today's vantage point, we can find an implicit continuity in the process that now allows us to travel to Mexico, but looking forward from 1300, that continuity had yet to emerge. We couldn't conceive of the possibility of a Mexico before the Spanish occupied the New World. Until someone came along and invented an internal-combustion engine, we couldn't have conceived of the possibility of airplanes. We could conceive of flying a kite or a place on the edges of a map where monsters exist, but an object that carried people through the sky at high rates of speed or to another land across the ocean? People would be unable to understand what we were talking about.

We are also reticent to question our models for fear that we will forsake what we think has made us unique among our competitors. The reality is that developments in many different domains have led to the possibility of that which was previously inconceivable. This progression takes place concurrently in two different ways. As technology develops, further technologies that were not previously even conceivable become possible. In addition, as we develop conceptual, symbolic, or metaphoric systems, new possibilities for ways of formulating ideas that weren't possible before come into existence. In mathematics, Newton's calculus could not have existed had there not previously been Euclidean geometry. New conceptual apparatuses make possible further conceptual apparatuses. On this continuum, history and experience provide a proving ground for theory, the fertile soil out of which something completely different from the soil itself can emerge.

Emergence and Novelty

What we find in retrospect is that in each stage of the process there is not only continuity but also novelty. When we transition to the next level in a hierarchical process, adjacent possibilities emerge and emergent novelty occurs. There is nothing in the process that even hints at it. Yet it is continuous with everything in the process that has led to it. In this manner, emergence is both continuous and novel. No one sits down in the evolution of mankind and decides let's have a written language. Language had to reach a certain level of development and complexity before this was possible.

In spite of the linear continuity that becomes apparent on hindsight, our ability as complex adaptive systems to interact and change each other is nonlinear and is further evidence of how we move from the complex to the more simple—what is referred to as "emergent phenomena." This seeming paradox has undoubtedly led to the misconception that what worked in the past will work in the future. In our postmodern, postindustrial world, there has been a confluence of radical change in both experience and technology, and they are intimately related. These radical changes, however, have not had a substantial impact on our thinking. It still remains much as it has been for the past three hundred years. Our thinking has become stuck in the rut of the fundamental assumption that we can always generalize from past experience to formulate future predictions or expectations. We're constantly moving toward a level of complexity in which something novel emerges. Not that something has been created out of nothing, but it is part of the nature of the process that is unfolding. We can't anticipate it.

If we try to think about what the process will be without recognizing the possibility of emergent novelty, we become stuck, repeating old thinking. This is not to imply that we cannot anticipate the future in all areas. We can, but if we do so, we can anticipate only insofar as we can imagine something that resembles what is and is therefore not novel, and only insofar as the process of generalizing will allow. Within the interactions of complex adaptive systems, we can apprehend a future, but that apprehension is very different from a prediction.

Past Generalizations, Present Orthodoxy

One of the major failings of business organizations is that much of their thinking and planning consists of nothing more than generalizing from what has worked in the past to some conclusions about what will work in the future. There is often an intervening step when we generalize in such a fashion. We observe what has worked. From that we generalize what will work and what will not work. We then provide an account as to why what worked did so, and why what worked previously will work in the future. We have assembled a set of metaphors that rationalize the decision, making it possible for everyone to understand it, be guided by it, and feel safe with it.

If what we do in the future on the basis of this generalization doesn't work, we rarely place the blame on the fact that we have uncritically made inferences from the past that we are now applying to the future. We tend to overlook that we have incorrectly assumed a stable structure between the past and the future. We assume it is the same world, market, and industry. We have failed to take into account that there might be something wrong with our metaphoric constructs, because we have explained organizationally why what worked in the past will work in the future. In so doing, we have made a whole network of assumptions that don't work.

When it doesn't work, we decide to redouble our efforts. We just have to do some tweaking. We didn't get something placed in the right way. We perceive that our failure was that we didn't do something effectively that we did effectively twenty years earlier. In truth, the problem wasn't that we didn't do something effectively, it was that we relied on the past. In essence, a double cognitive failure takes place. One is the assumption that we can, with confidence, generalize from the past, which at a certain level of abstraction is itself a major problem. The second failure is that we have relied uncritically on our formulations of the total situation, which almost by definition are tied to that experience from the past about which we are generalizing.

Cognitive failure occurs in the middle ground between past experience and future expectation. Only to the extent that we can recognize the reasons for the failure can we see how to correct it. How do we do that? We become intent on creating an environment within our companies in which inquiry and examination of ideas can occur productively and effectively. In addition, this environment must also allow for and nurture the possibilities of innovation.

Invariably, companies are the masters of their operations. Every company has an incredible range of skills in making whatever product it makes or providing whatever service it provides. They know a great deal about how to run a business reasonably, efficiently, and effectively. However, in the postmodern, or *hypermodern* (Spretnak's term) world, in which technologies are changing rapidly, as are the structure of the global world and our ideas about it, the one place we had better not get stuck is the cognitive. It is here that most companies don't know how to function well. They can make an airplane, but they don't know what constitutes the priorities within that cognitive area. When they are dealing with ideas and not the material stuff that they are fashioning in industry, they don't know how to look at the dynamics of how things work.

Whitehead implied that, to free our organizations we must look at the level of abstraction of all ideas or metaphors that we hold, where they come from, and the conditions and circumstances within which they have coevolved. We must make sure that the process of evolution is not just a technological process but that our metaphors and concepts are coevolving along with everything else.

As Peter Drucker suggested, it wasn't that Ford didn't know how to make an automobile when it came out with the Edsel. There was nothing wrong with the way they made it. Something went wrong in their thinking process. They generalized from the past to make a decision about the future, without asking any questions about how they were going about the process

Companies that get locked into their past can't diagnose the current situations or reformulate them to ask the necessary questions in such a way that the range of possibilities becomes broader. It is very difficult to anticipate what those possible solutions might be, because it is very difficult to disengage ourselves from what we have been doing and what has heretofore worked. The answer lies not in our paranoia of being consumed by the competition, but in the very nature of emergence.

NONLINEAR INVESTIGATION NO. 5: BUSINESS AS A COMPLEX ADAPTIVE SYSTEM

Once, when commenting upon Issac Newton's statement that "the purpose of the scientist is to sail the oceans of the unknown and discover the islands of the truth," [Jerome] Bruner impetuously burst forth with the claim, "Nonsense—the purpose of the scientist is to sail the oceans of the unknown and INVENT the islands of truth." • Bob Samples, *The Metaphoric Mind*

Learning: Human organizations adapt by learning. This means that they seek to expand and also to share understanding of their multidimensional interactions with their worlds.

1. How does our organization learn?

2. What are the indicators within our organization that learning—as distinct from reaction—is happening?

3. Does our company reformulate, whether by metaphor or theory, the events in its world?

4. How is learning shaped or constrained by the purposes of our organization?

5. What is the relationship between learning and information in our organization?
   - Is information in our company equated with data, reports, summations, and descriptions, or is there some larger sense of information to which each of these contributes?
   - To what extent is our information quantified?
   - Is our information located in a particular department or other place?
   - Is information someone's defined responsibility?
   - What are the sources of our information?

6. What is the relationship among learning, training, and information in our organization?

Ideas Are the
Geometries of Behaviors

Most paths . . . metaphorical, literal, or mathematical, take the form of an iterative equation, an equation where the values and events it produces are continually fed back into the equation again and again, influencing any future values it may throw out. Every action, then, no matter how small, influences every future action, no matter how large. • David Whyte, *The Heart Aroused*

In order to avoid cognitive failure, business must become more conscious of how it interprets the world it encounters. Politicians speak of "spin" as a way of supplying interpretations in order to shape a listener's opinions. In business, when we try to control the behaviors of those with whom we work, directly "spinning" the interactions within a predefined scope, we create an environment in which control becomes the limitation. The only success possible in an environment that treats ideas in this fashion is limited, to be followed by certain decline. Understanding the coevolutionary impact of our interactions is a critical aspect in sustaining success in any purposeful complex adaptive systems. Learning how to incorporate our ideas to harmonize with others' ideas becomes the integrating focus.

M odern, non-Euclidian geometries describe the curvature of space and the way angling shapes the behaviors of physical bodies moving in space. This process of shaping is typically called gravity. Before we understood the motion of things in space, before Newton ever bit from that apple and became dazed by its ramifications, Plato described the building structures of the universe as triangles. It was his view that within the arbitrary boundaries of space, once things are given shape, pattern, or order, they exist. Pythagoras, whose ideas influenced Plato, saw "magic" in geometry, feeling that it reflected the harmonies of the universe. If we were to describe magic as no more than a transformation by the unexpected, was Pythagoras far from complexity? The discussion that follows is not about figures and equations, but about how what we think shapes what we do.

Newton and gravity may be inextricably linked, but he was never really comfortable with the notion of action at a distance, in which two objects that did not have physical contact with each other actually affected each other. This was the case in spite of the precision of the predictions that detail where a particular body will be in public space at a specific time. If we look at ideas within this Newtonian model, the assumption is that behaviors, just like physical things, are determined by whatever is acting on the behaving body. This perception led to early attempts to predict social, historical, and individual behaviors on the basis of deterministic cause-and-effect relationships. Behavioral psychology's goal was that a psychologist would be able to predict the response to a specific stimulus, and, conversely, if he knew the response, to be able to infer what the stimulus must have been.

The problems with this approach continued to surface around the inability to integrate action at a distance into the fundamental theoretical framework of the system. This opened up a variety of mathematical explorations, including an approach that at first glance appeared very unlikely because it seemed to violate common sense: analyzing traditional geometries.

What If?

The new geometries of the nineteenth century were of the "What if?" variety: *What if* the world were assumed not to be the way we experience it, but to have other properties? What kinds of geometries would ensue? Geometry was a way of conducting theoretical and even simulated explorations of possibilities. It was not a descriptive science, but one in which the possibilities were provided neither by sense experience nor even by other theoretical systems. It is possible to speculate that these ideas may have led Einstein to a new way of thinking. In his epistemology, he criticized the rigid, presumed, deductive character of the way in which we assumed that our concepts related to our experience. As we know, he also criticized the idea that experience can lead to meaningful theory. He ended up with the perspective that our ideas were nothing more than the "free play of creative imagination."

This may have been because he was living in a world of geometries that were shaping *his* behavior. He may have found with excitement that these new daring ways of asking "What if?" kinds of questions could lead to something that was very powerful and usable. This is purely speculative. But, in spirit, if not in fact, he went beyond the predictable, deterministic calculational possibilities of a more traditional mathematics and primarily used what were called nonlinear partial differential equations. The use of these formulations is common in science today; they help shape today's scientific models.

Making the Shape of Behaviors Visible

Behaviors occur in the environment of space, and what makes them intelligible is the forms they take. We live and move in such a world, and our behaviors are a function of that world. Thinking Tools' John Hiles believes that many of the geometries that shape behavior are transparent, and that we must work to make them more opaque, "so we can see how [they shape] and [create] our experience. In spy and mystery movies, protagonists smoke a cigarette and blow smoke to expose the laser beam of the security system. The beam is invisible without the smoke. Our mental models are definitely there and are normally transparent because we look through them and cannot see things that later become surprises. If we change our mental models, we can take things that we would normally be blind to and use them . . . or at least anticipate when they are about to knock us on the head."

Behavior and Interpretation

It would be truly naive to assume that we ever have a direct experience of something and then act on the basis of that experience. Our experience

is always mediated by interpretation. The moment we have any sensations of any kind, what we sense is in part determined by what our interpretations allow us. We distinguish things. We have given them names,
contexts, and syndromes. It would be difficult to separate what we experience from our representations, ideas, and interpretations. How we react
to something is in large part determined by our interpretations, which are
nothing more than the ideas that we have of the thing. Our behaviors,
therefore, always occur within a context of interpretation.

As our organizations become more complex, interpretations play an
even greater role in the ways those entities behave. The interpretations
themselves become increasingly complex. We see a table. Immediately,
the very word conjures ideas we have of a table. Its uses and functions fit
within a network of entities that constitute our world as we understand
it. We have a sensation. We have a representation. We formulate an idea.
We behave in ways that are relevant to us and are programmed and structured by all of our ideas about tables—the network of relations that tables
have, the different kinds of tables, the reasons tables exist. Tables, however, are very concrete when compared with what business encounters.

The higher the level of complexity of an entity, the higher the level of
abstraction required for an adequate foundation of that entity. When an
organization engages with its world, it rules out as irrelevant its relationship to tables. As individuals, we have a greater relationship to tables,
because tables are in our offices. An organization operates on a different
level of abstraction. It may not "see" a table, but it recognizes markets.
There are markets in the world, and they are as real to the organization
as a table might be to an agent within the organization. A market can be
circumscribed and defined in ways similar to those used to define a table.

Does a table shape behavior? As an object, it does in very specific and
limited ways. The fact that a table is there means that if we walk from one
side of the room to the other, we must change direction to avoid bumping
into it: We can jump over it or go around it to the right or the left. The
table doesn't determine what those behaviors will be, but in some way it
defines a range of behaviors, it prescribes patterns of possible behaviors.
The sense qualities of the table, such as color or texture, are irrelevant to
this. The table occupies space, and if we are to move from one place to
another in space, we cannot occupy the same space at the same time as
the table.

Returning to the notion that a business is its ideas, these ideas eventually generate the infrastructure of the organization. This organization is

a mass moving in space, and by its nature as an entity in that space, it shapes the ideas of the employees who fall within the sphere of that organization. For example, an employee may see his or her job as providing service to the customer or he or she may see that job as generating profits for the company. These two views can lead to totally different behaviors supported by different kinds of infrastructure. One infrastructure may facilitate granting a refund to a customer when there is a breakdown; another infrastructure may be designed to prevent the issuance of refunds.

The organization has formed ideas about its world, the entities that make it up, and its relationships to other organizations. However, the ideas it has formed about itself are at different levels of abstraction. If the organization were to think of itself as a complex adaptive system, it would recognize that it needs to understand that it lives with the ideas of complexity just as much as it lives with a lot of other factors in its environment. Within the organization, we have to find some way of utilizing the ideas that facilitate adaptation and recognize those that don't. We must then focus our attention on those that do, prioritizing them while seeing the patterns of their relatedness to each other. Some ideas shape other ideas and provide access and entrée to those shaped ideas, because we can understand them as representations and formulations, in terms of yet more encompassing formulations and abstractions.

The more abstract the idea or formulation is, the greater the number of other ideas it can include. We can then select from those ideas those which can be used most effectively for successful adaptation. This adaptation, then, derives directly from the power of the abstract idea to generate a broad range of ideas and behaviors.

What we are suggesting is that a business look at the most abstract ideas it can conjure up about what it does. We have already seen how one abstract idea—providing service to customers—can lead to different behaviors than an abstract idea which holds that financial gain on each transaction is more important than service. This is the business's essence stated most simply. These larger ideas shape some of the smaller ideas. In looking at the pragmatic value of the idea, let us start with a simple idea (the more abstract an idea is, the simpler it is): that a business is a complex adaptive system. That is a very abstract statement about the way the business thinks of itself and subsequently behaves, one that shapes and forms everything that flows from it. We can refer other ideas back to it and ask whether they fit or don't fit. We can look to that idea for clarification or enlightenment. *This idea, by giving shape to other ideas, allows us to make distinctions between ideas that are relevant or important or those that are not.*

Behaviors at a Distance

As these ideas are being shaped, so too are our behaviors being shaped at every moment, at different levels of abstraction. This is an ongoing process in which ideas shape other ideas and also behaviors. Behaviors are ways of exploring, expressing, and exploiting various levels of what we do. As we pursue various behaviors, we find that some ideas will lead to dead-ends, some will require further exploration, and some are ready to exploit.

The assumption is that the organization works within a symbolic framework, in relation to which it understands its own identity and its own function and starts organizing its activities and its behaviors. It is partly a matter of prioritizing and determining what ideas make a difference and what ideas seem to be irrelevant.

Businesses tend to absorb the ideas that prevail in the society or industry in which they find themselves. This includes the value systems and histories out of which the ideas were formed. These outside forces provide the clues as to which ideas appear to be meaningful, useful, or relevant, and which ones do not. Within Industrial Age thinking, standardized mechanism was such a shaping force.

The idea of thinking of a business as a complex adaptive system, is a recent one and is not yet prevalent. It is derived from changes in the sciences that are slowly filtering down into the nonscientific sector of the society. An organization will learn this idea only if it is intentionally exposed to it. Someone may tell them what this idea is all about and how it relates to other ways of thinking that they may have, or they may read about it in a book.

An excellent example of ideas directly affecting behavior is offered by Alfred North Whitehead in his book *Adventure of Ideas*. In it he discusses the idea of slavery, and how it shaped society. He points out that if a society has a particular understanding of the nature of man, of a society, property, and warfare, the idea of slavery may be perfectly natural. It may never occur to that society to question its ethics.

If a government or society were to persist in behaviors consistent with its ideas of slavery, but did so at a time in which there were major changes in the environment, it would be holding on to an idea that was not very adaptive, one that would not lead the organization to adaptive behaviors.

In today's world, there are not many countries where the idea of slavery influences behaviors or where there are behaviors directed toward owning and managing slaves. In other environments and historical periods, slavery was normal and taken for granted. Behaviors existed that were shaped, first, by the idea of slavery and even more so by other more abstract ideas that reinforce the idea of slavery itself. As these ideas change, the behaviors change.

In India, in 1997, K. R. Narayanan became the first member of the "untouchables" caste to become president. In his acceptance speech Narayanan said his colleagues "had risen above the barriers of religion, caste, language, and region that separate us and reached out to the essential unity underlying this land of immense, diversities."[1] Narayanan recognized that the country is an immense, complex adaptive system, and that there had been a change in the ideas that were now shaping it.

New Shapes and New Ideas

In a comparable way, when a business thinks of itself as a complex adaptive system, realizing it is made up of an ongoing process of interactions between many agents, each of which is itself a complex adaptive system, it takes on a whole range of behaviors that have to do with the interactions and relationships with those other agents. One of those agents is called an employee.

The idea "employee" is shaped by an understanding of such concerns as human nature, the values of society, how people behave, and questions of control, motivation, compliance, instruction, performance evaluation, and compensation. All of these ideas are shaped by other ideas at different levels of abstraction, which in turn are shaped by a more abstract idea, the idea that we are a complex adaptive system. All of the behaviors flowing out of the abstract idea "we are a complex adaptive system" are totally different from those that come out of an organization with the idea that it is a mechanism. Unfortunately, the mechanistic metaphor is the prevailing idea that most businesses operate under. This idea leads to quite different organizations, with very different behaviors than that of a complex adaptive system.

For example, in the context of complex adaptive systems, the question "How do we control behavior?" might be irrelevant, but it is a very important question within a mechanistic context. John Holland's statement "It's complex adaptive systems all the way down" implies "We are going to be led to different behaviors, all the way down in our businesses." This starts with different ideas, new ideas that emerge, and how those ideas relate to the behaviors that relate to every one of those ideas. We are going to get different answers and behaviors to every question we ask about the idea of a business when we view the business as a complex adaptive system. Those answers will relate to everything from what people do, to how they go about doing it, how they should be compensated, how they work together, how they are to be evaluated, and what kinds of communications need to occur.

The world in which business operates today is as different from the world of the Industrial Age as our modern society is different from the Greek city-state. Just as slavery is now an obsolete idea, with no pragmatic value whatsoever, ideas from the Industrial Age regarding the conduct of business today are irrelevant. In light of this, it may be that an employee should no longer be looked upon as an employee, but as an adaptive agent. How does that idea shape new behaviors?

If we continue questioning, we will discover obsolete ideas related to the definition not only of employees, but of customers, marketplaces, profit, and of all of the fundamental ideas that shape the behaviors of most companies operating today.

The Ideas That a Business Has Shapes Its Ideas as a Business

The world of behaviors and experiences and the world of ideas both are continually developing. And, as we have suggested, there is also a constant cycling back and forth between these two evolving areas. They go on in parallel, but they are not independent of each other. Our behaviors and experiences are constantly modifying the way we think about them, and the way we think about them is constantly modifying those behaviors and experiences.

One of the peculiarities of this process is that although our behaviors and ideas are coevolving, they are not necessarily coevolving at the same rates. They are frequently out of phase with each other. Some of our ideas simply do not take account of and may not even coevolve with our developing experiences or behaviors. Therefore, our ideas may seem adequate to us because they relate to the set of experiences and behaviors with which we are familiar, but they may not stand the test of experiences and behaviors with which we are not familiar, that are not part of our existence.

For example, the idea *boss* meant something very specific to a slave. It is still used today to connote a superior. But, as we discussed previously, in a distributed system, in which people interact within the free exchange of ideas, the word *boss* has no meaning. This kind of distributed system was inconceivable to a slave in a Greek city-state.

Ideas have occurred and developed that people may not be aware of and to that extent their behaviors and experiences are not influenced by those ideas. The idea of the relationship between complex adaptive systems and business might be one. For people who haven't heard of these ideas, they simply do not exist. The constant evolutionary processes that go on in different domains may or may not be congruent, and may or may not fully exploit the possibilities of full coevolution.

This is why it is so critical for business to grasp the ideas coming out of science. What is missing in most businesses is a depth of comprehension of these ideas, yet they can turn out to be extremely relevant to newly developing experiences and behaviors that occur in the business world. Instead, organizations attempt to deal with new behaviors in terms of *old ideas*, missing the advantage of congruence between an agent and any other agent and therefore of a meaningful process of coevolution.

Throughout this book, we have characterized these new behaviors as "informational" as distinct from the old behaviors and experiences, which we characterized as mechanistic. These new behaviors have to do with several factors:

- The rapid development of new more complex and more far-reaching technologies, which alter the way things are done, thus altering behaviors and opening up people to new kinds of experiences.

- The emerging possibilities that computers represent.

- New ways of thinking have developed along with the computers.

- Increasing globalization.

- The coevolution of complex adaptive systems and nonlinearity.

- Changing views in relation to one's history, social structure, and value systems.

For emergence to occur, all of these and more must coevolve and keep pace with each other; otherwise the process is stopped and aborted. Meaningful change occurs only when there is a meeting of the experiential and the conceptual such that each contributes to the other. If each is not contributing to the other, there may be changes, but there isn't emergence.

Establishing the Ratio of Information to Infrastructure

If innovative change emerges from the interaction between our ideas and the behaviors shaped by them, it becomes imperative in today's postindustrial environment to maintain a high ratio of information to infrastructure. We can't speak of ideas in terms other than information. Information means the ways we repattern, restructure, reformulate, rethink, and reconceptualize all of the ideas we form. Those ideas, too, develop out of each other. There is a sense in which we don't need anything other than ideas to stimulate the development of new ideas.

But putting ideas into action means that they relate to events. We use the word *infrastructure* to refer to those events: the physical forms and structures that things take. Increasingly in postindustrial business, the priority and the direction of influence between information and infrastructure has been shifted. The question is, Where do these two cross and to what extent does infrastructure lead to new ideas, and new ideas influence the infrastructure? Complexity has prompted us to shape this relationship differently, increasing our focus on information as a foundation for operation. Today, more changes in infrastructure occur through developing information than occur through the infrastructure alone. This transference of priority from infrastructure to information is summed up well in a quote by the physicist Max Planck in his 1945 *Treatise on Thermo-Dynamics*. About the Second Law of Thermodynamics, or the law of entropy, Planck wrote,

> It would be absurd to assume that the validity of the second law depends in any way on the skill of the physicist or chemist in

observing or experimenting. The gist of the second law has nothing to do with experiment. The law asserts briefly that there exists in nature a quantity which always changes in the same way in all natural processes. The proposition stated in this general form may be correct or incorrect but whichever it may be, it will remain so, irrespective of whether thinking and measuring beings exist on Earth or not and whether or not, assuming they do exist, they are able to measure the details of physical or chemical processes more accurately by one, two, or one hundred decimal places.

The limitation of the law if any must lie in the same providence as its essential idea in the observed nature and not in the observer, that man's experience called upon in the deduction of the law is of no consequence. That is in fact our only way of arriving at a knowledge of natural law.

Planck is suggesting that developing information concerns the relationship of information to information within its own domain, independent of whether that information does or does not refer to any particular experience or sensation or behaviors. The validity of the information is determined by the relationships of ideas, concepts, or patterns of structure to each other, not to things.

The philosopher George Gilder further developed this idea. "The central event of the 20th century is the overthrow of matter. In technology, economics and the politics of nations, wealth in the form of physical resources is steadily declining in value and significance. The powers of mind are everywhere ascendant over the brute force of things."[2]

If we consider these two statements together, we see that business is operating in a context characterized by the decline of matter or infrastructure and the development of information. Matter as a metaphor for things continues to decline, as concern for the process, pattern, abstraction, and ideas increases. In any business in which more and more of the resources, tension, time, and energy are devoted to things (infrastructure) rather than to developing ideas (information), there is a hint that this business is becoming increasingly out of phase with the various environments in relation to which it is coevolving. When that happens, the business may start running into trouble.

How do today's businesses measure this ratio to assure they maintain a proper relationship? They don't. A relationship is dynamic. A measurement is static. Things are measured. Information is not matter. It doesn't have location, weight, or width. All we can do is look at the process and ask questions. This is one of the distinguishing features of working within an information structure as opposed to a mechanistic model. Information doesn't have the linear precision that would enable it to be measured. It becomes a matter of asking questions that will help us gain an understanding of what is occurring.

- Where are we as a business applying our financial resources?

- What are we investing in?

- Where are our key people focusing their attention, and how are they spending their time?

- If we look at e-mails and memoranda, what are we communicating?

- What are we communicating when we have meetings?

- What are we talking about?

We can pull these answers together and assess whether our resources, time, energies, or communications are spent on things (infrastructure) or ideas (information). All we can do is identify where we are focusing our attention.

Unfortunately, we can't draw a box called "information" and determine its size and what is in it and what isn't. In this sense, information might be analogous to the immune system: It isn't located somewhere specific in the body; all of the components of the organic system have a role in the system's operation. We can't segregate and separate out an immune system from any other system in the organism. The process of thinking, formulating, and interpreting ideas occurs everywhere throughout the system. Locating it in one particular centralized location only limits the possibilities of coevolution. The problem we face with information is in trying to apply spatial metaphors to something that by definition is not spatial. Information shapes space, but it cannot be quantified.

Another problem, pointed out by Applied Biosystems' Ken Prokuski, is that often people don't want to be responsible for thinking. Applied Biosystems' approach is to allow those who prefer maintaining the infrastructure to do so and those who are innovators to have their place, too. The key to making this work is to eliminate the competition between infrastructure and information, and see them as two parts of a reciprocal process, feeding back and furthering itself. The fact still remains that some people within any organization don't want the responsibility of thinking. This may be a remnant from having worked in an industrial mechanistic operation that was more comfortable with controlling ideas than eliciting them. But what if ideas do shape behaviors . . .

Business as a Purposeful Complex Adaptive System?

An organization that operated as a purposeful complex adaptive system would look very different from its mechanistic ancestor. First, we would look at the way the business organizes itself in terms of the agents that compose it, and how they can contribute to "adaptation" more effectively. This organization would undoubtedly be less rigid, with a greatly reduced command-type hierarchic structure. The communications would be more diffuse, less top to bottom and bottom to top. There would be more people talking to each other—whether peer to peer or between different levels—about more things. It would also be more "scientific" in the way it goes about organizing its inquiries and evaluating alternatives, with a much greater openness to the understanding of its own vocabularies and ideologies. It would always be open to new formulations to the extent that new formulations are more adequate. Businesses have been stuck in notions of their key behaviors, which go back unchanged to much earlier periods of time. A business as a complex adaptive system would recognize that these behaviors are no longer adequate or realistic in relation to concerns that have emerged in today's world. Would a worker be more willing to participate in the voices of such an organization?

Businesses operate around core ideas to which they attach all of the things they do and say. Some of those ideas are about the economy, industry, marketing, the consumer, and many other concerns. These ideas about the structural components of this world have not changed very much. Science has changed the meaning of some of its core ideas, but not many of the foundational or organizing ideas related to the conduct of business have followed suit. The time has arrived for business to do so too. In light of these new ideas, business needs to requestion, rethink, and redefine the meaning of supplier, employee, manager, worker, stockholder, and board of directors. For example, perhaps a supplier becomes a member of the board of directors, or functions like an employee at times. Perhaps an employee functions as if he or she were an outside supplier.

Oction, a leading Danish hearing-aid manufacturer, had lost its competitiveness and its innovative spirit. They decided to revision and restructure the company. In a bold move, they dismantled their hierarchical structure. People no longer had "jobs"; they had skill portfolios. Paper was eliminated and all communications were carried out person to person or electronically. There were no fixed workplaces for the employees, and to increase this fluid quality, what few possessions employees had went with them in mobile cabinets. Projects weren't management initiatives but emerged from within the organization, and they were internally advertised. Workers volunteered to participate in projects and were allowed to change project teams frequently. And much like Applied Biosystems' flocking, the system worked.

Team building is not new, but understanding how teams work as complex adaptive systems requires us to look at how those teams are assembled. We have spoken earlier about self-organization. The Prediction Company opened its doors with eight physicists who had never worked in a company before. Within a matter of a few years there were only two remaining. Doyne Farmer, one of the pioneers of chaos and complexity theories as well as artificial life experiments, was one who survived. "Building this company was like creating an artificial life experiment; we needed the right mixture of different stuff to make the company run. People who would know how to work as a team and get along. Personality became a very big part of the process. We had a few brilliant people come through that we decided would be a disaster to the organization. In an environment in which we are constantly trying to do more than we can, it's important that people get along and enjoy working together—it's what creates the emergent phenomena."

Perhaps the two terms requiring the greatest rethinking of our definitions are *customer* and *profit*. The old ideas of customer and profit still have a great deal of influence on behaviors in business. But these old ideas may be as obsolete as slavery.

Localized Action

As we have mentioned, in the mechanistic industrial world, it was not uncommon for a business to think of itself as an object or machine. It could draw a picture of itself, delineate its boundaries and its different functions, and see how they were separate from each other. It is increasingly difficult and irrelevant for a business to do that. Businesses can't draw pictures of themselves anymore because they structurally consist of embedded hierarchies of interactive agents, each of which contributes to the ongoing coevolution of the whole organization. Increasingly we are finding that everything that occurs is localized. There are so many regions and agents in the organization, so many interactions taking place, that localized fields are set up. Two people meet and talk. It is a conversation between person A and person B. It is not a conversation between person A and the organization or person B and the organization.

The local reaction creates a local perturbation, a concept from modern physics. It localizes the geometry. It shapes what occurs to the extent that what happens becomes part of that local event. Those shapings, in their aggregate and in their ongoing interactions, begin to delineate the shape of the organization. Anytime two agents interact—individual and individual—ideas get generated, as do interpretations. They are talking about something. They are not just talking about. There is a focus to the interaction that prescribes a meaningfulness for both of them. To the extent that any other agent is exposed to or becomes part of that field of interaction, it will be influenced by it too—not necessarily *determined* by it, but the agent must take account of the local interaction.

In order for an idea to shape behavior, the behaving entity has to have appropriated an idea. If it hasn't, that idea has no influence on it whatsoever. It is as if the idea didn't exist. Every behaving entity at any level of complex adaptive system has ideas and makes interpretations and formulations of those ideas. If we want to understand the behaviors, we can do so only in terms of the ideas it has accessed and represents. Behaviors cannot go beyond the paths structured by those ideas. If we want to change behaviors we have to add to the ideas, symbols, or formulations. We have to restructure and reshape them, introduce something new into the mix so that this complex adaptive system now behaves differently. Why would that make it behave differently? Because it has ideas that are different.

Identifying What Works

The big question is, How do we determine which ideas lead to the behaviors that are going to be successfully adaptive? Not just any idea will do—as Hawking stated, "It's the right idea." How do we find those right ideas and represent them so that they can contribute to the realization of whatever it is that the organization is seeking to "do"?

Unfortunately, right ideas can only be determined retrospectively on a purely pragmatic basis—what works. What works is what contributes to the capacity of the entity to realize the purpose, goals, and objectives for which it exists in the first place. If something doesn't contribute to what the company wants to accomplish, it is irrelevant.

A business exists for two reasons. First, it exists to provide the society with products or services that it has implicitly agreed to provide: automobiles, airplanes, haircuts, insurance, or management guidance. A business is not providing just anything. The nature of its product or service has emerged through time and expectations have been built up. If the business ceases to deliver to the society the products and services for which it has come into existence, it will not last very long. Ideas that further that delivery are pragmatically successful. Ideas that don't are not. As a corollary, the business has made an implicit agreement with the society to keep improving upon those products and/or services in terms of increased quality; increased operational capacity, to reduce the cost of those goods and services; and increased reliability and predictability. If those processes stop, the business is no longer fulfilling its function and it ceases to exist.

Business's second purpose is to develop and build the resources necessary for it to continue to perform the function it exists to perform, and to perform its function viably increasing its financial value through time. A company needs to expand those resources so that others invest, participate, share in the ownership, and are committed to the existence of the entity. Neither element can be neglected.

If we provide the service but do not build our viability as an entity, we're not going to survive. If we're assuring the viability, but we're not able to deliver products or services, then we won't survive. We have to do both. That's the unique character of a business organization. Sometimes, a business thinks it can sacrifice one for the other. Unfortunately, that doesn't work. Investors won't invest in a business that's not viable. Consumers won't buy products and services from a business that is not maintaining its quality.

This is the context within which right ideas must emerge

Distributed Management

Often in businesses stuck in Industrial Age thinking, decisions are made at the top and move down, without regard to localized interaction and feedback. What happens in a distributed system, in which there is little or no subordination and there are localized fields of influence? Who makes the decisions?

The prospect of this kind of uncertainty may seem like the ultimate terror for a mechanistic organization, but now we are talking about an organization that has been reshaped by the ideas of complexity. In such an organization, the answer to the question "Who makes the decisions?" is, surprisingly, the organization. Decisions emerge out of a very complex system of interactions with agents setting up many local fields. Those ideas shape the behaviors of the CEO fully as much as they shape the behaviors of any other agent in the organization. Technically, decisions may be made through a CEO, but the CEO is no more nor less free than any other agent in the company to make that decision.

The question we must ask of this process is: Does this happen in such a way that the organization as a whole is becoming more or less adaptive in relation to the environments with which it is coevolving?

Take the model of a jazz quintet as an example of a distributed system. By common consent all of the musicians in the quintet have agreed on the song they're going to play and the general description or orchestration of that song—its melodies and harmonic lines. They also agree to play their individual instruments to achieve those harmonies and melodies—the patterns they find in the music. No formal conductor is necessary, and all the players work together to shape the music, modifying and adapting themselves to the other players through their musical ideas. The music that results is in a continual state of coevolution, each agent influenced by the interpretations and improvisations (innovations) of the other players. They are all contributing to the music, but they are not necessarily playing the same thing. Every player understands that within the organization certain functions must be performed, and individuals assume those responsibilities. All listen to each other on an ongoing basis, and they all have a convergent interest—to play the song as well as possible and make great music *together*.

The individual agents bring their own technique, which becomes embedded in the group's mix. The jazz flutist and saxophone player Lew Tabacken likens this to being a samurai. He practices his technique endlessly, so that when he goes out onstage with his group he doesn't have to concentrate on what he's doing, but his reactions are right. "You don't react on pure instinct," Tabacken says, "you react through disciplined instinct." From this, improvisations soar and cohesion produces some-thing greater than any one of the agents.

In this complex adaptive system the individual agents cocreate the goal as they create an interpretation of an already existing framework. The one person who is not coevolving with the group is the original com-poser of the piece. The original music simply provokes a range of possible interpretations. It is the job of the quintet to self-organize to create an interpretation that meaningfully expands the understanding of the piece of music.

Business also creates its own score as it goes along cocreating its goals. The goals haven't been written down by a composer of goals—or if they have, the same creative process does not take place.

Solos and Jams

In traditional mechanistic organizations we tend to elevate individual fig-ures, such as a CEO, senior executive, or member of upper management or the board of directors. To what extent would that be done if the busi-ness thought of itself as a complex adaptive system? For example, the pos-sibility might exist in a complex adaptive system for a number of people to rotate the role of CEO. Then the organization wouldn't get stuck reflecting one person's biases and idiosyncrasies. This doesn't mean that within a complex adaptive system we can't have structures that perform specific functions. In the body, various cells don't take turns becoming a brain and then decide today they'll be the eyes. We are not suggesting a complete randomness to the system. But in the body system the heart is of equal importance as the brain, which is as important as the liver. The heart, brain, immune system, and liver all require and influence each other. Their boundaries are permeable to allow shaping from the outside, and through the nervous system they are interconnected in such a way as to provide instant and constant communication and feedback.

What role might a board of directors play in an organization that sees itself as a connected complex adaptive system? The answer might come from Aristotle. As science was birthed, Aristotle realized that in order to keep the ideas of science fresh, accurate, and relevant, those working within the science could not effectively evaluate its own axioms. He cre-ated a branch of science that would operate outside the science itself, whose sole occupation was to question the axioms of science. He called this science, metaphysics. It could be that the members of the board of directors of such companies might best serve the institutions they counsel as metaphysicians. This role would give them a way to constructively feed back into the system by examining the most abstract ideas of the business. Their task would not be to micromanage the system, but to take a more coarse-grained look at the business.

We Can't Know It All

Within the complexity of today's business environment and organizations, it would be truly presumptuous of any one person to think that he or she could possibly know everything required to operate a business successfully. More and more, organizations are discovering that to succeed and accomplish anything requires partnering and healthy relationships within all levels of operation. These localized fields of activity extend throughout complex adaptive systems and their embedded agents. Every physical body has a gravitational effect on every other physical body, no matter how infinitesimal. As Nobel Prize–winning physicist Murray Gell-Mann pointed out, even at the level of subatomic particles we must include the effect of gravity for our equations to make sense. Geometry shapes, and emergence, by its very interactive, coevolving nature, requires the interactive shaping of relationship and partnering for emergent novelty to arise.

If in fact all action within the system is local, not just general or simply reacting with something called the organization, this has profound implications for the decentralized character of innovation, organization, management, planning, and problem solving. Distributed management takes place throughout the organization at all levels, at all times . . . organically. We will explore this in greater detail in the next chapter, where we look at the powerful model of franchising and its built-in diversity of control.

NONLINEAR INVESTIGATION NO. 6:
AVAILABLE FEEDBACK

Feedback in [Norbert] Wiener's words, is the "control of a machine on the
basis of its actual performance rather than its expected performance."
In a broader sense feedback has come to mean the conveying
of information about the outcome of any process or activity
to its source. • Fritjof Capra, *The Web of Life*

Our models are only as accurate and effective as our available feedback. Feedback in living systems is often ubiquitous. By making feedback more accessible and more conscious, an organization can ensure that it is receiving the best available feedback. This feedback process is imperative for maintaining a high ratio of information to infrastructure. How an organization tests the quality of its feedback is the thrust of these questions.

Feedback: A special form of learning that is a unique feature of the business Information Age. It did not exist, except in very primitive forms, in the Industrial Age.

1. Does our organization tend to encourage or constrain feedback? How?

2. Is the process of giving feedback built into our operational activities?

3. If feedback does not support intended or expected results, what happens?

4. What are the various forms of feedback in our organization? Which are emphasized?
   - Conversations
   - Meetings
   - Reports (written or oral, individual or team)
   - Performance data
   - External media
   - Government

- Competitors
- Suppliers
- Other

5. Does our organization attempt to innovate or find new forms of feedback that are not currently available?

The Franchise Model:
Purpose in Action

*Franchising is the single most successful marketing
concept ever.* • John Naisbett

Models for business are limitless. They are always approximations of the principles out of which we operate. The model that comes closest to exemplifying a business as a purposeful complex adaptive system is franchising. While this way of doing business is influenced by factors in the various industries that practice it, overall it provides a framework that is applicable to every business. As we will demonstrate, franchising's success or failure is absolutely dependent on maintaining a high ratio of information to infrastructure and decentralized information implementation.

Within the open boundaries of our emerging universe, we find many different kinds of organizations occurring naturally—galactic communities, solar systems, and ant colonies. While the process of self-organization may be natural, purposeful complex adaptive systems are not. They are hand-made, imbued with human and social behaviors. In the previous chapters, we have looked at complex adaptive systems, both natural and purposeful, to understand how they enter into satisfying and successful coadaptive evolution with their environment. By definition, purposeful complex adaptive systems don't exist in isolation. They don't just happen. They grow in a specific environment because they have been put there. Their structure and function have been shaped within a human-designed context. What, then, are the features of a pragmatically successful landscape that enables a purposeful complex adaptive system to do what it does? "Do what it does" means delivering to the society the products and/or services the business has undertaken to provide—with a steady increase in the quality of those products, produced in a fashion so that the business viably sustains itself. In addition, it also makes it worthwhile for individuals, themselves complex adaptive agents within the system, to fulfill their own interests.

Within these criteria, we find clues to questions formulated upon the general understanding of how and why complex adaptive systems exhibit particular features and whether they relate to purposeful complex adaptive systems as well.

Are there universal features that constitute the minimally necessary conditions for successful adaptation by any complex adaptive system? Or, when we get into purposeful complex adaptive systems, is there a different set of characterizations? Does a purposeful, or nonnatural, complex adaptive system have the same conditions for successful adaptation as a natural system?

Our starting point in the developing sciences of complexity is to assume that there is one model that is adequate to the understanding of both the natural and the purposeful. It doesn't seek to segregate them. We shall see if that position turns out to be supportable as we proceed with the emerging process.

Of Language and Purpose

Everything we attempt to understand is approached through analogy, through metaphor—we deal with it as if it were something it is not. A purposeful complex adaptive system is not an organism, but we can speak of it metaphorically as if it were. Parenthetically, it is also not a thing, because a thing isn't a complex adaptive system. Yet there are times when we can speak of it as if it were a thing. As mentioned earlier, when we talk about the application of the science of complexity, we are talking in part about a shift in our metaphors from those derived from things to those derived from organisms.

We have discovered that when we talk about the behaviors of a business, it doesn't work as effectively to use *thing* metaphors as it does to use *organic* metaphors.

It is a matter of language. We move back and forth between several domains of languaging to get a sense of how we can communicate about and gain access to these organizations whose way of being in the world is very open and unclear. Interacting entities within an organization relate to each other around common understandings. We attempt then to look at those understandings in terms of the levels of abstraction we can understand ourselves. This means coming up with ideas that will encompass all the behaviors and data as compared to other formulations, which encompass only some of the ideas and behaviors.

This is very difficult, because traditionally we have approached organisms or behaviors through mechanistic science. We have dealt with these entities from the outside, as if we were an independent observer seeking to give an objective description about them. Further compounding our inaccurate point of view is the idea that the entity is unaffected by our observation and that we are unaffected by that observation as well. We attempt descriptions of those things. When we look at purposeful complex adaptive systems, however, we discover that we cannot disengage them from the environment of ideas that shape them, and from a history of how those shapings have emerged. From quantum theory we learn that there is no way of getting outside the whole system to look upon history as if we were not a part of it.

So what do our subjective observations tell us? We know almost a priori that purposeful organizations are not going to survive if they are monolithic. We can say this because these monolithic structures preclude interactions, blocking them by setting up barriers within the hierarchy. Their demise is almost predetermined by such behavior in that anything attempting to impede interactions adversely affects the health of a complex adaptive system. Anything that limits the openness also limits the possibilities for interactions.

The Setting of Arbitrary Boundaries

Another a priori feature of purposeful complex adaptive systems is that they have arbitrary boundaries. Where the business stops and something else begins is a matter of perception. The business exists within a larger environment of behaviors which may or may not be germane to the behaviors of the complex adaptive system we call the business. Nonetheless, this purposeful complex adaptive system, like all complex adaptive systems, is interacting with other systems that do not fall within its boundaries. Its boundaries have to be sufficiently open for interactions to occur, in order for the business to experience, form ideas, and be influenced by geometrical properties that other bodies in the environment exhibit, such as lifestyles. What happens in all the interactions that occur in our specific complex interactive system relates to all the embedded hierarchies in the environments that we find ourselves forming ideas about, and behaving in relation to.

For example, we see another company attempting to provide the same service and/or product that we provide, seeking to be viable under it's own name and identity just as we are. Within the context of our arbitrary boundaries, we call it a competitor. From another point of reference, we might also call it a collaborator. We have a common interest. We could share what we are doing. We could pool our resources. Ultimately, we may even merge and become one entity. We look at the other entities doing what we do. If we look at them from a different level of abstraction, we see a collection of many entities all of which have the same general orientation, disposition, and identity in relation to the world for providing a service or product as we do.

We also see an economy. We are interacting with systems of exchange—monetary systems and systems of value. These systems are also influenced by us, just as we are influenced by them. At the same time we are being shaped by ideas that we have of ourselves, and we are being shaped by ideas that we have of our external environments. We maintain our boundaries, but those boundaries are permeable, simultaneously permitting this shaping process to be ongoing. We are not cut off from anything outside our boundaries. In fact, we seek to understand those other businesses' ideas either to compete or to collaborate and make a decision. We try to locate who and what we are in relation to an industry, to an economy, and ultimately to a society. All of these are bounded in some way by boundaries that don't exist. They are ideational in character, yet nonetheless real.

So we know that the system cannot be monolithic or close off its boundaries and survive. What do these two principles say about the behaviors of these purposeful complex adaptive systems called businesses that might be conducive to their survival and successful adaptation?

The Franchising Model

To illustrate this more effectively, we are going to make a transition to a different area of discourse so that the features of these purposeful complex adaptive systems become more visible. The model we are offering, though different in principle from many business models, is, we think, applicable to all. It is the model of franchising, which prototypically embodies purposeful complex adaptive system features that are more apparent than in other forms of business. These features include:

- Autonomy of agents within its structure.

- A process of spreading responsibility.

- A process to distinguish specific kinds of responsibility within the larger system.

- Decentralization. The lack of centralized management control allows the system to move away from being monolithic.

In this regard, franchising lends itself to determining how businesses can most effectively and purposefully shape their behaviors. In so doing, the business receives what it wants those behaviors to produce.

Establishing Responsibility within Information/Infrastructure Relationships

As mentioned throughout this book, we are discovering in today's multiple environments a developing distinction between information and infrastructure. It is a distinction that would have made little sense during the Industrial Age. To a large extent it is engendered by the recognition of and necessity for new ways of thinking about complex interactions that are different from the ways we once thought about these activities. Behaviors, activities, and environments have changed. The ideas relating to all of them have changed, too. We need to find our way through this change to an intelligibility and order that makes sense of it all. We need to blaze a path that allows us to continue being productive, while extending our adaptive capacity on an ongoing basis.

This formulation of information/infrastructure is uniquely applicable to the Information Age. It is a way of labeling the shifting priorities we encounter. We can then contrast this model with the Industrial Age, and in turn with the Agrarian Age. Yet, the distinction between information and infrastructure is one that has existed throughout the history of our civilization in one fashion or another. Plato said that the two foundational principles of the universe are *reason* and *necessity*. He delineates what he means by reason, ending up with what could easily be translated into what we are saying about information. Necessity, in effect, could be translated into what we mean by infrastructure. For Plato, the interaction of reason and necessity brings about existence, process, and the sources of intelligibility for that process.

Another distinction, found in Aristotle in the fourth century B.C., that between form and matter, is similar to the distinction John von Neumann makes in the twentieth century between software and hardware. Von Neumann approached computers by distinguishing the thing that does the work from the logic that feeds it. The software has nothing to do with the structure of that which produces the results, but has to do with its own domain of logic, whether or not we find anything that can apply or make use of that logic. Obviously, this notion of information and infrastructure is an old distinction that has pervaded thinking throughout our civilization. As with all emergent processes, if we stop and look back at the steps taken within the Information Age, we find fundamental formative principles that have shaped Western civilization since its inception.

As Schrödinger said, "Science is thinking in a Greek way." Over the last twenty-five hundred years, little has changed within our governing principles. When we speak about information and infrastructure, we are saying something about our world, using vocabularies appropriate to *our* world, similar to what Plato said about his, with vocabularies appropriate to it.

The distinction taking place at the levels of behaviors and abstractions in which businesses occur is also a recognition that there is a role for ideas and abstract thinking that we haven't previously acknowledged. There is a shift of emphasis from the description of things to their interpretation, toward a growing recognition that what shapes our behaviors is indirect. Those interpretations are not accidental. They arise with certain continuities in relation to the ideas through which we make our world intelligible to ourselves.

It follows, then, that in order for a business to be successful, it must find a way of putting together reason and necessity, information and infrastructure, or the software and hardware of its business. These are the logics and ideas related to those logics. They are software that configures and shapes the behaviors of the system. A business is nothing more than its behaviors. They are not shaped by the hardware. They are shaped by what is put into the hardware—the logics and ideas. We are just on the verge, in this Postinformation Age, of understanding the implications of this perspective. Businesses are beginning to recognize that if they are to be successful, they need to ferret out the softwares they feed into the system themselves.

One area in which we see this ferreting process occurring organically is in the domain of franchising. None of the early franchisors designed it this way. Nonetheless, it emerged as a successful form of adaptation, and became a way of doing business in which the distinction between information and infrastructure was made quite differently than in other forms of business.

Franchising emerged out of the collective experience of the retail marketplace. Today, it represents 40 percent of retail sales in the United States, close to \$1 trillion, and provides 8 million jobs in sixty-five industries. By the year 2000, it is estimated that franchising will represent 50 percent of retail sales.[1] Franchised businesses have organized themselves to be intermediaries between the people who make objects and those who buy them.

The Franchise Approach

This is the commonsense experience out of which franchising is formed, and describes one format for franchising, that based on an existing business.

A businessperson recognized that someone down the street was providing the same products or services in the same way as he was. The businesses were open the same hours and often looked alike. There was not much of a distinction between them. Basically, they were using the same methodologies. Every dry cleaner is doing it exactly as the next, with minor variations. Even today, in most industries the variations between competing companies are very minor. The problems are in securing a share of the market, a niche, an identity, stability, and security. These are all things beyond the control of the business. It's difficult to say what is going on in the economy that is affecting the behaviors of people. We don't know what our so-called competitors are coming up with in the marketplace. They have a special on Tuesday, we have a special on Wednesday. Some of them are staying open longer hours, some are open on Sunday.

There are people engaged in those markets or industries who can see a way of changing it, of doing it better, or at the very least differently, but they don't know how to proceed. If they see a way of doing it differently and let it be known, it won't take long before everyone else will be doing it differently, too. Then the whole process has to start all over again. These innovators think, "Wouldn't it be great if, before people could learn about our different format, we could already have gotten it out, and be the first one to do it?"

But how does one do that? We could implement the new ideas in our shop if we understand the ideas well enough. We can change the shop tomorrow, but it wouldn't be very long before all our competitors within our immediate market would be doing it too, and the edge would be lost. However, if we could open a hundred such shops all at once, by the time the competition realized what happened it would be a fait accompli. Of course, we couldn't do that. We just have one shop. It cost us $100,000 to open this business. To open ten would cost $1 million. To open one hundred would cost $10 million. In contacting investors, partners, or borrowing money from banks, we'd have to tell them all our idea, and once again, it would be out. By the time we got around to doing it in our shop, it would already have become common knowledge.

But what if we could get other people to open shops and give them the right to use our format? We could teach them how to use it while maintaining the proprietary rights to the system. Our innovations, of course, would have to be complex enough so that when we explained it, they couldn't walk away and do it themselves. But what if we could find one hundred people, each of whom would spend $100,000 to do the work necessary to open a shop like ours in this newly conceived way? We wouldn't get the profit from each of those shops, as we would if we owned them ourselves, but we could charge a fee. We could get a percentage of the volume for the continued right to use our format.

Another format for franchising occurs when someone who has never been in the specific target business at all, someone from outside the industry, recognizes something within that industry that no one else sees. Entrepreneurs may not have time to open their own shops, but want to get moving. They take the idea as pure information, without any infrastructure at all, and then sell the rights to engage in that business to others. Some franchise systems started with nothing more than an idea from which people purchased franchises. Some of these succeeded and some did not. But then, too, some based on existing businesses succeeded and some did not.

There were abuses in the development of franchises in the 1940s–50s, when people concocted businesses they knew would never work. For this reason the Federal Trade Commission has very stringent definitions and procedures governing the offering of franchises, including requiring a prospectus for potential buyers. Still today, we find instances in which the information franchisors provide becomes the stuff of lawsuits: we already mentioned the problems of Mail Boxes Etc. In 1997 a $1 billion suit was filed against the Southland Corporation by two thousand 7-Eleven franchisees, who contended that there was a fraudulent misrepresentation to conceal Southland's allegedly precarious financial position.[2]

Midas International is an example of a successful company that was not originally a retail business, but came to understand the principles of franchising and the power of accurate information. In the early 1950s, Midas didn't have a shop in which to sell or install its mufflers. It was a manufacturer, making the products that the retailers were selling. It looked at the market and its system of distribution and realized that it was selling to thousands of auto parts stores, gas stations, and wrecking yards. The cost of servicing those customers was enormous. Midas had to maintain staffs of traveling salesmen, and, before computers, they had to track what was sold, bill each customer individually, and carry thousands of accounts. They had to check credit and collect payments. But they weren't developing a proprietary interest or brand. Their customers didn't have to buy their mufflers, because no one knew they existed as a specific brand of muffler.

In 1956 the manufacturer decided to change its method of distribution. Franchising already existed, but not for automobile mufflers. The idea was that if Midas opened a chain of specialized automotive shops that did nothing but install mufflers with the same name and identity in the marketplace, they would have only hundreds of customers to serve instead of thousands. They would also have an identity that was of great value. They didn't try to own everything. If they had they would have had hundreds of local bank accounts to contend with, thousands of employees to pay every week, and hundreds of landlords. It was the days before computers, and a paper record of every lease would have had to be kept along with its obligations and payment schedules. Midas would have had to carry a monumental accounting department.

Instead, they granted to others the right to set up a chain of stores and didn't have to use their own resources to open them. The franchisees would spend their own money and time starting the business. Midas provided the brand name, image, and product. They were also responsible for marketing, the design of the shops, directing the franchisees to the best equipment, and teaching them how to train employees. For franchise owners, Midas eventually looked for people who had never been in the automotive business before. In this way, the owners would have no preconceived ideas about the industry and would not resist new ideas as they emerged.

All Midas had to do was continue to make and ship mufflers, which was what it was already organized to do. It didn't have to create a new infrastructure. It's job was simply to disseminate information and be able to make sure that every one in the system understood it and abided by the rules of the game.

Midas quickly got into franchising without having to make a large investment or hire a lot of people. They opened about five hundred shops in the first five years.

Gradually they had to expand manufacturing and warehousing facilities, but they already had that existing infrastructure, and simply added to it. They didn't have to ask, How do we go about manufacturing mufflers? They opened more warehouses, but they knew how to lay out a warehouse. They didn't have to carry the infrastructure of the new system.

If they needed money to add to the warehouse space, this had nothing to do with the franchise program. It had to do with Midas's history with its banks, who were in the business of lending money to expand these facilities. If Midas had gone to the bank and asked to borrow a million dollars to open ten Midas muffler shops, the bank would have thought they were crazy. Midas had never been in the retail business before. It wasn't their core business. If they wanted to expand their manufacturing, which they had been doing for twenty years, that made sense. Over forty years later, there are more than two thousand independent Midas muffler shops worldwide.

Anyone who undertakes the franchising model has developed something novel that liberates the franchisees from the constraints and habits of that industry. Supercuts shops are open every day, seven days a week, twelve hours on weekdays, instead of nine-to-five, five days a week. Prior to this, every haircutting salon was closed on Monday, so it made sense that no one got a hair cut on Mondays. And since shops prior to Supercuts closed in the early evening, of course no one could get a hair cut at night. Those blinders were firmly in place and characterized the thinking and behaviors of the haircutting industry.

Supercuts was organized to be open every day, which was a major departure from the prevailing practice of the industry. Supercuts was organized to be open until nine on weeknights, again against prevailing practice. Supercuts didn't move just from experience to information. It was asking "What if?" questions, and those questions were answered prior to experience and were conditions of experience. Ideas shaped behavior.

Many franchise companies start out with one or more pilot operations that they mount quickly to develop a track record and that are used primarily as a selling tool. Supercuts opened a shop in Albany, California, which eventually was able to demonstrate to potential owners how the concept would work. Potential franchisees would make the journey to this northern California, Bay Area town and see a shop full of people between six and nine at night. The prevailing view had been that men and women wouldn't go to the same place. Men and women were both waiting. And on Sunday and Monday, there were people lined up at the door waiting, counter to the notion that people don't get their hair cut on Sunday or Monday.

The Information-Infrastructure Exchange

There are many ways to implement these systems. The important thing is that the form of business called franchising rests implicitly on the distinction that has emerged between information and infrastructure. The franchisor's job is to supply information, and the franchisee's job is to bring entities, which we call infrastructure, into existence. Franchisees look for locations, negotiate leases, buy equipment from vendors, hire contractors, hire employees, order inventory, and put the inventory away. The franchisor's job is to keep ahead of whatever anybody else was doing in the marketplace.

Creating Increasing Returns

When a business sees itself as a complex adaptive system, one of the adjacent possibilities it opens itself to is the opportunity to create increasing returns. *Increasing returns* is shorthand for describing the rewards of getting there first and locking in the market. In "What Is Evolutionary Economics?" the economist Kenneth Boulding writes, "The more we know, the easier it is to know more. The more we make, the easier it is to make more. The richer we are, the easier it is to get richer."[3]

The economist Brian Arthur, in a *Harvard Business Review* article, wrote, "Increasing returns are the tendency for that which is ahead to get further ahead, for that which loses advantage to lose further advantage. They are mechanisms of positive feedback, that operate within market businesses and industries to reinforce that which gains success or aggravate that which suffers loss. . . . Increasing returns can magnify disadvantage and the product or company or technology can go on to lock in the market."[4]

Franchising has emerged in the last fifty years as the form of business activity that can produce the highest level of increasing returns relative to capital expenditures. This doesn't mean that nonfranchise companies can't move into a position of dominance or leadership in the market, getting ahead of everyone and staying ahead. We've seen it with Microsoft, Starbucks, and Intel. But those business required greater capital expenditures to do so. Starbucks had to raise tens of millions of dollars in order to open its company-owned operations.

In contrast to the company-owned model, franchising comes into existence because someone has an idea and provides that idea to other people who implement it. The franchisor does not implement that idea, but focuses all of its time, energy, and attention on the continued formulation, refinement, and dissemination of everything related to that idea.

A franchisor is in the business of information. That is its nature. If a business consists of ideas, then the best example of such a business is a franchising company, because it is only ideas. Midas may have manufactured mufflers, but that was incidental. Those operations already existed. It formed a new business called Midas Muffler Shops, and that consisted only of information. It is no coincidence that increasing returns followed.

As the economy changes, more and more established companies are realizing that they have traditionally been in the business of making and distributing things, and it is no longer working for them. Increasingly, without necessarily choosing or designing it so, they find that their business is gravitating toward information. Increasingly, people are approaching these mature organizations not for their products but for solutions to problems in their businesses. If mature organizations can provide a piece of equipment that can be used in solving the problem, that is okay, but that's not the primary reason for the contact. Citibank's retired senior technology officer, Colin Crook, explains this by saying that in today's market, companies are "buying strategies, not products." When Crook bought equipment from John Chambers and Cisco Systems, Crook was investing in Cisco's strategy and ideas to solve his problems today and in the future, not just in its current product line.

An example of a small company moving from infrastructure to information is Bandelier Designs. For years, Bandelier designed and manufactured fabric-covered blank notebooks and journals, and other covered paper products. After a good deal of struggle with their manufacturing process, they realized they weren't a manufacturing company, but an idea company. They sold off their manufacturing process, and shrank their staff from fifty employees to six: accounting, marketing, design, reception, and the CEO. The result was swifter implementation of ideas and a broader market.

More and more companies are redesigning their business into franchise variations. They're slowly discovering that what they are really selling is information. In the parlance of complex adaptive systems, it's information all the way down. Even infrastructure-laden businesses are realizing, as they put together their manufacturing, warehousing, inventory control, and distribution operations, that all of their work depends on ideas. With this revelation, they start farming out some of their activities and the process repeats itself.

There are still many diminishing-returns activities and businesses. These do not function very differently from Industrial Age businesses, which were all of the diminishing-returns variety. Brian Arthur defines this kind of operation succinctly: "The assumption of diminishing returns, which has been the prevailing economic theory until very recently in this Information Age, is that products or companies that get ahead in a market eventually run into limitations so that a predictable equilibrium of prices and market shares is reached. The growth stops. It was roughly valid for the bulk processing, smoke-stack economy of [economist Alfred] Marshall's day. Western economy has undergone a transformation from those days from bulk material manufacturing to design and use of technology. From processing of resources to processing of information. The underlying mechanisms that determine economic behavior have shifted from one of diminishing to one of increasing returns."

It is important to reiterate that diminishing-returns companies still make up a good part of our economy. For most businesses, infrastructure makes up most of what we think of as the business. However, these infrastructure-heavy companies are finding out that a greater portion of their business is increasingly developing in the area of information. In fact, the majority of them can no longer perform their operations without massive information systems.

Information Is a Continual Flow

As we have said, a new franchise program starts with a high ratio of information to infrastructure. A franchisor wouldn't be able to attract either franchisees or customers without a uniquely distinguishing idea or business format. As the program develops, this ratio of information to infrastructure rapidly increases until it reaches a stable level. But the development of ideas/information *must always continue*. If it does, internally, increasing returns emerge. Good ideas lead to better ideas; good systems lead to better systems. This is analogous to increasing returns in the marketplace, in which increases in market share lead to more increases in market share; increases in brand recognition lead to more brand recognition. This is why this ratio is so important. If a franchise program neglects its responsibility so that good ideas aren't leading to better ideas, and good systems don't lead to better systems, this will be reflected in a slowdown in the rate of increasing returns out there in the world.

Increasing returns within the company and in the marketplace constitute a single continuous feedback mechanism: Increasing returns within the company means better ideas, which improve the quality of product, which leads to better products and/or services or even to improvements in infrastructure. These improvements lead to increasing returns in the marketplace, more revenue, more outlets, more customers, more recognition. These lead in turn to better ideas, processes, and systems. Increasing returns within the system and the marketplace cannot be separated: The recursive action between models and behaviors creates more and more innovation.

We see increasing return relationships in nonfranchised companies like Microsoft. Because of their brand name, they are able to keep their markets, even though their product might not always be best. Unlike other forms of business, however, franchising is uniquely founded upon and depends upon increasing returns.

Information is what drives increasing returns, not the product—the individual, infrastructural element of the system. In the ongoing conduct of the franchise system, this inseparable feedback process is never complete. The franchisor introduces new approaches within an industry. These approaches alter the industry and the marketplace, which means the franchisor requires further adaptation, learning, and innovation, which in turn alters the marketplace, and so on.

When the franchisor stops the information flow, the system will most certainly decline or even die. The process demands a constant readjusting and redefinition. The reality, of course, is that this is true for all businesses. If any business allows its information flow to decrease, that business is in trouble. It may not be as apparent as it is in franchising, but franchising is prototypical of what the ongoing adaptive process looks like.

Let us now summarize the essential features of this complex adaptive relationship between franchisor and franchisee. While reading these points, keep in mind that *these concepts can be formulated to represent nonfranchise business activities as well.*

1. The franchisor creates a business format and operational system or information for the distribution of its product or service in the marketplace. The franchisor may be expanding its already existing nonfranchise business or may be creating a new business. In either case, it always provides innovation within its industry, whatever that industry may be, sometimes to the point of virtually creating a new

industry. The franchisor may, in this process of innovation, create one or more prototypes.

2. The franchisor usually confronts a narrow window of opportunity for establishing itself in the marketplace before others imitate its innovative and new format. Rapid expansion is usually necessary to establish an increasing-returns position in the marketplace.

3. In a conventional business format, rapid expansion requires significant person power and capital. To develop these usually takes considerable time, almost certainly more time than the window of opportunity. Developing within this window of opportunity also usually requires considerable capital. For example, if one retail outlet costs $100,000, expansion to ten outlets would require a million dollars, and increasing returns may require opening several hundred outlets within the window of opportunity. The task of hiring and training hundreds of employees could take years. The creation of management and control systems and structures could also take years as well as substantial capital.

4. The franchisor can solve the problem of time and costs and achieve its goal of increasing returns by franchising its business format. The franchisee provides both management person power and capital. Its management and capital provide for rapid establishment of the infrastructure of the system, infrastructure that makes possible rapid introduction of the name and the marketing of the essential features of the system in the marketplace.

5. The franchisee can also achieve rapid identity in the marketplace, and even if the franchisee has never been in business nor engaged in this industry he can run his business effectively by simply following the franchisor's informational system. For example, the franchisor provides site-selection guidelines—information. The franchisee finds the site. This isn't always true, but many systems are structured in that way. The franchisor provides architectural design manuals and equipment specifications—information. The franchisee builds or improves the site infrastructure, providing both person power and capital.

6. In the process, both franchisor and franchisee realize the benefits of what neither could do without the other.

Franchising has flourished over the last fifty years because on the one hand, it has enabled small businesses with good ideas but limited staff and capital to grow by becoming franchisors, and on the other hand it has enabled individuals with limited business experience to establish a secure business in an unfamiliar industry, and to expand within their franchise system as a franchisee.

A Model of Distributed Management

An important difference between a franchise system and a business organized into divisions and departments is that the franchisee is not an employee of the franchisor. He or she is an independent businessperson who runs his or her own business autonomously within the agreed-upon informational structure supplied by the franchisor. This is accomplished within a framework of principles that is shared and communicated as a guide for the whole system. The principles exist within the prevailing models contained in the franchisor's operation manuals. These models may, as appropriate, change from time to time. Also, the few rules which are viable under the conditions of the franchisor/franchisee agreement are there to produce some commonalities of behavior within the system. The end result is that every outlet of the franchise system is essentially behaving consistently, providing the consumer a sense of dependability, familiarity, and integrity. When we enter a Wendy's, a Midas Muffler shop, or a One-Hour Martinizing dry cleaner, we don't have to be concerned that it will differ from other outlets in the same franchise system.

This is not to imply that the system doesn't change. It changes both because the franchisor is performing its informational function and because the franchisee, in autonomously implementing and applying these ideas, is providing constant feedback directly and indirectly into the system. The franchisor receives all the operating data of a franchisee's outlet as a basis upon which royalties are paid to the franchisor. It knows the volume, trends, and costs from the franchisee's financial statement. It gathers valuable feedback from that statement about the individual shop, the market, cycles during different times of year, and the micromarket within its larger market.

The other form of feedback the franchisor receives is the ongoing interaction between itself and the franchisee in the form of anecdote, story, and complaint. The significant distinction between franchise and company-owned operations is that this whole realm of feedback into the system comes through people who have the independence and autonomy to form their own information on the conduct of their own business and its interactions. This exchange of information takes place not only with the franchisor but with other franchisees—even with employees of one franchisee interacting with employees of others. For example, the franchisees send their managers to interact with each other at managers' conferences, where they share their experiences and observations. This is a level of information the franchisees don't necessarily have, except through feedback from the managers. This is an example of distributed management by autonomous agents all the way down.

If we were to move a level up from store manager to franchisee, we would find that there is no manager of the franchisees. There are people responsible for the integrity of the franchise system. These people, however, have no authority over the franchisee other than to ensure that the fundamental agreed-upon format of the system, as set forth in a franchise agreement, is being observed.

Unfortunately, attaining the same degree of feedback as in franchising is not possible for nonfranchise companies. The reason, based on observation, is that an organization cannot get independent, truthful feedback from a person hired to run an outlet who is concerned with job security, advancement, or image within the organization. A portion of that feedback always reflects what a manager thinks the system wants to hear. As autonomous agents, the franchisees have no such motivation to provide incomplete information. Thus, when it comes to feedback there is a true congruence of goals between the franchisor and franchisee. It is in the best interest of both to provide the best possible information throughout the system.

Establishing the Diversity of Control

Franchising has demonstrated that with complex adaptive systems, the diversity of sources of control benefits the organization. Industrial Age businesses have traditionally been organized around a central control that works its way down a hierarchy of roles in which people are told what to do. Their job is to comply. There is normally little structure for constructive feedback in this system. The shop manager of a company-owned chain system of shops does what he or she is told. In this fashion, a company-owned shop gets locked into being nothing but infrastructure. The system is closed, so there is little recursive action between information and infrastructure on which, ultimately, the health of the whole system depends. A franchisee, who is an autonomous franchise owner, performs an information function within his or her individual business. Because the information to infrastructure ratio must remain high, feedback with the store manager, the transfer of information from the franchisor, and the freedom to implement new ideas on a local level will prevent the franchisee from becoming bogged down in infrastructure.

In most company-owned models, the viewpoint is that the information structure belongs at the top. The company doesn't want its agents messing around with its ideas. For the most part, they also don't want feedback. The institution discourages that. Those businesses that are flourishing in this Information Age have found their way out of that kind of organizational constraint. We saw this in companies like Xerox PARC and Hewlett-Packard VeriFone, where the diversity of control, pushed to the periphery of the organization, provided the system the information it needed to continue growth and produce better service and products.

Establishing a system that favors diversity over centralized control is not an overnight process. Every business is afraid to relinquish control. In contrast to this, in the franchise model the franchisor relinquishes total control to the autonomous agents who run each outlet. It doesn't have a choice. The fear of what will happen if it doesn't relinquish control never comes into play. To repeat, this way of doing business is not an aberration; it accounts for 40 percent of American retail sales.

There is also another distinction between the franchise model and the company-owned model: In the former, the responsibility for staying in business, for profit and loss, is the franchisee's, not the company's. The franchisor's revenue is a percentage of the revenue of that entity. If that entity's revenue starts declining, as may be happening with McDonald's, the franchisor's revenue also declines. This is why the franchisor is motivated continually to provide novel innovation and information. If its ideas are not shaping the franchise successfully, the franchisor affects the whole system negatively. The franchisee is dependent on the franchisor's capacity to perform that information function, and if it fails to do so, there is little the franchisee can do but bite the bullet.

The franchisor's thinking is, "Our success is based on their success, which is based on the information we provide. In that regard, to a certain degree their failure is our failure, too, but our survival is not at stake." This is very different from an IBM in which the failure of a divisional system could threaten the survival of IBM. If a franchise unit fails, the franchisor has lost the revenue source, but has not risked a large amount of the money.

This is a big distinction. It is also the source for a major mistake made by franchise companies: to try and act like a franchisee and own stores. As soon as a franchisor, thinking it can make more than just royalties, decides to make all the profit itself by owning its own infrastructure, it has stepped outside the principles that govern the industry, and it is asking for trouble. Such franchisors now invest millions of dollars in locations and become absorbed with infrastructure issues. They effectively stop supplying information, which is their job, to the other franchise units. The result is a drain on the whole system, as the ratio of information to infrastructure falls. This situation occurred at Sizzler Steakhouse, Supercuts, and to a certain degree McDonald's. It has proved devastating to others who made this mistake.

Like a franchisor, a conventional company such as IBM has to recognize that in order to continue to grow and develop, it must find a way of relinquishing the centralized control that it holds on to out of anxiety and fear. It must provide for the kind of distributed management that makes real feedback possible. And it must recognize the responsibility of a distributed-management company to supply information. Without this commitment, it will spend its money and resources unnecessarily maintaining control mechanisms, which by their closed nature make it impossible to adapt quickly to local influences and succeed.

This does not mean that all control is neglected, but an organization has to rethink and reformulate what it means by control. The old idea of control is as obsolete as Newton's physics. Of course there is control: In a fundamental way, the franchisor controls the system. However, it doesn't control it as is classically defined in the history of business. The critical factor is that *control lies with information*. The organization controls to the extent that it provides ideas and formulations, which are the geometry that guides and shapes the behaviors. The lesson for all businesses to learn is that an organization's only control lies in its capacity to shape behaviors. This is done one way and one way only, through the formulation of ideas.

NLINEAR INVESTIGATION NO. 7:
FLOWS AND CONSTRICTIONS

It is the nature of man as he grows older . . . to protest against change, particularly change for the better. • John Steinbeck

Franchising within a traditional organizational structure creates a variety of different flows and interactions. This nonlinear investigation is designed to help you look at your organization's flows and constrictions to see how decentralized, semiautonomous franchise units might impact that flow.

Optimizing the Flow of Operations

1. What factors overwhelm your organization's current functional alignments?

2. What consequences arise when that overload takes place?

3. How does the organization react to these system overloads?

Realigning Interactions to Improve Flow

1. How would your organizational alignments look if they were reconstructed and re-formed as semiautonomous franchises within a franchised operation?

2. How would it change the relationships between departments and divisions?

3. How would it affect communication and feedback within the organization?

Command and Control

1. How would organizational administration functions change to accommodate a franchised structure?

2. Is your organization's administration willing to remove unnecessary restraints, or would a franchise reformulation simply create new ones?

3. What would be the benefits of these decentralized franchises in the short and long term?

Apprehending the Future

*When we are afraid of ourselves and afraid of the seeming threat the world
presents, then we become extremely selfish. We want to build our own little
nests, our own cocoons, so that we can live by ourselves in a secure
way. . . . Fundamentally, there is nothing that either threatens or
promotes our point of view. The four seasons occur free from
anyone's demand or vote. Hope and fear cannot alter*
the seasons. • Chogyam Trungpa, *The Sacred Path of the Warrior*

In one fashion or another, the unnecessary walls restraining our efforts
come down, whether through our concerted efforts or through
nature's continual renewal. We spoke earlier about the courage to discard
obsolete ways of thinking, and about the dynamics of a business as a purposeful complex adaptive system. We introduced the powerful relationship between information and infrastructure and how it affects what we
do at every level of our business. And within that ratio, we demonstrated
how ideas shape behaviors and how new ideas can emerge.

In his fourth-century B.C. treatise, *The Art of War*, Sun-tzu said that
"the way to defeat an enemy is to defeat his ideas." In today's postindustrial world, business's enemy is not lurking somewhere out there; rather
it is locked within the boundaries of the organizations we've constructed
to keep it out. The only way to outthink this insidious adversary, to defeat
its ideas, is to free ourselves from its outmoded ways. We've been stopped
over and over again by an overriding need to feel secure. Instability and
change are closely linked. As NeoRx's CEO Paul Abrams explained,
"Everyone wants progress. Nobody likes change." How, then, can our
businesses become comfortable with insecurity?

NeoRx, located just off Elliot Bay in Seattle, is a biotechnology company founded in 1984. It devised a process of using antibodies as targeting
vehicles, and then attached unique forms of radiation to them. The idea
was that these antibodies would accumulate on a particular cancer cell
and when the person was scanned with a gamma camera, it would help
diagnose cancer tumors earlier in their development and identify other
cancerous deposits in the body. When the process broke down and they

found that they weren't detecting otherwise undetectable tumors, they changed their focus. Instead of using the antibodies for detection, they used them for delivery of therapy. And it worked. They have since moved from producing primarily cancer-treatment products to include cardio-vascular disease treatments as well.

In a volatile field such as biotechnology, in which innovation and disappointment can cost millions in research and development, Abrams believes that "everyone is looking for security, but it doesn't exist. The real challenge is to make insecurity not seem as if it is unusual. If you surrender yourself to the uncertainty of the marketplace, in whatever endeavor you are talking about, you are saying you are willing to absorb negative outcomes, which most people are not. The constraining factor is insecurity. If we say, 'We need to let this process evolve,' as soon as there are any discontinuities, someone is going to get bent out of shape and will complain. Emergence may be a rational process, but you cannot see it at the time, only retrospectively, so it appears to be inherently irrational." For Abrams, getting people comfortable with this apparent insecurity takes a great deal of hand-holding.

The insecurity associated with making corporate change often starts with the individual. Reluctance to initiate change may not mean that someone doesn't see the benefit of it. Richard Rothwell, of the U.S. Postal Service, points out, "The opportunity to discredit yourself makes taking a risk hard. You have a lot of people who are willing to go after you. They may see the narrative you're providing is convincing others and they don't believe it, then they want to discredit you."

According to Rothwell, feeling insecure about stepping out with new ideas locks in older ideas. He points out, "What locks us in is ourselves. Each individual person gets locked in for fear of overstepping some invisible boundary. My first three years in the Postal Service I used to tell people several times a week to not stop doing something because they heard it was not allowed. Continue doing it. When there is an armed guard at the door forcing you to stop, call me, and we'll work on getting rid of the armed guard. These fears have been placed in people through years of getting their toes stepped on because they have tried to move forward a little faster."

Organizations also fear opening their systems because they think it will create uneasiness, often equating open with not having a direction. Allowing emergence to happen becomes seen as an organization's inability to settle on something. John Hiles at Thinking Tools equates this thinking to "Bronze Age man, who really wants to have a codified system that doesn't change. He wants to have a king and follow that king, even if that king is on his hands and knees searching for the path."

It seems quite evident that we think of this postmodern age as a time of insecurity, anxiety, uncertainty, and unpredictability. What we find, surprisingly, is that almost every activity and domain of human behavior has a predictability and certainty that has never previously existed. Prior to the Information Age, almost everything that human beings engaged in carried great unknowns. For example, in the Agrarian Age, a farmer planted a crop. Once it was in the ground there was no way of anticipating weather patterns, and little if any knowledge about chemical means for enhancing plant growth. Nor did the mechanisms exist that could affect the rate at which cultivating or harvesting took place. Today, most of the areas that were uncertain for the farmers of yesteryear are no longer uncertain. Reasonable predictions can be made in all of these areas.

In the case of medicine, if someone became ill, it was a matter of great uncertainty what the illness was, or whether it could be named and identified. There was then a great uncertainty about the possible remedies, what each would do, the timing for prescribing it and its side effects. It wasn't possible to look into the body using X-rays or CAT scans. There were no reliable chemical treatments, or radiation, or effective means for performing surgeries in which the patient's odds for survival were consistently high.

Whether we are talking about farming, medicine, transportation, or manufacturing, almost every process we engage in today is relatively predictable and thus provides a high degree of confidence that goes way beyond anything that earlier civilizations ever imagined possible. We send a spacecraft to another planet. We don't have to wonder what is going to become of it. We can predict where it will be at any designated point in time, even when it will arrive, to the second. We can predict with some certainty how to maintain communications with it and guide its progress. We can even perform repairs here on Earth to damages that may occur on the planet Mars.

All these things reflect expanding predictability. The paradox is that the more we know, the more we become aware of what we don't know. The ambiguities and uncertainties in medicine become highlighted. We fail to recognize that those highlighted ambiguities are minor relative to those that once existed. Today, we are also capable of questioning the process in a way that tells us where to look for answers and in what form they are likely to be accessible.

There is hardly any area of human endeavor that has not been so touched. It is not simply that new technologies have developed. It is that we have recognized the emergence of increasingly sophisticated logics, mathematics, languages, linguistic usages, formulations, and means and modes of communication, some of which are related to technology, but some of which are not. One of the ambiguities we see is that the flow moves as much from ideas to the technological outcomes as it does from new technologies to the ideas with which we structure our experience. To quote the distinguished mathematician and theoretical physicist Roger Penrose:

> There is . . . a feature which is completely unique to General Relativity, and not present at all in the Newtonian theory of gravity. That is that objects in orbit about each other radiate energy in the form of gravitational waves. These are like light waves but are ripples in space-time rather than ripples in the electromagnetic field. These waves take energy away from the system at a rate that can be calculated according to Einstein's theory. . . . [T]he accuracy with which the theory is known to be correct . . . makes General Relativity the most accurately tested theory known to science.

Penrose adds, "There is a moral in this story—Einstein's motivations in devoting eight or more years of his life to deriving the General Theory were not observational or experimental. . . . The theory was developed originally without any observational motivation."[1]

In other words, our knowledge of the structure of space-time as set forth in General Relativity, which reduces the uncertainty and ambiguity about the universe, bears upon our capacity to make incredibly accurate predictions. The theory's genesis did not depend on either observations or the new technologies that might make new observations possible.

Together, ideas and technology constitute what we call the Information Age. Contrary to popular sentiment, the net result has been a great reduction in uncertainty.

Oftentimes, uncertainty and insecurity are linked to issues of control and the diversity of control. How does an organization that has been locked into an Industrial Age framework and is now moving itself into a complex adaptive framework let go of the controls and mechanisms that once promised security, when what we are now looking at are more unpredictable processes?

If we were to look at an isolated individual Industrial Age business organization, it would be accurate to say that there was not a great deal of insecurity. They developed certain routines that were repeated over and over again. The outcome of those routines were known and the economy to which they were distributing their goods was fairly stable and predictable.

It is also true that they existed within a larger context in which an enormous amount was not under their control. This included their access to information, which could have a bearing on their viability and their ability to make plans and adjust their structures and behaviors. They did not have any information beyond that which was locally available. What they called the economy and the world were largely abstract concepts. What they had control over was their limited neighborhood, in which behaviors were reasonably predictable, changed slowly, and weren't influenced, so it was thought, from the outside.

Beyond the boundaries of these local landscapes, there were sources that produced enormous amounts of insecurity and lack of control in the world. Things happened that were completely unanticipated, like famines, plagues, hurricanes, tornadoes, and unexpected floods. What would the impact be if we had an industrial plant in an area which was gripped by a famine? The markets for distribution immediately disappear.

The ebb and flow of global events also contributed to this insecurity. The owner of a manufacturing plant in France in the 1800s wouldn't know what was happening between the governments of France and Germany, beyond the relatively slow dissemination of information by the daily press. Suddenly, we're in the middle of the Franco-Prussian War. The people we had counted on as a stable workforce are no longer available, because they have had to go to war. We lose a workforce that we assumed would be with us for years to come.

We might also run into a problem with access to raw materials, especially if any of those raw materials originated in enemy territory. A variety of events was going on in our world that we did not know about, did not have any information about, that we could not anticipate or plan for, or that placed our apparently stable, if local, environment in a much larger context of instability and unpredictability.

The Industrial Age broke down not just because new technologies were developed but because it reached an informational limitation. The constraints on this way of thinking were such that the reasonably stable industrial system could no longer continue functioning as it did, because of an increasing dependence on information.

The desired control that local industry was once seemingly able to achieve is similar to what modern businesses are looking for in terms of control, predictability, security, and the reduction of risk today. Unfortunately, it doesn't exist as it once did. Ultimately, we find ourselves in a strange paradox: The more reliably we can predict our world, the more insecurity is opened up. Another way of looking at this is that the more insecurity expands, the more obvious it becomes that we are able to control a great deal more about our world, our business, our industry, their environments, and even our economy than were our predecessors.

In order to make our companies more comfortable with this insecurity and uncertainty, we can no longer define control as we have in the nineteenth and for most of the twentieth century. Today, control lies for the most part in the capacity of a company to be informed. We control our business, industry, society, and economy to the extent that we can make what is happening intelligible within meaningful constructs like models. Once they are intelligible, by definition they are neither chaotic nor random. When we say that they are chaotic or random, it means in effect that we have no way of making them wholly intelligible or adequately intelligible to ourselves. Therefore, whatever happens is going to be as capricious as a drought in an agricultural area, which was a chaotic event. There was no way for the farmer who found himself in the drought to make sense of the drought as a phenomenon. There was no way that he could develop strategies for dealing with it. He was helpless, to the extent and only to the extent that he couldn't make any sense out of the occurrence. If he could make sense of it, the farmer would be able to produce a whole range of actions and strategies. His capacity to see a drought as a natural, recurring phenomenon may allow him to take precautions, to identify certain patterns and sources that give him a relationship to the drought that he would not otherwise have. What strategies does that involve? It may mean the farmer would do some contingency planning, like irrigation. He might have to reexamine the crops he was raising and plant crops that were less water-dependent.

The same could be said of medicine. In certain stages of medical history a disease like cancer was a totally chaotic, unintelligible phenomenon. We couldn't name it, classify it, or put it into a logical system in which it could be explained or accounted for. Cancer victims were helpless before it.

A company, too, has control only to the extent that it is not helpless in relationship to certain phenomena. Whether a situation is chaotic or not has to do solely with whether it can be dealt with within a system of ideas and understanding that make it intelligible. In making a phenomenon intelligible, we give it a form, in the absence of which it is nothing but chaos.

There is another issue at work here. Often, companies that are afraid to move out of what was once a safe place turn to rules as a means to maintain a control that no longer exists. We refer to this cycling between rules and behaviors as routines. They could be converted into statements of rules that work and produce predictable results. The problem with rules in today's organizational structures is that the interactions of component agents with each other change so rapidly that rules are not valid for very long. As we suggested earlier, rules are purely pragmatic moments of adaptation; we continue following the "rule" as long as it continues to deal with the issue successfully. When the issues or conditions change rapidly, one has to be willing to let go of the rule instantly. It may have had great relevance or value during the period of its existence, and may have helped make possible a transition that might not otherwise have been possible, but it no longer has relevance or value.

Holding on to rules after change has taken place is nothing more than a resistance to change. It's as if our security means more to us than being able to solve our problems. We think we can hide behind the rules and provide ourselves the illusion that everything is okay, because we are continuing to do things in the prescribed way. Unfortunately, this kind of thinking only constricts the system's life flow more and hastens decline.

Selling Complexity to the Organization

So how does a champion of a new way of thinking attempt to sell an idea like complex adaptive systems, with its inherent unpredictability, into an organization, especially one locked into rules and behaviors that are no longer serving the organization? We cannot go to our CEO or board of directors and simply tell them, "We've read this book by Sherman and Schultz. It has presented some good ideas in terms of how an organization needs to see itself and how organizations fundamentally operate. What it means in regard to our organization is that we are really going to have to look at ourselves very differently."

If that plan were followed there wouldn't be a great deal of incentive to change on the part of a board of directors or CEO, except maybe to start a search to replace the messenger. Whoever is responsible for selling this idea in must do some homework first. Richard Carlson has developed a process called the Perfect Sales Equation, which works, though he says it is neither perfect nor an equation (see Figure 6).[2] It is based on four fundamental ideas:

1. The Verified Need—What do we have too little or too much of that is contributing to the situation we find ourselves in? The answer is based on evidence and fact.

2. The Felt Need—Why is this situation intolerable? The answer is based on opinion.

3. The Verifiable Benefit—How will our proposal change the verified need? The answer is based on fact and evidence.

4. The Felt Benefit—What will be the long-term benefit of this approach? The answer is based on opinion.

To apply this formula successfully, answer the questions in order.

To determine the Verified Need, we might look at the insecurities of the company and the limitations of its capacity to understand what is happening in its world. The company's "world" includes its metaphoric climates, soils, weather patterns, seasons, and the extent to which the company does not understand a specific phenomenon that it cannot include in some pattern of intelligibility. Like all businesses, it is subject to events occurring on the outside over which it has no control and with which it cannot deal. It is constrained within the limits of its patterns of knowledge and information availability. Beyond that it is literally completely helpless. To use a biological metaphor: If an occurrence happens beyond the range of their medicine, they can be killed by it. They don't know what kills them or why they are killed or what they could have

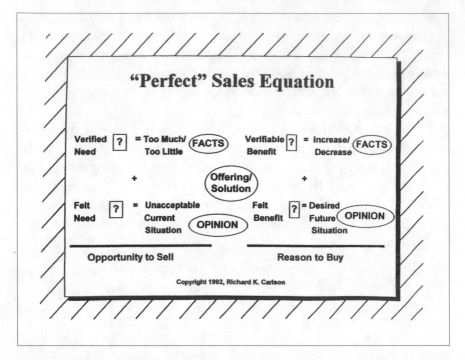

Figure 6.   The perfect sales equation

done to avoid it in the first place or to treat it in the second place. Their existence is a function of their cognitive capacities and their cognitive limitations. Document evidence of these limitations within the organization.

Then, gather the opinions of others as to why such a situation is intolerable. Before we can sell an organization on the benefit or a new way of thinking, we must first provide a reason to seek something new. Without the prior creation of this buy-in opportunity, no amount of benefit slinging will ever sell an idea. There's simply no motivation to do so.

To demonstrate a business as a complex adaptive system, it is important to show how today's organizations are just as helpless as any organization has ever been in relation to what it does not know, understand, or cannot structure in some meaningful form of intelligibility. Once the evidence substantiating this need for intelligibility is clear and there is sufficient emotion behind it, then a benefit can be brought forward. One might be that a company can broaden its range of intelligibility and enlarge its own capacity for viability and survival by structuring itself within the principles of complex adaptive systems.

We need to locate anything a business can do to enlarge its range of understanding. As we will see, doing so will enlarge the domain of the company's own predictable adaptability and success. For every business in today's world, there are cognitive possibilities that would expand its range of understanding and remove the limit of which most businesses are simply unaware. At their disposal are logics, metaphorical systems, symbolic systems, computer languages, and other sources of information with which few of them have had any contact. It is as if a farmer in the 1700s were subjected to all of the vicissitudes of agriculture, while in another part of the world fertilizers that would make an enormous impact on the quality and quantity of a farmer's yield, if he had access to them, had been developed. But the farmer doesn't know about it. These fertilizers don't exist for him. There is much in today's world that is possible, but is simply not accessed by many companies.

One of the first questions asked of those guiding the company is, Do you think you know, understand, and can make sense of everything there is to be known and understood about the nature of what we produce, as well as how we produce and distribute it? Do you think you understand everything about the way global markets are structured and work? The ways currencies relate to each other? The ways we may or may not be impacted by climates of legislative opinion and activity?

The cigarette industry is a good example of a failure to understand its own industry by asking such questions. If someone had gone to the CEO of Philip Morris twenty-five years ago and said, "I want to introduce us to a new way of thinking about our industry and our product. It is a way that involves taking into account more variables. It would bring in more information, by asking more and more fundamental questions that are not logistical but abstract. Would you be willing to invest in making this possible?" He'd say, "Hell, no! My problem is how to make cigarettes cheaper and sell more of them. I don't have any other interests."

There is no industry that is not to some degree in the position that the tobacco industry was in twenty-five years ago. The issues may not be health, dissemination of information, or governmental interference, but regardless of the issues, there is no business that is not going to be subject to unanticipated changes in the environment in which it operates. The problem with the tobacco industry was that it could not acknowledge that there could be changes in that environment. Medical, governmental, or social—all of those environments are open to change. The way they change and affect each other will have some bearing on the conduct of the industry.

In the environment in which business operates, there is no such thing as a closed system, being insulated from the ongoing interaction with all other environments. The question that must be asked is, What can the business do to enlarge the scope of its structures of understanding such that it can absorb these changes as they occur?

The Teamsters Union goes on strike against UPS, not on the basis of wages, but on issues related to job security. Ten years before, there was probably some executive at UPS who said there was no chance of a major strike: "We're paying our people well above prevailing wages." If we had asked that executive whether he thought the union would become pre-occupied with other issues, he would have undoubtedly replied, "Not a chance. What other issues? They are interested in wages. Everybody knows that unions are there to negotiate higher wages for their constituencies. We can anticipate that will happen almost linearly. Every X number of years, there is going to be a hullabaloo about raising wages. We can even start planning linearly and build into our internal plan, not for public dissemination, a Y percent of increase in wages every X years. It is a linear process."

To the extent that they are stuck with that snapshot of their business and respond linearly, they are not ready to deal with the changes in issues that are tagged to changing social needs, economic patterns, and perceptions. Consequently, they find themselves in a very costly strike, because no matter how it is settled, there is going to be a cost involved. This is just a symptom of losses that are due to cognitive limitations within the industry. How do we make this case to a CEO or board of directors? How can we drive home the high cost of cognitive limitations? It has nothing to do with our skill in increasing the number of cigarettes that we can make per minute, or the labor cost per cigarette. There are issues at work beyond the limitations of our boundaries, where monsters exist. We can't insulate against them. We can't treat our world as if it were a closed system. We have to open it up. And to the degree we open it up, we open ourselves to a continual process of feedback from the multiple environments we interact with. Through that feedback, we can enlarge our cognitive capacities, so less and less of what comes in from those places where monsters exist takes the form of chaos, and more and more takes the form of something that makes sense. This doesn't mean we necessarily agree with it; it means we can deal with it.

One of Paul Abrams's primary concerns about running his operations at NeoRx as a complex adaptive system was convincing his board of directors of its validity. "What I have tried to do is talk about the analogy between an organization and an organism, basically describing it as an amoeba. If an amoeba finds food, it moves in that direction. If not, it gets zapped, withdraws, and moves elsewhere. It is a constant interactive process. That has had some appeal, but the most acceptable concept is that of the learning organization. Still, the biggest, inherent problem is security. If I am going to be called upon to make a judgment, I want all the facts. I want to see what the future looks like. I may be wrong and the facts may be wrong, but I want all this because otherwise, I won't feel comfortable."

Abrams offers what he calls a "perfect example" of this kind of thinking, called the net present value (NPV) analysis: A pharmaceutical company has a product or one it intends to design, and it decides when it will introduce the product. In the pharmaceutical industry, because of all the government regulation and testing, that time may be five years down the road. The company figures out what the product will do, what its market is, what it will achieve, and what the investment is to get it to market. All of those numbers are run, and then a risk factor is chosen to discount it to present value. This produces a number. As Abrams points out, "That number has a false objectivity associated with it. It is objective only because it is a number. It is false, because it is built on a house of cards and assumptions, any one of which you change, changes the whole thing. The Europeans for many years called this the Anglo-Saxon contrivance. Now, they are going to business schools in the U.S. and doing NPV analyses on products. Why? What else are you going to do?" Boards are crying, "Give me a number, something that we feel safe with, in spite of the fact that it has no basis in any rational perspective."

John Hiles's approach at Thinking Tools to selling the idea of complex adaptive systems was to bring before the board of directors a stack of business magazines that were two to four years old and contained projections of great things. He told them, "This is what we all believed would happen. Look at some of the stuff we thought would happen and look at the things that *did* happen that *aren't* here. That is where you start."

VHA's Curt Lindberg's approach was to start small and build on success. Since VHA is an association of over fifteen hundred individual hospitals, selling these ideas required not going to a single board of
directors, but hundreds. "It was kind of like opening a school and seeing
what evolved with a small group. As that began to grow, people began
involving their colleagues first from within their organizations and then
from outside." They heard about complexity and complex adaptive systems through this talk in small groups. People then wanted to begin a
nucleus within their own organizations, so Lindberg's group enlarged.
The key was getting people to talk about what they were doing not only
among themselves but to people outside the group. Lindberg's group
was always open to new ideas and new participants. He wasn't concerned with creating a cult, or converting others, but with discovering
as a group what they could do to help the organization. It grew organically.

The Complex Adaptive Employee

Once a business recognizes itself as a complex adaptive system, what are
the job skills required of an employee in this new environment? At Xerox
PARC John Seely Brown looks for someone "who is passionate to have an
impact, willing to adapt and to pay attention to the world. Someone who
wants to get to the root of problems. Finally, someone who has great intu-
itions that are grounded in reality."

Curt Lindberg at VHA considers the ideal emergent employee to be "a
self-aware schizophrenic, someone who can be of two minds, to fill the
multiple roles and perspectives that a health system needs." He is also
looking for someone who is able to see "why there is novelty and possibilities and is able as well to work the status quo effectively."

At the Prediction Company, Doyne Farmer believes the core of any
organization is "having creative people. They get attracted to fields like
this because they are creative. Then there is the challenge to get people
both to be creative and to stay focused on the things that they have to do."

"Ego is very important," says Paul Abrams at NeoRx. "It drives pride,
authorship, and ownership." But he's also looking for the employee who
has ability to be "content with the fact that your 'discovery' may have
been luck, or maybe wasn't your discovery. It doesn't really matter

whether you did it or your colleague did it or the group did it. All of the are equal outcomes as long as the outcome is positive."

The running theme for an employee in a complex adaptive business is *creative*, a word that implies emergent, adaptive, and innovative. The Marine Corps's Colonel Tony Woods has a different take on this individual and his or her value to the unit. Woods's intensity increases as he speaks about these qualities in his Quantico, Virginia, office on the sprawling Marine Corps training campus. "The rarest resources are the creative contributors. They are an unusual set of men and women. That they are creative is not unusual, but that they are creative in a way that allows them to contribute is. The creative contributors are the people you need to find and enable.

"These are not creative hooligans or show-offs. The creative contributor is able to engender support and interest in what he or she is doing. They are an incredibly valuable group of people and they are not very common. The other thing about them is that they are easily killed. They have to be protected. You need to reward them, but more important, you need to protect them. They will continue to be creative and contribute whether you reward them or not, that is their nature. But you won't be able to use their ideas if you don't protect them, and you have to build a culture to do that, willing to listen. It is up to the leaders to take advantage of what the creative contributor is saying, and be willing to do so in the face of contradictions that the leader brings forward from the past." To get to these creative contributors, Woods believes, the system has to be far flatter. "They don't necessarily come up neatly," he says, "especially on the battlefield. We learned during Vietnam that there are lots of creative contributors. They were the small unit leaders, and today they're generals. Many of them left because of the nature of the times, but they made a lot of difference to the Marines who served with them. Those Marines are alive today, in most cases, because of them." Colonel Woods feels that for an outfit to be nimble, whether in military or civilian pursuits, the creative contributors need to be leveraged. The only way he knows to do so is to create a democratic infrastructure, flatten the organization, and thereby strengthen the values that are important to be competitive. In other words, improve the information flow.

John Hiles agrees with Colonel Woods. He believes these creative contributors are the ones who can see rules for what they are, and recognize

to be transformed. "The trainees that came in and
to a codified language of the company were not only
a nuisance to the people who had broken the rules
becoming effective."

Hiles calls the introduction of complexity into business Promethean—original, bold, and creative. "You are bringing back tacit knowledge into the light of day, meaning the codified system." According to Hiles, the bearers of this fiery knowledge are often mavericks within the organization, challenging the language, self-perception, and biography of the organization.

Everyone wants the creative employee, but few are willing to follow the advice of Colonel Woods in fostering and protecting the creative contributor. What often happens is that instead of providing more information to these people and opening their process up to greater possibilities, we slam the doors of control shut. "We have to contain these people. We can't let them fly off. That's not the way business is done." Out of one side of our mouths, we ask for creativity, while out of the other we do everything we can to snuff it out. We find this contradiction running throughout many organizations that see themselves as open, creative, learning organizations. Rather than protecting the creative contributor, knowing that the effect of the contribution will be to favor the organization, we often let our insecurity about the new reach out to squelch it. And then organizations wonder why they lose their creative people. This reluctance to embrace something new is very similar to the way many organizations approach the process of learning.

A Learning Organization Versus an Indoctrination Organization

In order to really understand our place in the system of things, we have to learn more and more about the world in which we operate. For innovation and novelty to emerge we need to create organizations that are learning organizations. These are based on receiving feedback and processing it in a way that furthers the learning process. What we find, however, is organizations that view themselves as learning organizations but, in fact, are indoctrination organizations.

Indoctrination is a symptom of the organization looking to the wrong sources for control and security: "We are a learning organization, and we will tell you what you need to learn." Companies that practice this approach don't understand that the sources of control lie not in indoctrination but in learning. Unless they learn this themselves, they will continue to act as if the sources of control lie in the predictability of behaviors and reactions of all the entities in the organization. One thing that can be predicted about this thinking is that the organization is going to pay a very high price if they don't break out of this tight pattern. As mentioned earlier, if we look at the forty-three companies listed in the book *In Search of Excellence*, we find that two thirds of the companies were no longer considered excellent after five years. How many of today's Fortune 500 companies were among the five hundred on the list five years ago? How many of them that are new to the list this year will be on it or even in existence five years from now?

In an open system, learning on a broad scale furthers the whole system. Being afraid that certain learning will somehow subvert the system, it subverts the system itself. It may be that only an enlightened CEO would have a broad enough perspective to have the capacity to effect the kind of organizational changes necessary for organizational viability. What we find, however, is that almost all CEOs are products of the old system, and tend to manage in the way that their businesses have learned to manage themselves. But one after another, companies are spitting out their CEOs. Why? Because nothing had changed. The CEO had learned to keep the system operating the way systems have operated successfully in the past.

Apprehending the Future

What we have been discussing up to now is what already exists, but contained within the latest emergent possibilities are the seeds for future emergence. Within the emergence of the Information Age are the first soundings of the Postinformation Age. Almost at the very moment that the new age begins, the successor to that new age emerges in reaction to it. Historically, the ink was hardly dry on Newton's *Principia Mathematica* when people like Kant began pointing out the limitations of the new science and the directions in which scientific inquiry would have to start moving. They called into question the very fundamental assumptions and categories of the new science before anyone had even heard of it. As soon as something starts to grow, something else is dying. Nature is fine with this.

Ionian science had barely come into existence when the Socratic-Platonic world was set into motion. No sooner had Socrates and Plato gotten underway than Aristotle introduced yet another new science.

Nonetheless, there are continuities. The Newtonian world supplanted Aristotelian science, but Aristotelian science has continued throughout the four hundred–year period since Newton. It served as the basis for biology until the time of Darwin. In many ways, Aristotelian thought is just as strong as it ever was. In fact, the Catholic church is thoroughly committed to the Aristotelian worldview. Aristotle doesn't disappear just because Newton comes along. Newton doesn't disappear just because quantum theory and general relativity come along.

The Information Age has supplanted the Industrial Age, but it doesn't mean that the Industrial Age has disappeared, nor does it mean that Information Age companies will stop trying to act like Industrial Age concerns.

Brian Arthur tells a story about the *Encyclopedia Britannica* that illustrates this well. In 1990, encyclopedias were finding their way onto CD-ROMs. What did Britannica do? According to Arthur, "They asked themselves, what is an encyclopedia? It is leather-bound volumes. What is our business? Selling leather-bound volumes to libraries and beleaguered parents. How do we do it? With a door-to-door hierarchy of salespeople." When CDs came along. Britannica interpreted these as very nice backups to leather-bound volumes and as further support, illustration, and extension of the Britannica volumes. "We have the best brand in the business. We have the best quality and writers, how can we fail? When we are ready for CD, we will do it and it will be an add-on."

A few years later, Arthur heard the CEO of Britannica being interviewed on the radio. He was asked why they had yet to get into CD-ROMs. He told the interviewer, "You have to realize that it would take two CDs to contain anything like Britannica's information." Arthur's immediate thought was "The fellow's right. You'd have to swap the A–K disc for the L–Z disc." Then he realized that there were already thirty-four separate volumes in the Micropedia, Macropedia, and index. If someone wants to look up something in the Britannica, it already takes five minutes. "I could have put twenty-five CDs in and out of my computer in that time," Arthur said. "They have finally done this, now, but along the way, they lost thirty percent of their sales in 1993, and another thirty percent in 1994–95, and they had to file Chapter Eleven. Why? Because they completely miscognized the business."

Finding that the future has passed us by not only is disconcerting, but it probably means that we're out of business. Bill Gates and Microsoft nearly made that costly mistake. A couple of years ago, Gates realized he was in the business of what was commonly referred to in the trade as "shrink-wrap apps"—that is, off-the-shelf products—and to his consternation, the market was indeed shrinking. He looked around and saw a lot of players sitting at another table where a new game was unfolding, the Internet and the World Wide Web. It was a game Gates wasn't playing in. What did he do? He gathered a small library of books about the Internet and the Web and went off to his cabin in the forests of Washington State. A few weeks later he emerged, as Brian Arthur described it, "like Moses with the tablets." Gates then made the pronouncement: "Microsoft is now a Web-based company." And they were.

During his retreat, Gates was able to leave the old model behind. To solve his problem, he did not try to use the same level of thinking that had caused it. He gave himself the necessary isolation to steep himself in this different culture, a different point of view, unprejudiced by those whose agenda may have been to hold the status quo, and he was then ready to step into the new.

The Photon Age—
Information-Bearing Light

As computers have pulled us firmly into the Information Age, we are now moving toward a totally different kind of technology, one we can hardly imagine but whose beginnings exist. An early example of Information Age technology is laser technology. This technology is capable of doing things that do not involve electronics, and it allows us to do certain things that we can not do electronically. In the not-too-distant future, we'll probably be recording information holographically. The hologram won't be about pictures, but about patterns, in which we look at the configurations of wholes rather than the elements that compose them.

Our forms of synthesis will be very different. For example, information may all be synthesized holographically rather than synthesized linearly or even in parallel. It will be recognized that within every level of this synthesis the patterns are the same. We may have a clue to this in the emergence of fractals, which repeat the same patterns no matter what the scale is, holographically.

We may not be far from a time when information is stored within and disseminated by light, or even by waves of gravity, as unlikely as it may seem. Einstein has already given us precise calculations for something called the dissemination of waves of gravity. These waves of gravity are as real as electromagnetic waves, but they have never been harnessed. They have never been used. They are considered relatively trivial by quantum physicists—who, however, can't do without them in their calculations.

Inevitably there will be new technologies. One day, our computers will be looked upon as unbelievably primitive and unnecessarily complicated. By the same token, today's businesses, their products and services, and the way they are organized will be looked upon as primitive as pre-electronic Industrial Age business. This is the nature of an emergent universe. Only from the current level of possibilities can we apprehend the adjacent level. Business has to take it one step at a time.

The competitive edge for business lies in developing its holographic visioning and being continually on the lookout for nonlinear adjacent possibilities. Maintaining a competitive edge is about being open and being willing to apprehend the future. As masters of our businesses, we can apprehend what the next step is likely to look like; even though twenty-five years ago it would have been inconceivable, now it is apparent. There is no way we can jump three steps ahead. *There are simply no shortcuts.* When Alan Turing put together the first computer, the "Turing machine," it would have been a waste of time for scientists to say, "Let's skip all this and focus our attention on voice-activated computers." First they had to work out the basic technology that would turn out to lead in that direction.

This emergent progression cannot take place within a closed system. If we choose to remain within the boundaries of this illusionary system, we are doomed to repeat ourselves. What was once innovative and productive becomes stagnant with intransigent repetition. Everything in our lives changes in a relatively short period of time, and those changes have always been based on prior changes, which in turn were based on prior changes. There are no huge leaps.

If you look at the way in which every area of science and technology evolves—whether it is computers, automobiles, aircraft, medical engineering, construction, or even abstract processes like mathematics—until the time of discovery, the next discovery not only cannot occur, we don't even know it is there. Once we have reshaped our behaviors into their natural form as complex adaptive systems, all we can do is keep opening up to the possible and the new.

APPENDIX 1

Postmodern Management—Integrating Beliefs and Methodologies

Developments in the sciences of complexity and relevant disciplines (such as mathematics, logic, epistemology, ontology, and information theory) tend to supplant the foundational belief systems of traditional science and the methodologies derived from them. In the left column below are some of the modern beliefs and methodologies that from the perspective of postmodernism can become obsolete and thus counterproductive. In the right column are the postmodern alternatives.

Innovative behavior in an organization can be characterized as a shift in thinking from the modern beliefs and methodologies given in the left column to the postmodern approaches in the right column. To facilitate innovation in a company, it can formally represent any modern belief of the organization and relate that belief to its methodologies. It can then examine the postmodern alternatives.

The paradox: This assumes that an organization can already recognize the linearity (or deterministic thinking) implicit in most beliefs prior to the exercise meant to reveal it.

The implication: This preanalytic recognition may provide the basis for organizational innovation.

Modern Approaches	**Postmodern Alternatives**
1. *Belief:* Methodologies are derived from beliefs. *Methodology:* Convoluted and covert apparatus for demonstrating that what *is* ought to be. Justification is transcendent mythology (frequently labeled "scientific").	1. There is no distinction between belief and methodology in the sense that beliefs are themselves methodologies, that is, pragmatic tools.
2. *Belief:* An explicit paradigm is necessary to provide a logical basis for understanding and explanation.	2. Metaphor replaces paradigm. Thus, creation precedes understanding and interpretation replaces logical demonstration.

Modern Approaches	Postmodern Alternatives
Methodology: Paradigm shifts, which beg the question of the paradigm of the paradigm ad infinitum, and ignore the necessarily nonexplicit character of background practices.	
3. *Belief:* There must be a vision in order for anything present to be acted upon, changed, developed, understood, validated, etc. New visions produce new actions.	3. There is no transcendent vision, because the notion is superfluous in any account of "change."
Methodology: Search for new "possibilities" in the organizational culture, development of techniques for culture shifts, begging the question of the vision from which such visions emerge. The use of normative language and the imposition of moral standards (the new vision becomes the form of what "ought to be"). Consequently, new visions repeat the prior dynamic.	
4. *Belief:* Linguistic distinctions provide a universe of discourse and inquiry and thus expand possibilities for knowledge and value.	4. Linguistic distinctions arise from an already biased value system and tend to perpetuate and solidify that system and its presumed "knowledge." Such distinctions also are grounded in a limited and distorted view of language in which definitions (the ultimate distinctions) are both necessary and desirable (for Wittgenstein they are not even possible), neglecting the unformed character of the background practices which linguistic usage always presupposes and from which it derives its communicability. Distinctions can at best be treated as provisional interpretations.
Methodology: Formalization of definitions as structural.	

Modern Approaches	Postmodern Alternatives
5. *Belief:* The future, or what we can become, determines and defines the present (thus, the focus on the not-yet-embodied: the paradigm and the vision). *Methodology:* Techniques for determining and formulating targeted "results" and "goals" and the formulation of strategic plans for reaching them. Formulation of related standards for performance and for evaluation of performance.	5. The future is a metaphor; its relationship to what we call the present is reciprocal (like all metaphorical relations), that is, each affects the other. Each is a way of speaking of the other. The future's metaphorical character is delineated by the new biology as "potential," by information theory as "news of a difference (futureness) that makes a difference," by quantum theory as "probabilistic," and by complexity as indeterminate, free, and open. If the future is indeterminate, the present cannot determine the future without eliminating it, and the future, being open, cannot determine the present. Result- and goal-oriented thinking, ironically, confine the future to the present and thus become self-defeating. "Futureness" in the metaphor reveals indeterminacy in the present itself. What we call the "present" contains an open "not yet," implying that the present is never complete, that it is always being formed. For postmodernism, management of an organization occurs in this open, indeterminate "not yet" of the present. Any attempt to fix what the organization is or ought to become is inimical to both its "present" and its "future." The task of the Information Age manager is to create both the "present" and the "future."

Modern Approaches	Postmodern Alternatives
6. *Belief:* Human behavior is "intentional" and requires "motivation." *Methodology:* Techniques of exhortation.	6. Heidegger's classic work in ontology, or the theory of being, definitively revealed the inadequacies of subjective, personal "intentionality" as a model for understanding, describing, explaining, controlling, or predicting human behavior. This made postmodern organizational thinking possible. The idea of "motivation" derives from the old Newtonian model of the universe, in which nothing happens to any entity until it is acted upon. In this energy, force, push-pull model, intentionality is nothing more than beliefs and desires in the mind acting on the entity to produce behavior. Without such conscious, subjective intrusions, the Newtonian model assumes that the Newtonian person would remain inert. In postmodern thinking, behavior neither requires nor is explained by a conscious subject acting upon itself. "Change," "results," "growth," "development" occur naturally without acting on or doing something to objects in the world, including one's self as such an object. The Newtonian-Cartesian distinction between two totally separate domains of subject/object or observer/observed or mind/matter becomes obsolete. For example, if mind is called thinking but unextended, and matter, extended and nonthinking, no

Modern Approaches	Postmodern Alternatives
	recursiveness is possible between them, and without recursiveness it is difficult to conceive of relevance to a world of human action. On such a model, for example, an absurd separation of individual and culture could be inferred, and such a model is still implicit in most modern organizational thinking. Postmodernism substitutes recursiveness for separation.
7. *Belief:* Anything that happens has a single cause. *Methodology:* Analysis of all processes as if they were linear in an attempt to limit the complexity of contributing factors. Search for an external (usually antecedent) event or circumstance that explains the presumed effect.	7. Linear causality is a thinly disguised substitute for ignorance. Such cause/effect distinctions tend to harden into beliefs. The universe and everything in it becomes unidirectional. Explanations assume determinism and order, rather than manifesting unpredictability, openness, and chaos. On this assumption of determinism, interaction, or recursiveness (such as multiple and mutual causality) between what is called cause and what is called effect is not possible. Postmodern approaches reject linear causality as inadequate and misleading.
8. *Belief:* Concepts and symbols have a rational relationship to whatever they represent. *Methodology:* Attempts to "figure out" this relationship and to formalize language systems.	8. The choice of concepts and symbols has a pragmatic, not a logical, basis. Concepts and symbols are chosen through what Einstein in his later years called "the free play of creative imagination." Rationality is meaningful only after the choice. The choice of concepts, symbols, and metaphors is thus free and flexible; their "test" is both aesthetic and pragmatic.

Modern Approaches	Postmodern Alternatives
9. *Belief:* All planning and thinking must be accurately representative of a preexisting and independently existing environment. *Methodology:* Techniques for objective data collection, measurement, and the organization of such data to correspond to that environment.	9. There is no indepedently existing environment to represent apart from its representation, as in quantum mechanics. For example, any presumed object of discourse and what is said or thought about that object share a recursive relationship and thus cannot be separated from each other.

APPENDIX 2

Arriving at Complexity

To understand how this new way of scientific thinking we call complexity has emerged, it may be beneficial to look backward, to see what happened when an earlier scientific bastion, Aristotelian thought, came tumbling down under the weight of a falling apple.

A Brief Historical Perspective

Not too long after Sir Isaac Newton received his apple-induced enlightenment, he put forward his most important work about how the physical world operated. His theories were built on scientific ideas that had first been ascribed to the early Greek scientists, but his viewpoint was very different from theirs. Newton's theories required a new perspective, a whole new mathematics—a new language to explain them. This language was calculus. As more scientists learned to speak this language, the concept known as the "mechanistic universe" was born. Everything and anything could be reduced, scientists told us, to their constituent bits and pieces. If we could *know* these parts, we could understand how all of them fit together, the object's, or system's, mechanics. Scientists believed that it was simply a matter of knowing the parts.

As a scientist, John Locke, a contemporary and friend of Newton, fully understood the power of an established, experimentally verified scientific theory—and as a philosopher, he developed its philosophical consequences.

In Newtonian physics, nature is understood as a system of physical objects located in a public infinite space. The essential philosophical question for Locke was, What is the relation between sensed qualities in sensed space (or the world as we experience it) and physical atoms in public (or objective) mathematical space? Locke's answer to that question leads to rigorous and persuasive conclusions about the nature of humans and their social and political institutions. An example of the direct influence that scientific thinking can have on social applications, including business, is that Locke's conclusions had an impact on thinking that led to the creation of the form of the government of the United States of America.

John C. Miller wrote in *Origins of the American Revolution,* "If any one man can be said to have dominated the political philosophy of the American Revolution, it is John Locke. American political thinking was largely an exegesis upon Locke, and patriots quoted him with as much reverence as communists quote Marx. . . . Indeed it is not too much to say that during the era of the American Revolution the 'party line' was John Locke. . . . The American mind of 1776 was saturated with John Locke."

Newtonian-Lockian thinking provided a "modern" approach to understanding a new political system. It also gave Thomas Jefferson a context in which to see the limitations of Aristotelian and pre-Newtonian political thought.

Jefferson, by way of John Locke, was able to recognize and formulate the basic principle for the newly forming American government: personal liberty. About the groundwork laid by pre-Newtonian political thinkers, Jefferson wrote:

> They had just ideas of the value of personal liberty, *but none at all of the structure of government best calculated to preserve it.* They knew no medium between a democracy (the only pure republic, but impracticable beyond the limits of a town) and the abandonment of themselves to an aristocracy, or a tyranny independent of the people. It seems not to have occurred that where the citizens cannot meet to transact their business in person, they alone have the right to choose the agents who shall transact it. . . . The full experiment of a government democratical, but representative, was and still is reserved for us. . . . The introduction of this new principle of representative democracy has rendered useless almost everything written before on the structure of government" (authors' italics).

Jefferson recognized that Newton and Locke had the principle—just ideas of the value of personal liberty—but nothing happened. The implication is that principles alone do not cause behaviors to issue forth. That occurs only through structure in the form of theories, models or metaphors, or patterns of possible organization. These involve imagination, design, and informing. They enable the process and localize existence—that place where it occurs and takes form. Jefferson is making the point that prior to America's Declaration of Independence, there were no models, what he calls "structures for the government best calculated to preserve." He had no prior model of such a government. Without the theories and models derived from Locke, this new possibility of government structure could not have come into existence.

This makes a very important point about the pervasive influence of science on all areas of human endeavor over the last four hundred years. Alfred North Whitehead explained: "This quiet growth of science has practically recolored our mentality so that modes of thought which in former times were exceptional, are now broadly spread through the educated world. This new coloring of ways of thought had been proceeding slowly for many ages in the European peoples. At last, it issued in the rapid development of science."

Whitehead later goes on to say, "The new mentality is more important even than the new science and new technology. It has altered the metaphysical presuppositions and the imaginative contents of our minds."

Whitehead is saying that everything is referable back to science, as if science creates legitimacy. Our worldviews, cosmologies, and epistemologies all come out of science. If any of those are to be different from that science, then they must contend with science at some point. For four hundred years, Galilean-Newtonian science has directly influenced human organization. We have already seen an extraordinary example of this is in the design of the American government.

Letting Go of Our Old Ways of Thinking

While many of Newton's concepts are still valid scientifically, there are some instances in which they have not been adequate. Newton's theories about the visible world—the world we see with our eyes, moving at speeds we can see—worked wonderfully. But things changed. It was discovered that the atom, thought by Newton to be the fundamental particle of matter, was made up of even smaller bits. Newton's laws and theories of the visible world couldn't accurately explain the activities of these subatomic particles. His theories also could not account for objects moving near the speed of light. Fortunately, Albert Einstein's theories could.

Like Newton's discoveries, Einstein's theory of relativity changed the way scientists looked at things. We needn't attempt to explain his special or general theories of relativity to note that they opened great holes in the Newtonian infrastructure and explained, among other things, objects moving at extremely high velocities. Like Newton before him, Einstein, to make this change, had to have a new frame of reference, essentially a new way of thinking. This does not mean that he ignored earlier work; as we have discussed in the context of adjacent possibilities, it was the work that preceded Einstein that opened what would otherwise have been inconceivable for him or anyone else.

In the late 1970s and early 1980s, another inconceivable series of events took place. Computers smashed the walls enclosing our information-processing capabilities. Thomas J. Watson, the cofounder of IBM, once said he didn't see the need for more than five computers in the world. Of course, the machines he knew were big, expensive to build, and slow. He was still locked in his Industrial Age mode of thinking. The computer-world maxim—that every time prices dropped by half, computer capability would double—hadn't emerged yet. Suddenly, computational equipment was operating at faster speeds with processors capable of tremendous capacity, and they were doing so not only in research centers and businesses, but in the home, too. A new way of thinking—moving from sequential to parallel processing—that never existed before has opened new possibilities: namely the transition from attention to parts and detail to patterns. Although this may be the way the human mind functions, the development of this capacity in the use of computers sheds new light on human mental activity as well as extending the range and capacity of computer applications. For example, the development of parallel processing in computer chess playing has finally enabled the computer to defeat a human chess master.

This increased processing power also made possible new ways of thinking about our existing frames of reference. In the light of this technological innovation, we saw something new: complex adaptive systems. Unmistakably, with this vast rush of computational information, scientists started seeing more than just the detailed mechanical bits and pieces of the universe. Increasingly they saw how the relationships of the parts affected the activities and evolution of the whole.

In the bright glow of this discovery, the understanding and emergence of complexity and chaos entered the spotlight. This time, however, the radiance of this new perspective caught the eye of a business world in desperate need of a new way of thinking. Industrial Age business theories could no longer account for the speed at which business was now traveling. Responding to these rapidly changing, unstable conditions required a new frame of reference.

Notes

A New Way of Thinking

1 Gerald Holton, *Einstein, History, and Other Passions* (Addison-Wesley, Reading, Mass., 1996).

2 John Holland, *Hidden Order* (Addison-Wesley, Reading, Mass., 1996).

3 Dr. Mario Laserva, quote from letter to Laserva from Einstein (Bogata, Columbia, January 8, 1955).

4 Interview with Bruce Abell, Managing Director, Santa Fe Center for Emergent Strategies, Santa Fe, N. Mex., April 1997.

5 Michael D. McMaster, *The Intelligence Advantage—Organizing for Complexity* (Knowledge Based Development, Ltd, London, England, 1995).

6 Stuart Kauffman, *Investigations* (The Santa Fe Institute, Santa Fe, N. Mex., 1996, p. 4).

7 Lynda Woodman, *"Barriers to Innovation,"* paper presented at the conference, Complexity and Strategy in Action, Santa Fe, N. Mex., 1996.

8 George Gendron, "Flashes of Genius," *Inc.* magazine, May 1996.

9 Paul Arthur Schilpp, ed., *Albert Einstein: Philosopher-Scientist* (Evanston, Ill.: Library of Living Philosophers, Inc., 1949, pp. 683–84.

10 James Collins and Jerry Porras, *Built to Last* (HarperBusiness, New York, 1997).

11 *Washington Post*, April 17, 1997.

Principles, Models, Rules, and Behaviors

1 Vaclav Havel, *The Art of the Impossible* (Knopf, New York, 1997).

2 Michael Polanyi, *Personal Knowledge: Toward A Post-Critical Philosophy*, 1958.

Demystifying Complexity

1 John Holland, *Hidden Order* (Addison-Wesley, Reading, Mass., 1996).

2 Michael D. McMaster, *The Intelligence Advantage—Organizing for Complexity*.

3 George Johnson, *Fire in the Mind* (Alfred A. Knopf, New York, 1995).

4 Chouinard quoted in *Business Ethics*, "Interview with Yvon Chouinard," May/June 1995.

5   David Lane and Robert Maxfield, "Foresight, Complexity, and Strategy" (The Santa Fe Institute, Santa Fe, N. Mex., 1995).

6   Peter Coveney and Roger Highfield, *Frontiers of Complexity* (Fawcett Columbine, New York, 1995).

7   John Holland, *Hidden Order* (Addison-Wesley, Reading, Mass., 1995).

Language, Narrative, and Metaphor

1   Flores quoted in Matthew Walker, "Being and Overtime," *San Francisco*, November 1997.

2   Thomas Petzinger, Jr., "Fernando Flores Says Entrepreneurs Are New World Leaders," *Wall Street Journal*, May 5, 1997.

3   Elie Wiesel, *The Gates of the Forest* (Holt, Rinehart and Winston, New York, 1966).

4   Galileo Galilei, quoted in E. A. Burtt, *Metaphysical Foundations of Physics* (Harcourt, Brace, New York, 1925).

5   Paul Arthur Schilpp, ed., *Albert Einstein Philosopher-Scientist* (Library of Living Philosophers, Evanston, Ill., 1949).

6   Timothy Ferris, *The Whole Shebang* (Simon & Schuster, New York, 1997).

7   Edmund Blair Bolles, ed., *Galileo's Commandment* (W. H. Freeman, New York, 1997).

8   William C. Taylor, "At VeriFone It's a Dog's Life," *Fast Company*.

Real-World Applications for Coevolving Metaphors

1   Loren Eiseley, *The Unexpeded Universe* (HarcourtBrace Jovanovich, New York, 1969).

2   George Lakoff and Mark Johnson, *Metaphors We Live By* (University of Chicago Press, Chicago, 1980).

3   Gemma Corradi Fiumara, *The Metaphoric Process: Connections between Language and Life*, (Routledge, New York, 1995).

4   William Irwin Thompson, *Imagining Landscape* (St. Martin's Press, New York, 1989).

5   Eiseley, *The Unexpected Universe*.

6   John Micklethwait and Adrian Wooldridge, *The Witch Doctors* (Times Business, New York, 1996).

7   Charlene Spretnak, *The Resurgence of the Real* (Addison-Wesley, Reading, Mass., 1997).

8   "McDonald's Returns to Its Roots for Sales Life," *USA Today*, July 30, 1997.

9   Sven Birkerts, *The Gutenberg Elegies: The Fate of Reading in an Electronic Age* (Fawcett Columbine, New York, 1994).

Ideas Are the Geometries of Behaviors

1 "Untouchable Is India's President," Associated Press, July 26, 1997.

2 John L. Casti, *Would-be Worlds* (John Wiley and Sons, New York, 1997).

The Franchise Model: Purpose in Action

1 Jeffrey L. Bandach, *Franchising Organizations* (Harvard Business School Press, Boston, Mass., 1998).

2 "Marriage of Franchiser to Owner One-Sided," *Chicago Tribune*, August 3, 1997.

3 Kenneth Boulding, "What Is Evolutionary Economics?" *Journal of Evolutionary Economics*, 1991, p. 14.

4 W. Brian Arthur, "Increasing Returns and the World of Business," *Harvard Business Review*, July–August 1996.

Apprehending the Future

1 Roger Penrose, *The Large, the Small and the Human Mind* (Cambridge University Press, Cambridge, U.K., 1997).

2 Richard Carlson, *The Prefect Sales Equation* (John Wiley, New York, 1994).

Glossary

Abstractions Any explanation that includes or goes beyond other explanations. "To be abstract is to transcend particular concrete occasions of actual happening (but to transcend an actual occasion does not mean to be disconnected from it)," said Alfred North Whitehead.

Agents Interacting entities that are constituents of complex adaptive systems. An agent is any such entity that interacts with other such entities. In complex human systems, such agents are purposeful, not simply reactive.

Authorized/Emergent Authorized behavior is what is prescribed, expected, or acceptable behavior within an organization. Emergent behavior is behavior that is not limited to what is expected or prescribed but that may fall outside the rules and regulations to achieve innovation.

Behaviors at a Distance In business, behaviors that exact a coevolutionary, shaping effect on others' actions and ideas. In physical terms, an example is the moon's gravitational effect on the tides.

Chaos Unpredictable and apparently random behavior in dynamic systems.

Coevolution A concept that organisms and their competitors evolve in relation to one another. To remain fit we must adapt to their adaptations, taking into account their effect on us and ours on them.

Complexity The behavior of macroscopic collections of simple units—complex adaptive structures—that have the potential to coevolve in time.

Computational Simulations An experiment conducted on high-speed computers to constrain a set of possible outcomes regarding the behavior of dynamic systems.

Deduction An inferred conclusion, usually within the rules of a given logic.

Decentralization The even distribution of responsibilities and actions within an organization, that allows each agent to act semiautonomously without necessarily requiring central approval.

Determinism Doctrine that our choices, decisions, and actions are decided by a cause that occurred prior to the choice, decision, or action.

Distributed Systems A way of operating a business by spreading out its operations and responsibilities from centralized control to autonomous or semiautonomous units or agents.

Diversity of Control A form of organizational decentralization in which no one entity or agent within the organization has complete command and control. The organization is thus more open to the innovative potential of generative relationships.

Emergence Complex systems are not inert. They become, are in process, change, develop, and grow. Emergence refers to the occurrence of properties at any level of development not found at simpler levels, arising out of the depths of complex interactions.

Emergent Novelty The appearance of something new and unexpected that has become evident only as a function of the last level of possibilities that emerged.

Epistemology The study of the nature of knowledge and how knowledge occurs.

Fitness Objectives Fitness is a measure of an individual's (or group's) success in a given environment. Fitness objectives would be the criteria for such success.

Franchising A business formulation in which a parent company supports semiautonomous outlets which duplicate the model of the original.

Generative Relationships A form of interaction evolving from group behavior that cannot be understood or predicted by looking at the individuals alone.

Hermeneutics The science and art of interpreting texts, under the assumption that any text says what it means or means what it says.

Interactions A complex system can be understood only through the interplay of its constituent, simpler complex systems, not through a study of the "parts" in isolation from one another. Without such interactions there is no complex system.

Interpretation/Description Interpretation is the act of applying meaning to information. It is a subjective act that implies history. Interpretation is distinguished from description, which is merely an account of something. It is presumed that every description already has built into it some interpretation and is itself a form of interpretation.

Languaging To express ideas in a fashion that transmits them from one agent to another.

Localization Process whereby interactions at decentralized localities—at specific times and circumstances derive meaning from immediate situations in which they occur—generate at-the-source problem solving and decision making.

Metanarrative Founding story, which in business may often be held above reproach, considered sacrosanct, and which tends to lock in certain assumptions and beliefs that can limit the ideas of an organization.

Nonlinear Dynamics A system is nonlinear if the behaviors or properties of the system cannot be obtained by simply adding together the behaviors of its constituent parts. Dynamic systems change over time. Dynamic models of such systems look at changing not static patterns.

Novelty A new or unusual thing or occurrence.

Organic-Evolutionary/Mechanistic Adjectives describing the fundamental distinction between complexity and Newtonian science. Organic-evolutionary implies adjacent possibilities out of which phenomena emerge and which are not predictable. Mechanistic implies that if we can understand the individual parts we can comprehend the whole. Whitehead said, "A thoroughgoing evolutionary philosophy is inconsistent with materialism (mechanism). The result has been that the nonevolution of matter has been a tacit presupposition throughout modern thought."

Phenomenology The investigation and description of the visible or directly observable.

Postmodernism The cultural era that follows modernism. According to French philosopher Jean-Francois Lyotard, postmodernism was an "incredulity towards metanarratives." The management guru Peter Drucker defines postmodern as postindustrial, implying a shift from the modern Cartesian worldview to a new universe of pattern, purpose, and process.

Principles The most abstract, least likely to change, formulation of a system's identity.

Purpose A conscious activity, with a specific, defined objective, shaped within a human-designed context and based on multiple strategies.

Recursive Characterizing an interactive repetition of events that can be either nonchanging or coevolutionary.

The Second Law of Thermodynamics The principle of increasing entropy, in which ordered energy may be collected into disordered energy, i.e., heat.

Self-organization A collective that can catalyze its own formulation.

Speech Acts An occurrence of the use of language.

Tautologies The same things said twice using different words.

Theory A supposition or system of ideas explaining something.

About the Santa Fe Center for Emergent Strategies

The Santa Fe Center for Emergent Strategies facilitates the emergence and realization of new possibilities for business performance.

We liberate strategic processes from the unexamined beliefs and assumptions (what everybody knows) that have become barriers to achieving intended results. By doing so, we reveal new possibilities for both ideas and behaviors and facilitate new levels of performance.

1. We approach businesses—within the context of the interdisciplinary sciences of complexity—as complex adaptive systems. Such systems are characterized by change, responsiveness, innovation, and coevolution.

2. We examine with managers the core principles, models, and rules of the system, especially as they relate to how business formulates its identity, values, purposes, and priorities.

3. We look upon the sources of any instance of business performance as essentially cognitive, not merely behavioral or motivational. That is, we look at ideas as foundational, influencing the way a company and its complex activities are organized and managed. In this sense, behaviors can rarely go beyond what ideas—as models—make possible, but models can and do go beyond prevailing behaviors.

4. If the behaviors are robust, that is, generated by models not by rules or habit, then the behaviors will provide feedback which extends and modifies our understanding and formulation of the models. Models and behaviors then resonate. Unexpected strategies emerge. This is the source of successful adaptation and of corporate innovation and growth. We facilitate such growth.

5. We look at the relevance of a company's core ideas to today's multiple environments.

Our programs include: consulting, or formal facilitation; public seminars and conferences; in-house seminars and workshops; networking, through a structured membership program, "The Forum"; and publications.

The Santa Fe Center for Emergent Strategies
2 Chamisa Drive North, Suite A
Santa Fe, New Mexico 87505
Phone: 505/466-7901
Fax: 505/466-4012
email: info@santafe-strategy.com

Index

Abell, Bruce, 72
Abrams, Paul, 188, 189, 199, 200–201
Abstraction, 27, 44
Adaptive organizations, 74–76
Adventure of Ideas (Whitehead), 149
Agrarian Age, 32, 190
Allen, Catherine, 83
Ambiguity, conditions of, 4–5
Anderson, Philip, 80, 81
Apple Computers, 20, 29
Applied Biosystems, 84–85, 108, 122, 155, 157
Aristotle, 44, 63, 94, 129, 161, 171, 204
Arthur, Brian, 116, 177, 179, 204, 205
Art of War, The (Sun-tzu), 188
Aspen Mountaineering, 80
Assumptions, questioning, 136–138
AT&T, 23, 31–32

Bailey, James, 81, 88
Ball, Brad, 129
Bandelier Designs, 178
Barker, Rodney, 126
Barr, William, 30, 83
Behaviors, 8, 21, 47
  adaptive, 158–159
  ideas and, 149–150, 151–153
  interpretation and, 146–149
  objects and, 115–117
  rules and, 54–55
  See also Principles, models, rules, and behaviors
Bellcore, 30, 83
Bertalanffy, Ludwig von, 88
Birkerts, Sven, 135–136, 137
Boss, idea of, 99, 152
Boulding, Kenneth, 177
Boundaries, arbitrary, 169–170
Breakthrough thinking, 63
Brown, John Seely, 27, 132, 200
  new ideas, 101–105
Built to Last (Collins and Porras), 51–52

Business, purposes of, 35, 159
Business Design Associates, 92

Campbell, Christina, 127–128
Capra, Fritjof, 163
Carlson, Richard, 195
Cartesian model, 6
Chambers, John, 178
Champy, James, 14, 15, 26, 39, 44
Chaos, 19–20
  understanding, 68–69
Chouinard, Yvon, 79–80
Cisco Systems, 178
Citibank, 4, 25, 34, 73, 83, 178
Closed system, 10, 35, 98–99, 121
  myth of, 2–7
Coca-Cola, 73–74
Cognitive failure, 14, 87, 140, 144
  peril of, 26–27, 29
Cognitive success, 127
Collective unconscious, 116
Compaq, 25
Competition, 75
Complex adaptive systems, 17–19, 30, 142, 161–162, 206
  arbitrary boundaries, 169–170
  concepts of, 180–181
  demonstrating, 194–200
  employees as, 150–151
  language and purpose, 167–169
  purposeful, 108–109, 156–157
  See also Franchise model
Complexity, 7, 8, 10, 11–12
  in action, 69–78
  comprehending, 62–64
Complexity thinking, 16–17, 30, 47, 53, 68
  allowing emergence, 79–81
  flocking (swarming resources), 84–85
  generative relationships, 81–84
  importance of, 20–22
  self-organization, 85–87
  in the workplace, 78–81

227